THE COSTS OF WAR

INTERNATIONAL LAW, THE UN, AND WORLD ORDER AFTER IRAQ

BY RICHARD A. FALK

Routledge
Taylor & Francis Group
New York   London

Routledge
Taylor & Francis Group
270 Madison Avenue
New York, NY 10016

Routledge
Taylor & Francis Group
2 Park Square
Milton Park, Abingdon
Oxon OX14 4RN

Printed in the United States of America on acid-free paper
10 9 8 7 6 5 4 3 2 1

International Standard Book Number-13: 978-0-415-95509-6 (Softcover) 978-0-415-95508-9 (Hardcover)

Library of Congress Cataloging-in-Publication Data

Falk, Richard.
    The costs of war : international law, the UN, and world order after Iraq / Richard Falk. -- 1st ed.
        p. cm.
    ISBN 978-0-415-95508-9 (hardback : alk. paper) -- ISBN 978-0-415-95509-6 (pbk. : alk. paper) -- ISBN 978-0-203-94070-9 (ebook)
    1. Iraq War, 2003---Law and legislation. 2. International law. I. Title.

KZ6795.I73.F35 2008
341--dc22   2007011625

**Visit the Taylor & Francis Web site at
http://www.taylorandfrancis.com**

**and the Routledge Web site at
http://www.routledge.com**

For Hilal

Life partner in love and all else that matters

Contents

Acknowledgments

Most of my professional life has involved a struggle with political realists who viewed the world through a prism of power, with morality and legality assigned to the outer margins of policy and decision. It has also led to tensions with many in the international law community who shared this realist vision, although often calling themselves liberals due to their abstract enthusiasm for international law and the United Nations. Concretely, for such liberals this meant accepting a subordinate role for law and the authority of the UN Charter when it came to matters of war and peace engaging the United States. The debates surrounding the lawfulness of the Vietnam War was the most illuminating test of this fundamental normative tension, and was the maturing moment for my own approach to world order.

With the rise of the neoconservatives to governmental ascendancy in this country, especially in the period following the 9/11 attacks, the locus of debate and concern has moved so far to the right as to make me feel unexpectedly nostalgic about the good old days when the primacy of realism shaped American foreign policy. At least realists acknowledged the limits of power, and prided themselves on the geopolitical virtue of prudence, regarding their main undertaking the maintenance of countervailing military capabilities with the goal of *avoiding* war. In contrast, neoconservatives conceived of their mission as the global spread of American values, expressed to be sure in self-serving terms relating to the interests of big business, military dominance, and energy geopolitics, with centrality accorded to unilateral war making conceived as a necessary and appropriate enterprise. International law was treated as irrelevant, indeed law in general was so treated, with limitless and supposedly unaccountable power to play the security card allegedly vested in a post-9/11 wartime presidency of imperial pretensions. While law was made irrelevant, lawyers were not. Lawyers of neoconservative persuasion twisted and turned respected constraints of law to such an extent as to shock even the hardened sensibilities of realists, and to make liberals previously compliant with the ways of the power into radical critics of government policy.

It is against such a background that this book looks at international law and UN authority in the twenty-first century within the context of the American debate on security policy after 9/11. In fundamental respects, my central argument is that historical circumstances, correctly interpreted, are such as to reverse relations between power and law, making adherence to international law the most reliable discipline for the exercise of power even if the dominant criterion for policymakers is the pursuit of national interests. Such a view is especially persuasive in the current global setting where American power is unchecked by countervailing power, but is still subject to the sorts of resistance that makes its use productive of national ordeals (such as Iraq) rather than occasions of political and military victory. In short, geopolitical wisdom in this new century counsels a law-oriented foreign policy for the United States. This is the main message of this book.

The writings in this volume are anchored in responses to the somewhat contradictory challenges posed by the Kosovo War in 1999 and the Iraq War that started in 2003. Most of the chapters draw on previously published material written during the first years of this new century. There is some overlap because of the attention given to these two wars from a variety of perspectives. No undertaking of this sort would be possible without the support, insight, and inspiration of colleagues throughout the world. I want to acknowledge and thank only those few who were particularly influential in this recent period: Georges Abi-Saab, Asli Bali, Upendra Baxi, Amy Bartholomew, Alison Brysk, Hilary Charlesworth, Fred Dallmayr, Ahmet Davutoglu, Michael Doyle, Howard Friel, David Ray Griffin, Irene Gendzier, Stephen Gill, Mary Kaldor, David Krieger, Lisa Hajjar, Robert Jay Lifton, Saul Mendlovitz, Chandra Muzaffar, Balakrishnan Rajagopal, Amin Saikal, Andrew Strauss, Rob Walker, Paul Wapner, and Burns Weston.

This book was written entirely during my period of affiliation with the Program of Global and International Studies of the University of California at Santa Barbara. In this regard I wish to thank Richard Appelbaum, Giles Gunn, and Mark Juergensmeyer for their interest, support, and most of all, for their friendship. Many others at UCSB have made this an enjoyable, congenial, and stimulating atmosphere, especially Avery Gordon, Chris Newfield, Jacqueline Stevens, Elisabeth Weber, and Howard Winant. My close relationship with David Krieger, and the Nuclear Age Peace Foundation, has also strengthened my appreciation of the importance of getting governments, particularly our own, to respect law and morality for the sake of human survival and the well being of the earth community.

Finally, my wife, Hilal, to whom this book is happily dedicated, has shared all of these concerns with grace and humor, while making me feel more than ever that life is a sacred gift and that the future needs to be preserved for the sake of our precious children and grandchildren, and for the benefit of the born and unborn peoples of the world. It will take more than law and morality, but it cannot be done without a dramatic deepening of this collective normative consciousness of humanity.

Introduction

By now there are many valuable books about the Iraq War. There are several excellent accounts of how and why the United States government decided to invade Iraq, including Tom Ricks's *Fiasco: The American Military Adventure in Iraq* (2006) and the Woodward bestsellers, *Plan of Attack* (2004) and *State of Denial* (2006). There are also some convincing books on how and why to get out. One of the best written from an antiwar perspective is Arnold Arnove's *Iraq: The Logic of Withdrawal* (updated 2007). A more mainstream set of proposals aimed at ending the war was published under the title of *The Iraq Study Group Report* (2006). It was the work of a bipartisan commission of eminent persons chaired by James Baker and Lee Hamilton.

Far less attention has been devoted to the normative costs of the Iraq War. We do have several studies written from the perspective of international law, including the highly readable *Lawless World*, by Philippe Sand. But there is little in print on the broader costs to world order that are associated with the Iraq War, and more generally an evaluation of the neoconservative blueprint for U.S. foreign policy from the perspectives of world order. Despite all that has gone wrong in Iraq, the neoconservative "fix" seems to involve "staying the course" in Iraq, and possibly expanding the war zone to include Iran and maybe Syria and Lebanon. So far, despite the opportunity for a graceful reversal of policy in Iraq provided by the Baker–Hamilton report, President Bush has given every sign of keeping faith with the now wildly unpopular neoconservative game plan. Its latest phase, announced early in 2007, combines a "surge" of troop strength in Iraq, especially Baghdad, and an escalation of war talk relating to Iran.

This book's main concerns relate to the fraying of world order: the weakening of international law and international morality; the eroding of the authority of the United Nations; the disappearance of respect for and the legitimacy of American global leadership on matters pertaining to the global public good (e.g., global warming). Beyond critique is an implicit argument that respect for international law matters more and more in our globalizing world, which is experiencing growing pressure to make fundamental behavioral adjustments. I also believe that strict adherence to the guidelines of international law, especially with respect to war, serve the national interest in the twenty-first century, and definitely the human interest as well. The guidance of law in any political setting can never be treated as absolute, but in relation to international law, departures should be convincingly justified by special facts and sustained by principled reasoning without any reliance on deceptive manipulation of intelligence reports.

Among the many disturbing features of the Iraq experience has been the absence of debate on these facets of American foreign policy. The American people, with eyes wide closed, passively stood by watching the decisions to wage aggressive war against Iraq take shape during 2002 and the first months of 2003. The media, including its most trusted organs of news and editorial opinion, basically orchestrated support for the war, seriously questioning only issues of cost and feasibility. The cautionary lessons of Vietnam were completely ignored. The lingering trauma of 9/11 was allowed to make the Iraq War into a street-corner shell game with no one daring to look at the emptiness underneath the counterterrorist card. War was undertaken in violation of international law and the United Nations Charter, in defiance of world public opinion, and without a proper mandate as required by the U.S. Constitution. It was precisely recourse to aggressive war of this character that was punished at the Nuremberg Judgment after World War II, and declared the supreme crime in international law as well as constituting the core commitment of the UN Charter.

But times have changed. The instrument of war was cut loose from a legal net of constraints. The United States government situated its policy choices relating to the use of international force in a realm above law. Mainstream opinion followed rather blindly. Such respected journalistic voices lent their support. Tom Friedman influentially endorsed an attack on Iraq as an example of what he called "wars of choice," which were to be distinguished from "wars of necessity," defensive wars impelled by an enemy attack. Although such voices have been temporarily muted by the failure of the Iraq undertaking, similar arguments are again being made, this time with Iran in the gun sights, by such hardcore neoconservatives as William Kristol and their academic henchmen such as Bernard Lewis. And once more the only arguments against such war that reach the general public address consequential concerns about Iran's retaliatory options and the extent to which the United States can bear the financial and military burdens of an expanding war zone. There seems surprisingly little willingness to ask whether recourse to war against Iran is consistent with international law and morality. The argument of this book is that the exclusion of these normative objections from debate and decision diminishes the quality of American democracy, undermines American legitimacy on the global level, and makes hypocritical American promotion of the rule of law for foreign societies. Additionally such war talk implicitly advocates killing others without weighing the human costs of war.

A young U.S. Army officer, Lt. Ehren Watada, refused in 2006 to be deployed in Iraq, and was prosecuted under the Uniform Code of Military Justice for deliberately missing the order to deploy (Art. 88) and, by making public antiwar comments, for conduct unbecoming an officer and a gentleman (Art. 133). In the court-martial proceeding held at Fort Lewis in the State of Washington, Lt. Watada's attempt to present testimony that supported the reasonableness of his belief that the war was illegal was disallowed, as was any judicial consideration of his claim that speaking in public against the war was within his rights to free speech as an American citizen. Such penal charges confronted this military officer, and indirectly all military personnel, with a dilemma. According to the Field Manual 27-10 that governs behavior of members of the Army, an aggressive war is a Crime Against Peace (Art. 498), and military personnel are instructed to realize in this setting that "members of the armed forces are bound only to obey lawful orders." (Art. 509(b), with reference to Art. 92). Whatever Lt. Watada might have done, he would be in violation of the law: either he engages in the Iraq War and knowingly contributes to what he believes to be an illegal war of aggression, or he refuses such an unlawful order and faces punishment for disobedience. This puts Lt. Watada deep in Catch-22 territory.

One finds greater receptivity to the role of international law and the authority of the United Nations among the leading European countries, with the partial exception of Britain. The European Union has itself emerged as a zone of peace in which the member countries seem highly unlikely to consider war as a suitable remedy for any regional dispute. Such a culture of peace has emerged only after centuries of recurrent and devastating warfare. But even Europe, while skeptical about the merits of the Iraq War, is reluctant to insist on the implementation of international law or the Nuremberg Principles in relation to the Iraq War. Only the mobilized forces of civil society seem to be moving toward a genuine commitment that points an accusatory finger at the leadership of the United States and Great Britain. On February 15, 2003, demonstrations of eleven million against the Iraq War were held in some eighty countries. Never before in history had there been such a massive outcry from all corners of the planet to stave off an impending war, but it was to no avail. After the onset of the war, a worldwide set of civil-society initiatives investigated allegations that the Iraq War was an illegal war of aggression and that its architects and perpetrators were criminally accountable. Some twenty separate events were organized in a variety of countries, and the overall endeavor became known as "the tribunal movement." The culminating expression of this movement was the World Tribunal on Iraq held in Istanbul during June 2005. The Declaration of Conscience issued by the tribunal clearly concluded that the American attack on Iraq was a war of aggression and that individuals and organizations associated with the war, including during its occupation phase, were indictable for war crimes and Crimes Against Peace.

These peoples' tribunals found it particularly dispiriting that even moderate states and the United Nations have maintained a stony silence while the most basic norm of international law is flagrantly violated and a member state is devastated in the course of an unlawful occupation that has unleashed a deadly civil war already responsible for civilian deaths numbering at least 100,000 in Iraq, as well as many more wounded and displaced.

This book argues that we need to appreciate the normative costs of this silence, and that as citizens of democratic societies we have a duty to speak and act, and to insist that elected leaders follow international law in foreign policy or face the consequences of their criminality. An elite, bipartisan political culture in this country resists such an argument and effectively relegates concerns of law and morality to domestic political life or considers such normative arguments as tools sometimes useful for mounting propaganda campaigns against foreign enemies. It is acceptable to criticize foreign policy in public as mistaken or as tragic, but not to contend that it is illegal and criminal. If atrocities come to the surface, as has occurred in Iraq, high-level efforts are made to contain the damage. It is treated as a public relations problem. At most, low-ranking military officials, the supposed "bad apples" of Abu Ghraib, will be singled out for prosecution, while their leaders will continue to be treated as honorable men and women who, even if responsible, should be granted impunity given their service to the country. President Bush's reelection in 2004 was interpreted by many observers around the world as an expression of approval by the citizenry of America for the excesses of Abu Ghraib and Guantanamo. Perhaps such a perception is unfair or exaggerated, but it does illuminate the unwillingness of the leadership cadre in this country to regard U.S. foreign policy as subject to the constraints of international law in relation to issues of war and peace. And so long as that unwillingness is unchallenged, the situation will persist, especially given the huge investment in maintaining an American military presence of global scope, with navies on every ocean, with foreign bases in as many as sixty countries, with control of the entire earth from space a strategic priority, and the entire structure sustained by a powerful military-industrial-academic establishment. It never occurs to such elite institutions as the Council on Foreign Relations to question American foreign policy on grounds of international law and morality, but only to argue about the costs of policy or whether a given course of action can be sold to the American public. Such blinders on discourse are signs of pervasive civilizational decadence at the highest levels of society.

This set of circumstances is not new, but it was definitely aggravated by the end of the Cold War and the associated collapse of the Soviet Union. The United States emerged from the long ideological and geopolitical struggle as undeterred, robust economically, dominant militarily, and psychologically confident. The absence of a countervailing power might have prompted the U.S. government to urge disarmament and other moves to strengthen global governance under the auspices of regional organizations and the United Nations. But instead American leadership mainly promoted an expansive economistic mood in the 1990s that focused on spreading the neoliberal gospel to all corners of the earth as "the only game in town." Behind the emphasis on trade and investment existed a seductive temptation to administer global security from a Washington headquarters. This project was launched somewhat diffidently during the 1990s, lacking sufficient military vigor to satisfy neoconservative zealots. With the election of George W. Bush and 9/11, the climate suddenly became supportive of this global dominance project, rather explicitly set forth in the authoritative document *National Security Strategy of the United States of America,* issued by the White House in 2002, updated in 2006. This document makes clear that international law and the United Nations were only useful to the extent that they could be used to promote these grand strategy objectives. This essentially means that international law and the United Nations are not allowed to limit American discretion, but are to be used to stigmatize enemies and to lend normative weight to whatever the United States undertakes.

This situation of unresponsiveness to law is not likely to change rapidly. Even if the occupation of Iraq is brought to an end and war with Iran is averted, there is no basis for confidence that future leaders of the United States will conceive of American power as constrained by international law and respect for the United Nations. But without such constraints and respect, the United States government is unlikely to rethink its militarist approach to world order, which is likely in the future as in the past to induce extremely wasteful and self-destructive foreign policy initiatives. Such a pessimistic understanding, if correct, means more illegal warfare in the future, as well as a continuation of an overinvestment in the military phases of security and a potentially catastrophic underinvestment in the urgent imperatives of human security (including climate change, alternative energy, disease control). If change is to come about, it will require the cracking of the elite culture, including its bureaucratic hold on what Peter Dale Scott calls "the deep politics" of the state. It will involve struggle and political education. It will depend on the example and awakening impact of many brave individuals like Lt. Ehren Watada. It may require courts in other countries to call American policies into account under the rubric of universal jurisdiction — namely, that Crimes Against Peace and Crimes Against Humanity are indictable and punishable wherever and whenever they occur. As with many struggles against dysfunctional practices and outlooks, the prospects do not now look favorable, but history has a cunning that eludes human comprehension. No one expected the abolition of slavery, the overthrow of colonialism, the end of Soviet oppression, the overcoming of South Africa's racist regime, when such movements were launched by lonely individuals who most often were ignored or punished until their sun rose and suddenly their roles were appreciated, then celebrated. Nelson Mandela embodies that path that led from prolonged imprisonment to the pinnacles of political eminence and public moral authority. The way forward may seem blocked today, but it is not an option to be discouraged.

The quality of world order at this stage of history is largely determined by the effectiveness of the rule of law with respect to the most powerful political actors. As there can be no enforcement against these actors, the effectiveness of law depends on patterns of voluntary adherence, especially by dominant sovereign states. As matters now stand, the positive law is itself deformed by the extent that it incorporates exemptions and exhibits practice tainted by double standards. The basic criterion of legality for any political order is the equal treatment of equals. The UN Charter, and even more, the primacy of geopolitics in controlling UN practice, by the veto power given to the permanent members of the Security Council and by its unwillingness and inability to move against major states, summarizes the current weakness of the rule of law. Nothing better exemplifies this anachronistic geopolitical logic than the so-called "war on terror." Similarly, the selective implementation of the Non-Proliferation Treaty regime, allowing some countries to retain nuclear weapons while others are precluded, is a tribute to inequality, accentuated by the degree to which the nuclear weapons states ignore their obligation to seek nuclear disarmament in good faith and defy an Advisory Opinion of the International Court of Justice that unanimously endorses such a legal duty. The Iraq War and the coercive diplomacy being used against Iran express the continuing erosion of world order reflecting the priorities of a lawless geopolitics. As this book argues, such lawlessness has become dysfunctional, imperiling even the civilizational and survival prospects of the human species. Recognizing this dysfunction and making suitable adjustments are, as yet, an unacknowledged challenge that makes the deepening crisis of global governance seem impossible to resolve.

This is a time when realism and idealism are increasingly fused in their call for a future world order based on law and justice, but this cannot be made to happen without the engagement of the peoples of the earth acting as detribalized citizens without borders. In a globalizing world, experiencing acute ecological stress, no political actor, including those individuals who act on its behalf, should be above the law. We who are citizens of the United States have a special responsibility to make our leaders accountable to international law and the authority of the United Nations for our own sake and for the sake of others around the world currently victimized by American lawlessness.

1

International Law
Power, Justice, and Stability

The thesis of this book is simple: there exist rising costs associated with the disregard of international law and the authority of the United Nations. These rising costs diminish the quality of world order from the perspective of stability and sustainability, and to the extent incurred by a global leader diminish respect for and deference to its leadership.

The history of international law has been decidedly mixed. It has functioned for several centuries mainly as a sword for the strong, but occasionally, and increasingly, as a shield for the weak. It has developed over the course of modern times, stretching back to the Peace of Westphalia in 1648, as a regulatory, cooperative, and aspirational framework for the interplay of sovereign states.

Throughout this history the juridical logic of equality among sovereign states that is at the core of international law has been consistently subordinated to the geopolitical framework of world politics based on the logic of relative power. The same ratio of law to power pertains today. This means that the quality of world order is very dependent on the prudence, wisdom, and legitimacy of the global leadership provided at a given time and in various settings by the main geopolitical actors.

During the early stages of the Cold War this leadership was provided mainly by the United States, with the Soviet Union in a defensive and reactive pattern. Under this leadership the United Nations was established, the Nuremberg/Tokyo war crimes trials were held, and the Genocide Convention and the Universal Declaration of Human Right (UDHR) were adopted. Each was a major *geopolitical* acknowledgement of the importance of strengthening the hitherto feeble role of the normative side (that is, law plus morality) of international relations. This strengthening related to three major world-order deficiencies that had been disclosed by the great devastation of the two world wars, and the human suffering associated with oppressive regimes: establishing authoritatively the unlawfulness of war and international uses of force except in self-defense narrowly defined (Articles 2(4) and 51); holding political leaders accountable for crimes of state (Nuremberg and Tokyo Judgments, as supplemented by the Genocide Convention); and challenging a central tenet of the Westphalian ethos that views whatever takes places *within* the territory of a state as a matter of sovereign right and not subject to external review. Such initiatives were tentative and provisional steps with little indications of an intention to implement, but looking toward wide horizons of possibility, which have remained despite many disappointments. These initiatives were from the outset somewhat hypocritically endorsed, and were subject to major qualifications and regressive moves in geopolitics that occurred throughout the Cold War. At the same time such steps gave grounds for hope that future world order might turn out to be an improvement over the past. The essence of this improvement would be a greater effort to reconcile international law with global justice. This hope, while often crushed by persisting geopolitical Machiavellianism, has remained important as an inspiration and source of legitimation for normatively inclined governments and visionary elements of civil society. Even when states have cynically cast aside or defied these normative promises of the Charter, Nuremberg, and the Genocide Convention/UDHR, civil-society actors have done their best, especially in war/peace and human rights situations, to show respect for these higher expectations. The sad truth remains that international law operates in the war/peace domain as an essentially *voluntary* system of constraints for major states, and is selectively, and often selectively and arbitrarily only enforced in relation to weaker states. The nonproliferation regime governing development and possession of nuclear weapons illustrates both sides of this dynamic: exemptions for the powerful; enforcement for the weak.

The United Nations Charter and practice is a major arena within which these tensions were expressed. For instance, the Charter affirms sovereign rights in rather unconditional terms, declaring that the UN shall refrain from intervening in matters "essentially within the domestic jurisdiction of any state" (Article 2[7]), which effectively nullifies any prospect that international human rights will be implemented in relation to abusive governments. Going further, it seems clear that the only reason that the UDHR could have been agreed upon in the first place was the tacit understanding among the main participating governments that it would *not* be enforced. But civil society took more seriously the norms contained in the UDHR, and found ways to convert this instrument from the statist intention to set forth a list of pieties into a viable political project that has had positive impacts on the oppressive practices of some governments. This political project took hold as a result of pressures exerted by an array of transnational human rights organizations founded and funded by civil society, and given historical relevance in the course of a variety of struggles against oppressive rule. Such struggles included those in East Europe and Latin America, as well as the variety of movements to realize the right of self-determination in the many colonized nations of Africa and Asia. This sense of legitimate goals was also at the core of the global anti-apartheid movement. In this sense, states, including geopolitical actors, *rediscovered* human rights as a useful instrument of world order *after* these norms of political behavior had been first taken seriously at the level of civil society.

In a sense, the same dynamic is manifest with respect to the legacy of the Nuremberg/Tokyo tradition. This tradition suffered from the taint of victors' justice, which had exempted from legal scrutiny such wartime atrocities of the winning side as the indiscriminate bombing of German and Japanese cities, and the initiation of the nuclear age with the atomic bombs dropped on Hiroshima and Nagasaki. At Nuremberg it was declared that the standards used to judge the defeated Germans would only be vindicated in the future if those who sat in judgment accepted accountability by reference to the same legal constraints on the behavior of sovereign states. This "Nuremberg Promise" was repeatedly broken by the subsequent official crimes of the World War II victors. But the promise was not entirely forgotten by representatives of civil society. In the course of the Vietnam War, in the United States antiwar Americans committed many acts based on their reading of Nuremberg that sought to implement over the heads of the geopoliticians norms of limitation associated with the prohibition of aggressive war and the obligations of international humanitarian law with respect to the conduct of war. The impact of these acts of civil resistance are hard to assess, but it would seem at the very least that they contributed to the delegitimation of the Algerian War and the Vietnam War, and, when coupled with battlefield failures, led to the eventual repudiation of these wars even by policymaking elites.

The Bertrand Russell War Crimes Tribunal, set up in 1967 on the basis of civil-society concerns about the criminality of the Vietnam War, had a similar effect, engaging the participation of the leading European intellectuals of the day (Jean-Paul Sartre, Simone de Beauvoir) and later inspiring the formation of the Permanent Peoples Tribunal in Rome, which has for more than twenty years relied upon the progressive elements in international law to assess the injustices, wrongdoing, and crimes of leading geopolitical actors that are met with silence by the state system and even by the United Nations.

The Charter itself embodied the contradictory impulses of international law and geopolitics. On one side, principles of nonintervention, self-determination, equality of states are affirmed, as well as the prohibition of all nondefensive uses of force to resolve international disputes. On the other side, no legal obligation to disarm or to submit disputes to the International Court of Justice is imposed. The five permanent members of the Security Council (picked from the winners of World War II, plus China) were given a veto power, which in effect exempted them from the duty to respect the UN Charter. Such deference to political realism is an explicit acknowledgement that international legal authority cannot yet be imposed upon leading political actors. In practice this exemption, combined with the geopolitical stalemate in the Cold War and the refusal of either superpower to go forward with the Chapter VII (Articles 39–49) arrangements designed to establish procedures and capabilities enabling collective security in the face of aggression, doomed the effort to end recourse to discretionary war by geopolitical actors and their friends. Again, to the extent that this normative expectation has been kept alive, it has been a result of the action of world citizens and peace movements that base their demonstrations and other initiatives on an unconditional acceptance of the outlawry of aggressive war for all states, big and small alike.

What is evident, then, over the course of the last century is a difficult, largely unsuccessful, struggle to curtail the primacy of geopolitics and territorial sovereignty as the pillars of world order. This struggle has had ebbs and flows. Its positive results often depend on some sort of convergence between the demands of civil society and either the moderation or weakness of geopolitical forces. Its negative experiences usually reflect the impact of extremist geopolitical orientations and related militarist orientations toward the fulfillment of geopolitical world-order goals. This pattern has been given great prominence in the period since the end of the Cold War. The next section examines the optimistic mood of the 1990s associated with the first normative "revolution" in world politics that raised hopes as the millennium approached despite some discouraging developments during the same period. The third section focuses on the return to regressive geopolitics as a consequence of the American approach to the pursuit of grand strategy goals in the aftermath of the 9/11 attacks. A final section discusses prospects as of the early twenty-first century for reviving the normative revolution, taking some account of three impinging trends: the growing dysfunction of war and militarism as a geopolitical instrument; the tightening energy/ecological squeeze that will require a complex and dangerous transition to a postpetroleum world economy during the decades ahead; and the growing need for a more institutionalized and democratized form of global governance to cope effectively and fairly with the growing interdependence and fragility of the world.

NOTES ON THE NORMATIVE REVOLUTION OF THE 1990s

The period immediately following the Cold War seemed to present strong opportunities for global reform, giving the West lots of political space in which to take initiatives to make the world safer and more equitable. It was a moment of liberal-capitalist global ascendancy in the aftermath of the Soviet collapse, with a virtually worldwide acceptance of only those forms of political governance based on a combination of a strong market economy and constitutional democracy. Additionally, the decolonization process had been virtually completed, with only South Africa and Palestine remaining important remnants of the colonial era at the start of the 1990s. The United States emerged as the undisputed global leader, claiming for itself a special role in the Clinton years as the "indispensable nation" (according to its secretary of state, Madeleine Albright), given the geopolitical background of unipolarity. In such a favorable context, the United States might have encouraged several promising world-order initiatives, either on its own or in concert with other leading governments: serious nuclear disarmament and negotiated demilitarization (e.g., a worldwide 1 percent of GNP ceiling on military expenditures for national security); a permanent UN peace force funded by an independent revenue base; limitations on the use of the veto in the UN Security Council and mandatory reference of contested policy issues before the UN to ICJ for quick resolution according to international law; and serious and balanced diplomatic efforts to promote a fair settlement of the Israel/Palestine conflict.

Unfortunately, rather than taking advantage of the favorable atmosphere to lay the foundation for global governance, the geopolitical energies of major states were mainly devoted to global economic growth along neoliberal lines, producing both a prevailing sense that "globalization" was the basis of a "new world order" and an antiglobalization backlash by those social forces around the world that believed that they were being victimized by this latest phase of predatory world capitalism. The intergovernmental basis for reformist action lacked any forward energy. The prior image of a "new world order" as explicitly proclaimed in 1990 by the first George Bush consisted of an opportunistic packaging of recourse to a specific war against Iraq. Bush referred to a new world order to help mobilize support for a coalition formed under a UN mandate to push Iraq out of Kuwait. This call was never meant to be anything more than a temporary effort within the United States and the world to validate a somewhat dubious war that was intended to be controlled from Washington but backed by the United Nations. In this sense, rather than the *new* world order, it was a dramatic reminder of the resilience of the *old* world order with the geopolitical ventriloquist making an effective use of the UN as compliant puppet.

Despite this disappointing failure to take advantage of the global setting to introduce needed changes for the sake of global governance, the 1990s did produce some notable developments that were based on the potentially constructive contributions of international law to global justice and *humane* global governance. In all instances — and this is a dramatic expression of the rise of nonstate, civil-society actors — these developments reflected the rise and creative influence of global civil society as a political force acting either autonomously or in collaboration with those state actors that wanted to restrict sovereign rights and geopolitical discretion. These two elements of Westphalian world order were historically the two main *international* sources of human wrongs and war making. International law played a central role in giving substance to these undertakings and confidence to activists. Several of these initiatives can be mentioned to show the continuity that existed with the earlier global reformist surge evident after 1945: to restrict war making, to hold leaders criminally accountable for violations of fundamental rules about the use of force and with respect to the treatment of persons under sovereign control, and to move toward the *international* protection of the fundamental human rights of vulnerable peoples subject to severe abuse from territorial governments or other causes internal to the state. Despite the forward movement in each domain, there were also major setbacks and contradictory tendencies, but overall the result was a widespread appreciation that these efforts led by transnational activists to globalize liberal legality were improving the quality of world order.

Several significant legal developments involved moves to restrict certain tactics in relation to warfare over the opposition of geopolitical actors. Two illustrations can be given: "A new internationalism" involving a coalition joining large numbers of transnational civil-society actors to moderate governments around the world. This blending of Westphalian and post-Westphalian political actors managed to produce a treaty that was rapidly negotiated and widely supported by most governments to ban the use of antipersonnel landmines. Such a move was impressive symbolically, as it suggested a certain new political space for rapid global reforms even in the face of American opposition. At the same time, the success was somewhat misleading. It is likely of only marginal relevance to modern warfare, as the dependence on antipersonnel landmines was only a matter of cost efficiency and effective military substitutes exist to achieve similar battlefield results.

More challenging was an initiative of the General Assembly, responsive to well-orchestrated civil-society pressures in the early 1990s to refer to the World Court the question of the legality of nuclear weapons. Once again, with greater resolve than in relation to landmines, the United States government used its political leverage to oppose this initiative, and again failed. This failure was reinforced when the World Court in 1996 issued its legal opinion, which cast grave doubt on the legality of almost every contemplated use of nuclear weapons, and which challenged strategic thinking in the nuclear weapons states from the perspective of international law. The World Court also unanimously reminded nuclear weapons states of their solemn obligation under Article VI of the Nonproliferation Treaty to pursue in good faith nuclear disarmament. This set of World Court directives, while completely ignored by the nuclear weapons states, did contribute to the general climate of illegitimacy, even criminality, associated with any future threat or use of nuclear weapons. In this respect, the gap between an objective reading of international law requirements and the attitude of nuclear weapons states encourages two quite divergent lines of interpretation: on one side, the inability of international law to overcome the priorities of geopolitical actors with respect to the most urgent of war/peace issues; and on the other side, the importance of future collaborations between non–nuclear weapons states and antinuclear civil-society forces in seeking the implementation of international legal standards with respect to these weapons of mass destruction. If the Preamble of the UN Charter "to save succeeding generations from the scourge of war" is ever going to be taken seriously as a challenge to entrenched militarism, this new internationalism will have to become more robust in both its political will and tactics.

Perhaps of more immediate substantive impact was the unexpected revival of the Nuremberg tradition of accountability of leaders. The victims of the Pinochet regime in Chile had been particularly active around the world for many years, seeking some kind of justice in response to their experience of abuse, but few held out much hope that anything would happen. Then in 1998 Pinochet was dramatically detained in Britain because of a request for extradition that came from Spain, where a controversial and daring prosecutor was ready to prosecute the former Chilean dictator for torture and other international crimes. The extended litigation in British courts that followed gained media notoriety, focusing world attention for the first time on this issue of international criminal accountability of heads of sovereign states. Although Pinochet was eventually allowed to escape prosecution in Spain and returned to Chile, because he was deemed by the British government medically unfit to stand trial, a strong follow-up process was encouraged. All at once great enthusiasm was generated throughout most of the world for moving quickly to establish a permanent international criminal court, as well as to extend the authority of domestic courts throughout the world to enforce international criminal law, exercising authority on the basis of what is called by international lawyers "universal jurisdiction." Again, a global coalition of civil-society actors and moderate, reform-minded governments was effective in generating a process that produced an innovative international treaty. To the amazement of many skeptical observers of world politics, the Rome Treaty establishing the International Criminal Court (ICC) received the required sixty ratifications by governments to enter into force in 2002. Whether such an institution established to administer legal accountability is able to operate effectively in the face of intense current American opposition remains to be seen. This opposition has taken various forms beyond the unwillingness to become a party subject to the jurisdiction of the ICC. Among the most obstructive of these tactics has been for the U.S. government to negotiate a large number of bilateral agreements with governments to exempt its citizens from ever being turned over for prosecution. It requires only a touch of irony to appreciate that it is American policymakers and commanders that currently would stand in the great jeopardy of indictment and prosecution if an international criminal procedure of the sort foreshadowed at Nuremberg were allowed to go forward in the early twenty-first century and have the capacity to extend its reach to those who acted on behalf of *all* states, and not just as at present, the leadership of weak or defeated states. As its strong support for the criminal trials of Slobodan Milosevic and Saddam Hussein demonstrates, the U.S. government is not opposed *on principle* to the Nuremberg legacy if narrowly confined to American adversaries. Its opposition is directed at the extension of criminal jurisdiction relating to crimes of state to the activities of dominant geopolitical actors and their friends.

A third kind of initiative during the 1990s was associated with "humanitarian intervention" in circumstances where a vulnerable population faced catastrophe. The first major attempt to move in this direction involved the breakup of the former Yugoslavia, with some earlier halfhearted and pathetically ineffectual efforts under UN auspices to avoid ethnic cleansing in Bosnia in the early 1990s. A second early humanitarian effort involved Somalia, where the UN was tasked with alleviating a massive humanitarian crisis brought about by governmental collapse, and a subsequent international undertaking in the setting of what was being described as "a failed state." The initial role of the UN operation in Somalia was restricted to providing emergency food and medical assistance, and the mission enjoyed success, including a welcome from the Somali people. However, when this clearly humanitarian mission was followed in 1993 by a more ambitious UN peacekeeping undertaking, led by the United States, to reconstitute governmental authority in the country, troubles ensued. The UN formal presence was viewed as a fig leaf for American geopolitical ambitions and designs, giving rise to armed resistance by Somali political leaders whose power base was threatened. American casualties resulted, and the operation was rather abruptly ended by a decision made in Washington. International forces were irresponsibly withdrawn despite the persistence of chaotic conditions in Somalia. The United States, in particular, was eager to avoid any deeper involvement in factional struggles that were ripping the country apart and making the goal of restoring stable governance seem unattainable at an acceptable cost. The difficulties encountered in Somalia that led to failure there later contributed to an American-led unwillingness to allow protective action by the UN to go forward despite clear evidence of a slide toward genocide in Rwanda during 1994, and the probable capacity to have saved many hundreds of thousands of lives with a relatively small expansion of the UN presence in the country. This show of global apathy under such conditions was also widely condemned as failure. It was followed shortly by the ignominy of UN peacekeepers standing by while Muslim males in Bosnia were slaughtered in the thousands in the supposed UN safe haven of Srebrenica in 1995. These three developments discredited the United Nations in settings of humanitarian crisis.

Humanitarian concerns converged with some geopolitical priorities a few years later, generating political backing for humanitarian intervention in Kosovo under NATO command in 1999. In effect, substituting NATO for the UN raised the stakes of involvement, making it more difficult for Washington to accept failure as an outcome. The United States was, at best, ambivalent about experiences that diminished confidence in UN capabilities, but it was deeply concerned about sustaining the reputation of NATO as a valuable strategic instrument despite the ending of the Cold War and the collapse of the Soviet Union. The Kosovo initiative, although criticized at the time for bypassing the UNSC and thus weakening the UN and defying international law, was politically supported by most European governments and welcomed by the overwhelming majority of the Kosovar population as an alternative to oppressive Serbian rule and a credible menace of ethnic cleansing. The intervention did successfully avert what appeared to be a new cycle of ethnic cleansing in the region, as well as give the Kosovar struggle for self-determination a major push forward. The effectiveness of this response, as compared to the Somalia and Rwanda failures, certainly reflected a major geopolitical commitment to the use of sufficient force to succeed in Kosovo, and thereby demonstrate the persisting role of NATO in establishing European security and showcasing the continuing seriousness of American involvement in European affairs. Part of the message was to remind Europeans that only collective military force under American leadership can achieve desired political results at acceptable costs. In other words, the geopolitical stakes associated with the post–Cold War credibility of NATO combined with a display of a continuing American commitment to European issues to ensure that humanitarian concerns would not be shortchanged if difficulties emerged. And indeed difficulties did emerge, as the bombing campaign did not lead Belgrade to accept NATO demands for Serbian withdrawal from Kosovo nearly as quickly as had been expected.

Some serious criticisms of the NATO approach were also made: it encroached upon the proper UN role with respect to global peace and security, as well as violated the sovereign rights of a member state; the aerial bombardment from high altitudes by NATO aircraft shifted the main costs of the war from the intervening military forces to the civilian population of Serbia and Kosovo; inadequate steps were taken in the immediate postconflict setting by NATO or the UN postwar reconstruction administration to protect Serbs from Albanian acts of revenge; and insufficient resources were devoted to restoring Kosovo to social and economic normalcy. The Kosovo War remains a normatively ambiguous experience in which the role of global civil society was marginal, partly because civic attitudes were not in agreement about whether or not the intervention as carried out was justified, differing especially on whether the geopolitical stakes overshadowed the humanitarian challenge. Prominent critics such as Noam Chomsky and Edward Said derided the Kosovo War as a dangerous expression of what Chomsky called "military humanism."

The Kosovo precedent is also ambiguous with respect to international law. It definitely seemed to authorize an evasion of the supposedly total authority of the UNSC over nondefensive uses of force, setting an unfortunate precedent that looks even worse in retrospect, particularly in light of some reliance on it by advocates of the invasion of Iraq. But there were also favorable results vindicating those who believed it was possible to rescue an endangered population at an acceptable cost. The NATO bombing campaign, despite the flaws that have been mentioned, did rescue a vulnerable population from what definitely seemed to be imminent catastrophe. The massive immediate return of most Kosovars from Macedonian refugee camps was an impressive demonstration of fear prior to the intervention and confidence after Serb control was superseded by joint NATO/UN administration and de facto independence. The interpretation of these developments is contested. Critics of the war argue that the threat of ethnic cleansing was manipulated, if not contrived, by violent Albanian Kosovar forces (the Kosovo Liberation Army or KLA) acting to provoke an anti-Serb intervention, and that the outflow of refugees from Kosovo was not caused by the Serbs, but by the prospect of NATO bombing.

It is doubtful that such issues will ever be resolved in a manner overcoming the continuing debate. Nevertheless, the NATO Kosovo War definitely illustrated the degree to which a convergence of perceived normative and geopolitical priorities has the capacity to produce effective action. By such reasoning there also emerges what might be called "the lesson of Kosovo," that such a convergence is a necessary foundation to achieve a successful humanitarian intervention. Moral imperatives and legal authorization are not sufficient, unless reinforced by relevant strategic interests. If strategic interests are present, as in relation to Kosovo, then it may be possible to legitimate a use of international force even absent a proper legal authorization, although this absence clouds the precedent.

The 1990s gave rise to additional efforts to improve the quality of world order. The decade saw an unprecedented number of moves to redress historic wrongs either by apologies, commissions of truth and reconciliation, and the tender of reparations and compensation. Long-suppressed issues involving the victims of Japanese and German abuses during World War II (slave labor, comfort women, confiscated assets) or the dispossession of indigenous peoples in various settings around the world suddenly received meaningful official attention. There was a definite trend designed to bring international law into closer conformity with the requirements of global justice, as well as to set limits on the sovereign rights of states to act within their own territories. At the same time, these moves toward normative revolution were generally of a preliminary and largely symbolic character, and as subsequent developments have made clear, quite reversible due to a series of adverse geopolitical developments, especially associated with the American response to September 11. The developments in the 1990s, although notable, did not challenge the persistent centrality of geopolitical actors in the shaping of world order. This top-down pattern of world politics is inconsistent with aspirations to achieve a bottom-up, more democratic world order, but it is not necessarily malevolent. It depends on the orientation and behavior of the dominant geopolitical actors. It is instructive to compare the relatively constructive role of the United States in the period immediately following World War II with its behavior after the September 11 attacks. One can illustrate this comparison by pointing out the degree of congruence between global reform and the strengthening of international law and institutions in 1945, and the hostility toward these same goals since 2001. This latter pattern is addressed in the next section.

AMERICAN LAWLESSNESS IN THE TWENTY-FIRST CENTURY

The U.S. government has long adopted double standards when it comes to respecting international law, especially in the setting of national security issues. It promotes a generalized respect for the rule of law in world politics, is outraged by violations of international law by its adversaries, and chooses selectively when to comply and when to violate, especially with respect to the use of international force. This pattern can be traced far back in American history, but it is convenient to take note of American violations of international law in the setting of the Vietnam War, as well as periodic and frequent interventions in Central and South America. I would argue that this pattern has diminished the United States' global reputation and capacity for leadership, as well as worked against its own national interests, particularly in recent decades.

It seems clear that the United States, and the American people, would have benefited over the years from a foreign policy carried out in accordance with international law. If the U.S. government had abided by international law, the dreadful experience of the Vietnam War would never have occurred. More recently (this observation will be discussed further below), upholding international law would have avoided the fiasco of the Iraq War. Contrary to popular belief, respecting the restraints of international law better serves the national interest of a powerful country at this stage of history far more than does a sovereignty-first attitude, so prevalent in neoconservative circles that has largely shaped American foreign policy since 9/11. This more nihilistic conception treats international law in the context of security geopolitics as mainly inconvenient, unnecessary, unwise, and completely discretionary (except so far as its adversaries are concerned). From neoconservative perspectives, national and global security for the United States depends on the discretion and willingness to use international force to promote "values" as well as to defend "interests," thereby downplaying the relevance of prudence. It is this enlargement of the discretion claimed by realists that makes so extreme the neoconservative approach characteristic of the Bush presidency.

It is important to understand that the restraints embodied in international law have been voluntarily developed on the basis of international experience and changing attitudes toward war by diplomatic representatives of sovereign states acting to uphold the realist interests and professed values of their governments.

The substance of international law, particularly with respect to recourse to and the conduct of war, has been overwhelmingly shaped by practical considerations, and has generally resisted aspirational or idealistic pressures for legal standards that go beyond what governments can be expected to abide under pressure. The core principles of international law encode the wisdom of diplomacy accumulated over the course of the last several centuries, including the terrible experiences of destructive warfare during the last century. International law is of particular importance in relation to uses of force as an instrument of foreign policy, and more generally, as it bears upon issues relating to security, especially war and peace. The U.S. Constitution declares in Article VI(2) that "duly ratified treaties are the supreme law of the land." This formally puts the key rules and principles of international law on a par with Congressional acts within the American legal system. The Supreme Court has ruled that in the event of an unavoidable clash between these two sources of legal authority, the last in time should prevail, but that to the extent possible both forms of legal authority should be reconciled by way of interpretation.

The basic argument in favor of a foreign policy that is respectful of the constraints of international law deserves to be expressed vigorously: in a globalizing world of great complexity, it is overwhelmingly in the interest of all states, large and small, that their relations be reliably and peacefully regulated by international law. Such a generalization takes on added weight when the potential destructive impacts of weapons of mass destruction, especially nuclear weapons, are taken into account. This observation has long been acceptable as applicable to most of the daily operations of the world economy and many other types of international behavior, including maritime safety, environmental protection, tourism, immigration, disease control, and criminal law enforcement. The stability of international life depends on a closely woven fabric of law as providing a needed foundation of reliability for almost all recurrent activity that partly or wholly takes place outside and across the borders of a sovereign state.

What is a cause for deepest current worry is that the United States government, along with supportive academic authors, has seemed determined to repudiate this elementary understanding of the relevance of law to the establishment of world order. As suggested, this regressive attitude toward international law is not entirely new, although it has not in the past been as boldly theorized. Deviations from the restraints of international law run like a great river throughout the entire course of American history, but it has taken a deeply ideological turn for the worse during the Bush presidency, especially in the aftermath of the September 11 attacks. Even prior to the attacks, the foreign policy of the Bush administration made it a point of pride to disclose its disdain for widely respected international treaties, seemingly as an expression of its recognition of a new freedom from the constraints of legality given the realities of a unipolar world. The Bush White House contended that existing and pending treaties limited its military and political options in undesirable ways. In the early months of the Bush presidency the White House announced its opposition to the Comprehensive Test Ban Treaty prohibiting nuclear weapons testing, its withdrawal from ABM Treaty design to avoid an arms race in space, its unwillingness to submit for Senate ratification the Kyoto Protocol regulating greenhouse-gas emissions, and its defiant and gratuitous withdrawal of the American signature (in the final days of the Clinton presidency) from the Rome Treaty establishing the International Criminal Court. Such a pattern of unilateralist and undisguised hostility to international treaties and multilateral cooperation was unprecedented in American history. Normally friendly governments were clearly disturbed by this strident display of unilateralism and international nihilism by the new American president in the early months of 2001. This American repudiation of widely endorsed multilateral treaty arrangements also upset large segments of world public opinion. These treaty arrangements dealing with important matters of global policy had generally been regarded as important contributions to a peaceful world, making their repudiation seem contrary to common sense, as well as dangerous for the overall well being of the peoples of the world. These expressions of unilateralism by the United States to global policy issues did not involve violating existing international law. What was exhibited was a diplomacy based on an outmoded and neoconservative opposition to almost any form of multilateral undertaking in the security area other than by way of alliance relationships such as NATO or the aggressive partnership with Israel. This unilateralism limited the American capacity to make constructive use of its status as global leader in the aftermath of the Cold War. It also places an excessive reliance on military approaches to problem solving and encourages immensely wasteful expenditures on overinvestment in unusable military hardware. In effect, the overall pattern of neoconservative advocacy weakens, rather than strengthens, the capacity of the American government to achieve sustainable security at home or abroad.

Not all blame should be laid at the feet of a neoconservative presidency. The U.S. Congress, and the American public, also bear a heavy responsibility. It was in Congress, even before George W. Bush came to Washington in 2001, that militarist pressures were brought to bear in such a way as to oppose beneficial multilateral treaty constraints on United States policy. The Senate refused to ratify the Comprehensive Test Ban Treaty in the Clinton years, and it was so strongly opposed to the International Criminal Court and Kyoto Protocol that there was no prospect for such treaties to be approved by the required two-thirds vote if they had been submitted to the Senate for ratification. The Bush approach to international law was mainly distinguished by two further developments: its alignment of the executive branch with an anti-internationalist set of policies; and its avowedly ideological and emphatic repudiation of treaty instruments in order to signal a unilateralist approach to foreign policy that relied more overtly upon military dominance and interventionary diplomacy. It was this aggressive geopolitical posture by the Bush leadership that frightened world public opinion. Before September 11 a rising crescendo of domestic and international opposition to the Bush policies led to mounting criticism of this approach to world affairs, which hardened the perception that Bush's credentials as president were already unusually weak given his contested electoral mandate and lack of prior foreign policy experience. Many observers who scrutinized the results in 2000 believed that a fair count of the votes in Florida would have resulted in Bush's defeat and victory for Al Gore, with some similar, although less-substantiated doubts clouding the outcome of the 2004 Republican victory over the weak Democratic Party challenger, John Kerry.

This concern and opposition has dramatically intensified outside the United States since September 11, because the Bush White House has moved from these earlier expressions of hostility to multilateralism to a posture of pronounced unwillingness to abide by fundamental international legal rules and standards that this country, along with other constitutional democracies, had previously accepted and applied as a matter of course. These rules include humane treatment of prisoners taken during armed combat, unconditional prohibitions on torture and assassination of political opponents, and the duty to protect civilians in any foreign territory under occupation. The most important of all these legal restrictions on foreign policy is the rule of international law prohibiting nondefensive uses of force without a mandate from the UN Security Council. In his 2004 State of the Union Address President Bush told the Congress that the United States would never seek "a permission slip" in matters bearing on its security. But it is precisely a permission slip that international law, and the UN Charter, requires if force is used outside the scope of self-defense *against a prior armed attack*. This strict limitation on recourse to war was written into the Charter largely at the behest of the U.S. government after World War II. The basic hope back then was to bind the states of the world to a legal framework that unconditionally prohibited wars of aggression, or what have more brashly been recently called "wars of choice" to remove the opprobrium implicit in the word "aggession." German and Japanese leaders were sentenced to death at war crimes tribunals in 1945 because they were adjudged to have initiated and conducted aggressive wars, a precedent not entirely lost on the peoples of the world, especially as revived in a number of settings, but especially in relation to the crimes of states associated with the breakup of the former Yugoslavia.

The Iraq War is a notorious example of an aggressive war (or war of choice) that violates this fundamental rule of international law set forth authoritatively in Article 2(4) of the United Nations Charter. As such, according to the Nuremberg Principles embodied in general international law after the conviction of

German leaders for their criminal conduct, the invasion of Iraq in 2003 constitutes a crime against peace. The American prosecutor at Nuremberg, Justice Robert Jackson, famously said to the tribunal, " . . . let me make clear that while this law is first applied against German aggressors, the law includes, and if it is to serve a useful purpose it must condemn, aggression by other nations, including those which sit here now in judgment." It is this Nuremberg Promise that has been repeatedly and defiantly broken by the United States and Israel, thereby undermining any prospect for peace and normalcy in the world.

The pattern of illegality associated with the Iraq War, and subsequent occupation, continues to shock the conscience of humanity. American officials have strained to redefine "torture" so as to authorize its personnel to engage in interrogation practices that the rest of the world, and common sense, understand to be "torture." The abuse of prisoners detained in Guantánamo, Abu Ghraib, and elsewhere has severely damaged the United States' reputation in the world, as well as discredited a genuine and necessary struggle against extremist enemies engaged in terrorism. Government lawyers and their neoconservative supporters in society have argued in favor of assassinating terrorist suspects in foreign countries, and have justified under the terminology of "extraordinary rendition" deliberately handing over suspects to foreign governments notorious for reliance on torture as their normal mode of prisoner interrogation. The detrimental impact of American lawlessness on the protection of human rights worldwide and within the United States has been set forth in great detail by such respected civil-society organizations as the American Civil Liberties Union, Amnesty International, and Human Rights Watch. This record of American abuse has badly undercut the credibility of any U.S. government pressure on other governments to protect human rights, making it easy to dismiss such pressure as suspect and hypocritical. A quality of incoherence is associated with neoconservative public diplomacy that adopts a highly moralizing tone in emphasizing commitments to liberty and democracy while adopting policies that are so repellently incompatible with upholding human rights or abiding by international humanitarian law.

The events of September 11 produced a patriotic surge within the United States that gave the Bush administration the political space it needed to embark on an assertive foreign policy aimed at "geopolitical preeminence," which, despite protestation to the contrary, was only incidentally concerned with the defeat of Al Qaeda and the containment of transnational terrorism. This ambitious and disguised foreign policy agenda of the neoconservatives was clearly set forth before September 11 in the report of the Project for a New American Century published in September 2000, and prepared in the two prior years, under the title of "Repairing America's Defenses," and endorsed by many individuals who later became leading advisers to the Bush presidency. This wider grand strategy was explicitly embraced, contextualized to fit within a counter-terrorist agenda, and set forth in detail, subsequent to September 11, in the important White House document entitled "The National Security Strategy of the United States of America" (2002). This latter document has been reaffirmed and updated in a subsequent document released by the White House in 2006 with the same title. In the present atmosphere of intense domestic opposition to the Bush presidency, centering on criticism of its approach to the Iraq War, it is doubtful that the White House would now reaffirm this grandiose worldview.

In other words, violating international law, including embarking on wars of aggression, has been integral to the realization of preexisting American global ambitions that were *politically* nonviable before September 11. To sustain a climate of acquiescence, if not support, within the United States, the leadership in Washington has had to rely on a manipulative politics of fear and anger associated with the September 11 experience that until the public turned against the Iraq War late in 2006 led to a suspension of mainstream criticism by the media, an absence of debate reinforced by the passivity of the opposition Democratic Party and the U.S. Congress. In this crucial respect, the Congress had been failing in its constitutional duties by its unwillingness to exert principled pressure on the executive to uphold the rule of law by demanding compliance with international law. The public outrage associated with the derelictions of governmental duty in the setting of Hurricane Katrina in 2005 seemed temporarily to have finally opened a space for challenging the legitimacy of the present government, but this critical mood quickly vanished, even though the Bush presidency has been steadily losing popular support. We now see some indication that Congress and the public are finally ready to cancel the blank check issued to the Bush presidency in the setting of foreign policy in the feverish atmosphere following September 11. The election of a Democratically controlled Congress in November 2006, followed by the refusal of the Bush administration to alter its basic approach in Iraq, has stiffened the backbone of the opposition, but with what impact remains unclear. Despite all that has happened, it still appears that it is politically viable for the U.S. government, in collaboration with Israel, to embark upon new aggressive warfare in the Middle East, expanding the war zone to encompass Iran and possibly Syria. Whether such an extension of the war would quiet or agitate opposition cannot be foreseen.

This focus on American behavior obscures the larger framework of argument. It has become a requirement of a constitutional democracy in the twenty-first century for a government's foreign policy, as well as its domestic behavior, to be conducted in a manner consistent with the discipline of international law. In a globalizing world the extension of law to international activity almost always serves the national interest of even powerful states. The constraints of international law keep the leaders of democratic states from undertaking dangerous and costly geopolitical ventures that would not be supported by an informed citizenry. The refusal of one state, particularly if it is seen to be a leading state, to abide by international law creates a precedent that gives other states a reciprocal right, as well as political encouragement, to violate their legal obligations.

Finally, adherence to international law in matters of war and peace is in the interest of the peoples of the world. There may be humanitarian emergencies or dangerous threats of attack that might justify recourse to war as the UN Secretary General's report "In Larger Freedom" and as the UN High-Level Panel on Threats, Challenges and Change recommends, but such recourse to war is only legally valid if it is authorized by the Security Council. America and the world will be better off when nondefensive warfare requires in every instance the issuance of "a permission slip." The bad American example should not confuse political leaders around the world. It will be beneficial for the peoples of the world to strengthen the global rule of law, and to encourage a pedagogy of peace and security that emphasizes that respect for international law is an indispensable to achieving a peaceful, equitable, and sustainable world order. Perhaps the perceived disadvantages of lawlessness in this period from the perspective of American self-interest can encourage a global swing by other political actors back toward lawfulness, thereby emulating the broad tendencies toward law-oriented global policies associated with the European Union. It would be helpful if leaders in global civil society would give greater attention to the importance of effective legal regimes to regulate many sectors of international life, and move to reinforce efforts to hold criminally accountable those who are responsible for aggressive warfare and abusive conduct. The world is now far too morally sensitive and politically integrated to ignore or tolerate the commission of Crimes Against Peace or Crimes Against Humanity.

CONCLUDING COMMENTS

International law is likely to remain subordinate to geopolitics for some time to come, and thus the quality of global security is shaped to a considerable extent by the priorities and prudence of the leading political actor at a given historical interval. This overview is not the entire story. International law, especially as embodied in Nuremberg, the UN Charter, and the UDHR, as well as the many recent rulings by the World Court, also offers and encourages resistance to geopolitically driven projects destructive of human values and to particular abuses of sovereign rights, as well as encourages the rethinking of geopolitics so as to incorporate rather than repudiate the constraints of international law.

The emergence of global civil society actors represents a further geopolitical challenge in a number of domains of international life. The World Tribunal on Iraq, organized as a civil society undertaking in 2005, and held in Istanbul, confirmed the unlawfulness of the American and British invasion of Iraq and its subsequent occupation, and implored global institutions to hold those responsible for these policies criminally accountable in the Nuremberg sense. Such a decision by a civil-society tribunal, now spread to all parts of the planet via the Internet, definitely contributes to a climate of illegitimacy surrounding the persistent war policies of the United States and Israel, although the tribunal is unable to implement its "legal" findings in a manner that would directly alter behavior of these political actors.

Several developments suggest an important potential role for law in shaping the future of humanity on a global scale:

- accepting the practical need for agreed patterns of order amid complexity and fragility of many aspects of transnational activity;
- acknowledging the growing evidence that warfare and military expenditures are dysfunctional means by which to pursue political ends associated with national and global security, and that adherence to legal standards and procedures offer promising alternatives with far lower risks and costs;
- meeting the challenge of globally delimited problems such as global warming, polar melting, mass migration, energy and water shortages, decline of ocean fisheries;
- recognizing the success of the European Project in providing a model of post-Westphalian political order on a regional scale that relies on regional law, procedures, and institutions to address conflict and has managed to instill an impressively durable culture of peace among the participants.

While these encouraging signs should be noted, this potential role of international law can only become actual if the United States renounces its role as rogue hegemon. To do so the government needs to change its approach toward these issues, becoming less unilateralist, abandoning the pursuit of global empire, and moving toward an acknowledged appreciation of the benefits *for itself* of a law-oriented foreign policy in which self-discipline accomplishes much of what law enforcement requires. The prospect of an American defeat in Iraq, and the frustration of the main neoconservative plan to export "democracy" to the Middle East by freely elected secular leaders who rush off to Washington to pledge allegiance once in control, may soon open enough space for alternative visions of regional and world order to become relevant. Before such an adjustment occurs, we are likely to experience a downward spiral that will diminish still further respect for the core norms of international law. In the regional crisis that took place in the summer of 2006, Israel, with the backing of the United States, undertook a large-scale border-crossing military action to attack the whole of Lebanon, unconvincingly claiming that this recourse to war was justifiable "self-defense" in view of Hezbollah's prior border provocation. Of course, it was nothing of the sort. The media went along with the confusion. It is correct that a state subject to a military attack of any kind is entitled to make an appropriate response, but unless the attack is of a scale to qualify as "an armed attack" across a border it does not give rise to a right of self-defense by the attacked government, but only a legal option of retaliation in kind, limited and focused. Even if self-defense is claimed, the use of force must be *proportionate* to the provoking attack, which in this case was a border incident with single-digit casualties on the Israeli side. What was further discouraging, although not surprising, was that Turkey immediately invoked what its foreign minister called "Israel's precedent in international law" to frame an argument about a comparable Turkish right to intervene militarily in northern Iraq to deal with an allegedly mounting Kurdish threat to Turkey.

But civil-society actors need not be merely reactive with respect to international law. It would seem quite appropriate to frame a future world order by two different, although complementary, legal directives: (1) the affirmations in Articles 25 and 28 of the Universal Declaration of Human Rights that everyone enjoys "the right to a standard of living" adequate to meet basic human needs and that "everyone is entitled to a social and international order" that realizes all of the specific enumerated human rights in the document. For such strong normative affirmations to be contained in an intergovernmental document is almost too good to be true, and however aspirational in intention, does provide civil-society actors with official criteria by which to legitimate their vision of and struggles to achieve global justice and humane global governance; (2) to articulate and act upon a new globalist ethos of human solidarity that informs a concept of responsible global citizenship, mindful of specific overlapping national and regional identities, but dedicated to the *whole* rather than to its *parts*, whereby "global law" comes to anchor world order rather than Westphalian "international law." In an illuminating respect, the "realist" constraints of international law with respect to recourse to international force can be contrasted with the "idealist," even utopian, norms set forth in the setting of human rights.

2

The Surprising Revival of the Just War Framework

As the modern state system evolved during the centuries before the seminal event of the Peace of Westphalia in 1648, international law gradually displaced just war doctrine in providing guidelines for permissible uses of international force. During this process international law absorbed the basic just war guidelines, building a bridge of continuity between the religious outlook of medieval Europe and the emergent secularism of the modern state system. In this respect, modernity and secularism went hand in hand. Just war thinking, which is rooted in the religious traditions of the West, especially Christianity, is usually grounded in the fifth-century writings of the great Catholic theologian St. Augustine. In contrast, international law has freed itself from direct religious authority in stages. By the nineteenth century, international law was tied to the consent of sovereign states, an expression of statist secularism, and the legacy of the rationalism and scientific ethos associated with the triumph of the Enlightenment in the West.

This legalist approach to war, intervention, and force reached its climax in the period immediately after World War II. The Nuremberg Judgment punished surviving Nazi leaders for Crimes Against Peace, the United Nations Charter made an unconditional prohibition on the use of nondefensive force its core commitment. Nuremberg also punished Crimes of War and Crimes Against Humanity; namely, acute legal violations associated with *conduct* as distinct from *recourse* to force, paralleling the just war distinction between *jus ad bello* and *jus in bello*. International law became an entirely autonomous source of authority with respect to the use of force and the exclusive guideline for statecraft, although theologians and moralists on the sidelines continued to debate appropriate limits on force from a just war perspective. In some versions, just war thinking was more permissive toward the use of force than international law, in others more restrictive.

How, then, can we explain this just war revival in discussions about the use of force during the Cold War, and especially in the period after September 11, 2001? The essential explanation lies in the revolutionary changes in the technology of warfare, the nature of conflict, and the doctrine of territorial sovereignty. These changes burst the bounds of international law and gave rise to the search for ways of thinking about force in international affairs that avoided the extremes of sterile legalism and political nihilism. International law had temporarily seemed to lose much of its legitimacy as an acceptable source of guidance for the leaders of liberal democracies, which were the only states that were somewhat inclined to orient their behavior by reference to these legal constraints. Even here, it is easy to exaggerate. U.S. leaders after World War I, partly under the dual influences of Woodrow Wilson and antiwar public opinion, seemed to endorse a law-oriented approach to issues of war and peace; however, this was severely attacked by such prominent realists as George Kennan and Hans Morgenthau as paving the way to World War II, emboldening aggressor nations while inducing the democracies to fall into a condition of geopolitical slumber. Realism prevailed in the period of the Cold War, but was variously interpreted in specific instances as disclosed by intense debates among realists in relation to whether the Vietnam War served United States national interests. Given these circumstances, it was mainly in civil society that international law became a focus for opposition to "illegal" uses of force. This dynamic reached its peak during the latter years of the Vietnam War.

But then why did the just war tradition reemerge? It reemerged because international law no longer seemed sufficient, and at the very least needed to be reinforced by ethical constraints, as an instrument of persuasion in civil society. Ethics has its deepest roots in the just war tradition in regard to international issues. More specifically, the limits imposed by international law seemed to be unable to accommodate the development of nuclear weapons. The revival of just war thinking can be traced back to Nuremberg. It might also have been appropriate to raise questions about the massive, indiscriminate bombing of German and Japanese cities in World War II. The question was whether a goal of war can justify relying on such apocalyptic weaponry that flagrantly violates the moral and legal imperative to target discriminately so as to avoid direct harm to civilians. International law, caught between its endorsement of wars based on defensive necessity and its vague rejection of excessive and indiscriminate force in deference to the law of war, was helpless to respond. The most important formulation on these issues from the just war tradition was a widely influential 1983 Pastoral Letter by the Catholic Bishops of North America addressing the question of the role of nuclear weaponry in the Cold War context of mutual deterrence.

International law interestingly followed suit in the aftermath of the Cold War, in the form of an Advisory Opinion of the International Court of Justice issued in 1996 as a response to a question put to it by the UN General Assembly as to the legality of nuclear weapons. The whole engagement of international law with this vital issue was brought about by a strong civil society effort that won the support of a group of moderate nonnuclear states, and proceeded to win General Assembly approval over the determined opposition of the United States government. The advisory opinion, although expressive of the views of only a slim majority of the fifteen judges, followed a line of legal reasoning that rather closely resembled the just war thinking of the 1983 Pastoral Letter, although the historical context formed after the collapse of the Soviet Union meant that deterrence was much less of a concern, and the World Court focused its attention on carving out a *possible* narrow domain of potential legality for these weapons if the survival of the state was genuinely at stake. It is worth noting that three judges refused to join in such an interpretation, believing that international law required a conclusion of unconditional illegality. The majority opinion made it clear that a conclusion of legality was not a foregone conclusion even in the special circumstances where a state using nuclear weapons could demonstrate that it was reasonable for its leaders to believe that the survival of the state was at stake.

JUST WAR AND HUMANITARIAN CLAIMS

It was not until the 1990s that the relevance of just war thinking to claims of humanitarian intervention became apparent. Here, the challenges to international law were developments of a normative character, such as legal standards, global ethics, and the changing balance within the United Nations between upholding sovereign rights and protecting peoples victimized by human rights abuses. As widely understood, international law disallowed all nondefensive uses of force by states, including those motivated by humanitarian concerns, unless they were authorized in advance by the UN Security Council or consented to by the territorial government. Furthermore, the United Nations as an organization of states accepted as a basic principle in its Charter a broadly formulated prohibition on intervening in the internal affairs of states for purposes other than international peace and security. The pressure to intervene came from four different directions: the rising prominence given to the implementation of fundamental standards of international human rights, the multidimensional erosion of sovereignty as the basis for ordering the relations between state and society, the media-induced awareness (referred to as "the CNN factor") of humanitarian catastrophes, and most of all, the globalization of political life. Three consecutive UN secretary generals, most vigorously Kofi Annan, issued strong statements supportive of humanitarian intervention in extreme cases where genocide was taking place or credibly imminent. These UN leaders argued that while the sovereignty of states should still be respected and even honored, it was no longer an absolute bar. Increasingly, internationalists insisted that there existed moral and political imperatives to protect vulnerable peoples facing acute threats to their collective existence that, when and where necessary, took precedence over deference to the territorial supremacy of sovereign states.

In practice, the United Nations authorized "interventionary" protection of the Kurds in northern Iraq after the Persian Gulf War of 1991, as well as extensive missions in response to the failed state of Somalia and ethnic cleansing in

Bosnia. Both the United Nations and the United States were sharply criticized for their failure to do more to prevent the 1994 genocide in Rwanda. International law offered little guidance as to what conditions needed to exist to make intervention permissible. To the extent that legal guidelines were followed, they inhibited undertakings that reflected emerging moral and political imperatives associated with human solidarity and a human rights culture. International law had to either be recast, which was a political impossibility given the sensitivity of China and many ex-colonial states to any infringement of sovereign rights, or ignored if humanitarian claims were to be satisfied to any degree. Neither alternative seemed satisfactory.

KOSOVO: LEGALITY VERSUS LEGITIMACY

These issues reached a boiling point with the controversy generated by the 1999 NATO war over Kosovo. The United States, working within a NATO framework, organized a regional response to the mounting evidence of a credible threat of imminent ethnic cleansing by Serbia in Kosovo. The governmental sponsors of the invasion avoided seeking approval from the UN Security Council, foreseeing vetoes by Russia and China. This was a clear case of nondefensive force being used without UN authorization, thus in violation of international law. Yet the intervention was urgently needed in Kosovo to avoid reproducing the human tragedy that had occurred a few years earlier in Bosnia. The dilemma between legality and legitimacy was highlighted by the massacre of several thousand Muslim men at Srebrenica in 1995 while UN peacekeepers looked on as spectators, grotesquely respecting their pledge of impartiality rather than responding to the elementary dictates of humanity to lend necessary protection. Of course, too few peacekeeping soldiers had been assigned to protect the Bosnian safe havens, so at the time of greatest danger nothing effective by way of protection could have been done. But neither before nor after did the major governments take steps to design the UN peacekeeping mission so as to be able to protect endangered civilians.

After the Kosovo War, the Swedish government appointed the Independent International Commission on Kosovo in consultation with the UN secretary general. The commission's goal was to sort out the issues being debated and evaluate the precedent that was created. In its report, it concluded that the intervention was "legitimate, but illegal." It was legitimate because the evidence supported the claim of a humanitarian emergency. The results from the use of force did prudently improve the future prospects of 90 percent or more of the Kosovo population for a peaceful and humane life. It was illegal because there was no way to reconcile such a use of force with international law and the UN Charter. The Commission enumerated a series of guidelines to give support to its sense of legitimacy, including adherence to international humanitarian law governing the conduct of such an operation and reliance on force as a last resort. Although these guidelines were not phrased as such, they can be best understood as a rewriting of just war thinking to fit the beneficial actuality of humanitarian intervention in the contemporary world, while at the same time providing a framework that would restrict the use of force as much as possible. The just war approach is attractive in such situations where the legal framework seems ill-adapted to changing values and conditions. The vagueness of just war criteria that invites criticism in other contexts becomes a strength when the perceived need is for greater flexibility in interpreting the constraints on the use of force.

The Kosovo Commission did recognize that this gap between legality and legitimacy was not desirable, and should be regarded as a temporary stopgap. Some advocates of the intervention had agreed either with Thomas Franck that it was preferable to violate international law accompanied by a principled explanation or with Michael Glennon that the Charter view of international law governing the use of force was obsolete beyond repair, given the existence of strong moral and political pressures in favor of humanitarian intervention and other nondefensive uses of force. Glennon's widely discussed alternative to UN legality was to entrust such interventions to "coalitions of the willing," which would seem to give a green light to the geopolitical powers to use force whenever their converging interests so decreed. As with the legality/legitimacy solution, Glennon also regarded coalitions of the willing as a temporary expedient, awaiting a reformulation of the procedures and norms of international law that better reflects the new realities of the global setting. The Commission rejected such proposed adjustments, arguing instead for legal reform to the extent attainable, especially within the setting of the United Nations. The reforms that the report recommended were either a voluntary or mandatory suspension of the veto in instances of humanitarian emergency, or a UN Security Council or General Assembly directive allowing uses of force to protect human rights in circumstances that involve a humanitarian emergency. As a practical matter, such a closing of the gap is not likely to occur in the near future. There remains a distinct break between those states that favor this sort of limited interventionary option, both within and outside the United Nations, and those that insist on a stricter adherence to the letter of the law as it was written more than a half-century ago, when the sovereignty of states was uncontestable on human rights grounds.

A third closely related attempt to bridge this chasm between beneficial policy and war prevention resulted from the efforts of a second international initiative, the International Commission on Intervention and State Sovereignty. Its report, *The Responsibility to Protect*, made a distinct effort to overcome the harshness of the Kosovo debate by substituting the language of "responsibility" for that of "intervention." In such a shift the locus of decision making becomes the international community rather than the state that is the target for intervention under certain conditions. The international community, then, is declared to have a responsibility to protect vulnerable peoples facing tragedy. Drawing connections between international law and just war thinking, the commission report tried to restrict interventionary uses of force by identifying as narrowly as possible "just causes" for military intervention to two broad instances: "large scale loss of life, actual or apprehended, with genocidal intent or not, which is the product of deliberate state action, or state neglect or inability to act, or a failed state situation; or large scale 'ethnic cleansing,' actual or apprehended, whether carried out by killing, forced expulsion, acts of terror or rape." This responsibility approach leaves much room for subjective interpretation of whether a particular case warrants intervention or not, but does vest authorizations for any use of force in the Security Council. Some discretion is unavoidable, but it makes the credibility of the process depend more heavily on the trustworthiness of the procedures of inquiry, and suggests the importance of minimizing the role of geopolitics, whether within the United Nations or outside it.

JUST WAR AND NEOINTERVENTIONISM

The preoccupations of the 1990s have been superseded by controversial and largely unsuccessful uses of force since September 11, 2001. The relevance or obsolescence of international law has become a matter of serious concern, and relates to whether the just war framework provides a solution for those who seek to bring a more principled discussion to the debate than is provided by reliance on international law. There is no doubt that the initial centrality accorded to the conflict between the Al Qaeda network of political extremists situated potentially everywhere, but at the same time without a definite territorial locus, and the United States, the preeminent state that has designated the entire world as a battlefield, makes it difficult to conceive of international law as providing regulatory guidance. A conflict between a loosely and uncertainly linked transnational network and a global state involves a new kind of war waged between nonterritorial actors, whereas international law emerged in the modern world to regulate relations of war and peace among sovereign states operating within and beyond national territorial space.

In this setting, the more flexible notions of permissible use of force associated with just war thinking seems as if it might be helpful, and was relied upon by a group of prominent, conservative intellectuals to express their support for President Bush's line of response to September 11, 2001. They sought to place the attack within a broader moral, cultural, religious, and humanistic framework. This endorsement, acknowledging the novelty of this encounter, as well as emphasizing the need to defend against the assaults of megaterrorism, grants to the U.S. government an overgeneralized open-ended mandate for the neglect of prior legal restraints while countering counterterrorist threats. This mandate is conferred without making a convincing case for principled departures in the name of "defensive necessity" as compared to what uses of international force were previously authorized by international law. In the earliest phases of the American response to September 11, the expansion seemed justified as applied to the prospective war against Afghanistan, which merged arguments associated with the need to destroy the Al Qaeda headquarters and training center with the 1990s rationale for humanitarian intervention without an explicit UN mandate to remove an oppressive regime. The political language of the twenty-first century emphasized "regime change," but the justification strongly stressed the abysmal human rights record of the Taliban regime as grounds for disregarding its sovereign status as representing the state of Afghanistan. The fact that only three states accorded diplomatic recognition to the Taliban as the government of Afghanistan lent weight to the disregard of its political legitimacy, especially as two of three broke relations after September 11. Under these conditions intervention seemed justified, or as in the earlier language used to justify the Kosovo War, or at the very least "legitimate," and possibly even "legal." The question of legality revolved around whether international law governing self-defense could be stretched to fit the new circumstances of defensive necessity. There was some incoherence with respect to the rationale for attacking Afghanistan, the main lines of justification hovering indistinctly between claims associated with security and those arising from the existence of a humanitarian emergency in the country arising from an impending famine combined with an abysmal human rights record.

But when the case for military intervention and regime change shifted to Iraq, the problematic character of the earlier just war approval of the conservative signers of the "Letter from America" became more apparent. First of all, there was a lack of evidence establishing defensive necessity, including any plausible linkage between the secular tyranny of Saddam Hussein and the Islamic extremism of Osama bin Laden. A tenuous argument for humanitarian intervention existed, but it was far weaker than in prior years, especially during the late 1980s; there was no current urgency, the governments now urging intervention had previously supported the Baghdad regime during its period of worst atrocities, and there were grounds to suspect that humanitarianism was invoked as a pretense designed to hide the pursuit of oil and the military establishment of regional control. When the war in Iraq ensued over the opposition of the UN Security Council and the validating claim of removing improperly possessed weapons of mass destruction turned sour, the Bush administration began to emphasize the liberating impact of its intervention. The claim to intervene was increasingly refuted by the growing evidence of a widely based resistance to and even-wider unpopularity of the U.S.-led occupation of the country. It is here that the vitality of international law remains valuable, prohibiting on the basis of authoritative law such wars of choice, and the limits of the just war approach become evident, allowing for flimsy and self-serving justifications for an illegal war to possess a façade of credibility.

NEW FRAMEWORK FOR INTERVENTION

This leaves us more confused than ever about the realities of global politics. Several levels of interaction each have an appropriate logic of justification relating to the interventionary use of force. On the level of state-to-state relations, wars of choice fought for strategic gain should remain under the prohibitory mantle of international law and the authority of the United Nations. From such a perspective, it is correct to reinforce the wide rejection of the war in Iraq by world public opinion and by the legal considerations used to condemn recourse to aggressive war by Germany and Japan before and during World War II.

On the level of the distinct challenge posed by Al Qaeda, a dual approach needs to be used at this point, combining a rationale based on just war thinking with the possibility of altering the parameters of defensive necessity under international law. To the extent that the new imperatives of security are relied on to expand the right of self-defense via an argument for "preemptive war," the facts and procedures must confirm the magnitude and imminence of the threat, and *post hoc* justification by way of humanitarian intervention is unacceptable. On the level of humanitarian intervention, the debate over law and justice remains unresolved, with a persisting tolerance for interventionary uses of force in response to an impending humanitarian catastrophe of the kind associated with genocide, Crimes Against Humanity, and mass suffering arising from disease, famine, and natural disasters. There is, however, a strong preference for UN authorization, and at least a regional endorsement, as well as a convincing argument that a forcible intervention without the consent of the territorial government is necessary (without diplomatic alternatives) and is a genuine last resort.

The discussion of conceptual frameworks available to lend or withhold approval from interventionary uses of force challenges us to find ways to walk the shaky political tightrope between humanitarian action and war prevention. As matters now stand, the United States, acting under the banner of a war against terrorism, claims the unilateral prerogative to fight wars of choice that violate the guidelines embedded in modern international law after a long struggle by seasoned diplomats to outlaw war to the extent possible for the mutual benefit of peoples and governments. Preseident Bush in the 2004 State of the Union drove this point home with his provocative statement that "America will never seek a permission slip to defend the security of our country." At the same time, the last decade of the twentieth century gave rise to a new humanitarian diplomacy seeking to protect those facing humanitarian catastrophe. The most pressing challenge in this setting is to endow the world community with the capability to address humanitarian emergencies without weakening the bonds of restraint that restrict war-making by states. One promising initiative that would help restore a positive balance would be the establishment of a voluntary peace enforcement capability within the framework of the United Nations, activated by a two-thirds decision of the Security Council, four-fifths recommendation of the General Assembly, and an expression of approval by the secretary general enunciated in an explicit public document. Such an operation should also, to the extent possible, be funded by either voluntary contributions or a global tax imposed on multinational corporations and banks. The objective would be to loosen the bonds that now tie intervention to the vagaries of geopolitics, encourage democratic debate on issues of intervention, and give to the organized international community a decisive role and responsibility in both redefining the relationship between human rights and state sovereignty, as well as in defining those rare circumstances in which military action should be authorized to achieve humanitarian goals. Perhaps such a proposal seems utopian in the present global climate, but it is no less relevant than the dystopian opening of the floodgates of "wars of choice," a euphemism for "wars of aggression" or "Crimes Against Peace," that currently threaten to undermine a logic of limits, whether derived from international law or the just war tradition. This logic of limits as a counter to the destructiveness of modern warfare cannot be separated from a more fundamental and sweeping struggle of the human species to survive in the face of multiple threats to the sustainability of complex forms of social existence on this planet.

3

Reviving Punitive Peace
The Sanctions Regime (1991–2003)

The preoccupation in recent years with the Iraq War should not obscure the importance of the preceding period, when a harsh sanctions regime was imposed on Iraq while the country's infrastructure was devastated in the aftermath of the 1991 Gulf War.

This regime, carried out under the auspices of the United Nations, punished Iraq's entire civilian population, causing many deaths and much suffering. It is part of the longer narrative that reached its climax in March 2003 with the unprovoked invasion of Iraq in flagrant violation of the United Nations Charter and international law. Such a pattern raises many questions about the motives and goals of this effort led by the U.S. government. This chapter focuses on the interval between the two Iraq wars (1991–2003).

What accounts for the obsessiveness of American policy toward Iraq over the course of more than fifteen years? Was it another Vietnam in the sense that the U.S. government can again not bring itself to acknowledge the failure of its approach to Iraq in the years after the end of the Gulf War? After all, Baghdad withstood comprehensive sanctions, a variety of covert assaults, and repeated American harassment from the air without flinching. Was it the pique at the White House and Pentagon associated with the electoral removal from the scene of Bush Sr. contrasting with the persistence of Saddam Hussein, posing an implicit filial challenge to Bush Jr.? Was it some sort of Freudian response by the younger Bush in retaliation for Saddam Hussein's alleged plot to assassinate his father? Was it the long-deferred payback to Israel for staying on the sidelines during the Gulf War, despite several Scud missiles being fired from Iraq? Was it a matter of securing U.S. control of the oil reserves being linked to periodic displays of regional dominance, especially through the denial of weaponry of mass destruction to those states in the Middle East that might seek at some point to deter or challenge the United States or Israel in some future crisis? Or was it part of the American empire-building strategy that viewed Saddam's Iraq as an obstacle but also as providing an opportunity to demonstrate the extent of military dominance possessed by the U.S. government and its political will to deal harshly with states that stand in the way? Or was it the new cover story, frequently repeated by Bush and senior political aides, that the Baghdad regime had become more dangerous since September 11 because it might enable Al Qaeda at some future time to obtain weaponry of mass destruction that would then be used against American targets?

Undoubtedly, there is no single correct answer, because different members of the Bush neoconservative inner circle were drawn to various combinations of these lines of analysis and advocacy that seem mutually reinforcing in any event. But what is beyond doubt is that American policy toward Iraq since the ceasefire in 1991 that ended the Gulf War has violated the most basic precepts of international law, including the UN Charter, and the fundamental economic, political, and social rights of the Iraqi people.[1] To the extent that the UN Security Council has endorsed American policy, it has weakened respect for and impaired the legitimacy of the UN around the world. In 1991 Iraq was defeated in a war and accepted humiliating conditions for a ceasefire, which effectively encroached upon the basic sovereign rights of Iraq as a state. In the ensuing period, Iraq has not been offered any kind of protection by the international community even when it was faced with an increasing prospect of an unprovoked armed attack by the United States. Such an attack when it came constituted both a violation of the UN Charter prohibition on recourse to aggressive war and a crime against peace in the sense delimited by the Nuremberg Principles.

This chapter discusses the changing context of U.S. policy toward Iraq, then considers sanctions and war threats under international law, and concludes with a criticism of the approach taken by the United States and by the United Nations over this period of more than a decade. The international community, as dominated diplomatically in this period by the United States government, imposed an extremely punitive peace on Iraq, and in the process neglected the lessons supposedly learned as a consequence of the disastrous effects of the punitive peace imposed by the victorious powers on Germany after World War I. These lessons were self-consciously and successfully applied to Germany and Japan to promote the recovery and restored normalcy of these defeated countries in the aftermath of World War II. In retrospect, it seems reasonable to wonder whether these "lessons of Versailles" were only meant for "civilized" countries in the North, and were not meant to be applicable to the South. The South, subordinate in any event, has remained fertile ground for indefinite punishment of a political actor that challenged the established geopolitical order. Iraq, formerly a strategic junior partner in the maintenance of such an order during the Cold War, especially during Iraq's long war with the Islamic Republic of Iran during the 1980s, became the archenemy, challenging the post–Cold War American design for the region. After the 1991 ceasefire Iraq faced a variety of dire threats of invasion and attack that were unabashedly discussed by American political leaders, with various plans for a military operation debated in mainstream media.[2] The debate focused only on the feasibility of the means being proposed, their probable degree of effectiveness, and their anticipated costs and risks. In the public discourse the acceptability of the ends was taken for granted or treated as irrelevant, despite the fact that any invasion of Iraq would amount to a stark violation of the most basic rules of the UN Charter prohibiting recourse to nondefensive force in the setting of an unresolved international dispute. Looking sympathetically at the plight of Iraq as a beleaguered state should not be confused with an endorsement of the Baghdad regime, or be viewed as a display of impunity with respect to the brutal and bloody past behavior of its leaders, both with respect to neighbors and its own internal adversaries, whether the Kurdish minority or the Shiite majority. In this regard, there is little doubt that Saddam Hussein and his entourage were indictable for Crimes Against Humanity and Crimes Against Peace, although only in a manner that conformed with international due-process standards. But the criminality of a head of state or of official policies pursued does not by itself impair the sovereignty of that state, nor does it provide grounds for suspending the application of international law in relation to hostile acts or threats and uses of force by outside states. The reclassification of Iraq as "enemy" and "rogue state" that occurred in the 1990s was purely a consequence of altered geopolitical priorities in Washington, as the worst excesses of the Iraqi government were committed years prior to its attack on Kuwait and at those earlier times led to no abandonment of U.S. strategic support.

THE CHANGING CONTEXT

From every perspective except that of geopolitics, American policy toward Iraq since the end of the Gulf War had been a disaster. The imposition and retention of comprehensive sanctions for more than a decade after the deliberate destruction of the Iraqi civilian infrastructure during the Gulf War has resulted in hundreds of thousands of civilian casualties, more than a million according to some estimates.[3] Reliable international sources have abundantly documented such a disturbing assessment. Those most acutely afflicted were the very young and the poorest sectors of the Iraqi population.[4] Although sanctions were regrettably formally backed by the United Nations through a strained interpretation of Security Council Resolution 687, with some modifications in recent years, the sanctions had a cruel impact that so appalled several of the most senior international civil servants of the UN entrusted with administering oil-for-food programs as to prompt that rarest of bureaucratic impulses, successive resignations by the lead administrators on principle![5] The political objective of this highly punitive diplomacy was justified as a way to destabilize and contain the repressive regime of Saddam Hussein, but the evidence clearly indicated that, as the years passed, the government in Baghdad gathered political strength while internal and external opposition among Iraqis came to seem ever more inconsequential. It was mainly ordinary Iraqi people who were paying the price for this continuing encounter between Hussein's regime and the United States government.

Throughout this period, as well, American and British planes continued to patrol extensive no-fly zones that had been established in the north and south of Iraq, initially justified by the U.S. government as indirectly authorized by Security Council Resolution 688 as a way to protect endangered Hussein's domestic enemies but later maintained as a way to challenge Baghdad militarily on a daily basis, exhibiting its helplessness as a sovereign state to uphold its territorial integrity. Unlike sanctions, these military incursions lacked clear Security Council authorization, gradually becoming quite unconnected with their original protective function benefiting the Kurds in northern Iraq and the Shia so-called "marsh Arabs" in southern Iraq during the immediate aftermath of the Gulf War, during which period Baghdad was seeking revenge against those elements in the Iraqi population that had sided with the American-led military campaign and had been encouraged to mount an uprising against the Baathist regime.

At issue all along was the UN mechanism, the United Nations Special Commission (UNSCOM), that was imposed on Iraq after the ceasefire in the form of an inspection mechanism that claimed extensive rights to oversee the destruction of existing Iraqi stockpiles of weaponry of mass destruction and ensure that no activities were continuing secretly to acquire such weaponry in the future.[6] Much controversy surrounded UNSCOM activities, associated with alleged Iraqi evasions and denials of access, but also countercharges by Iraq contending that the inspection procedure was being used for espionage purposes and to harass and humiliate the Iraqi government. After several years of controversy Iraq refused to grant further access to UNSCOM, creating a new pretext for intervention and the resumption of war, as well as producing debates about whether such inspections, however extensive, could ever provide confidence about Iraqi compliance with the stringent conditions of disarmament imposed by UN Security Resolution 687. During the initial period of the presidency of George W. Bush many high-level assertions were made that without more rigorous inspection a preemptive war would be needed and justified to ensure that Iraq did not pose a threat to the United States in the future. Some neoconservatives, including Dick Cheney, also asserted that inspections, even if restored and intensified, could never provide sufficient confidence to obviate the need for a military attack designed to achieve the desired regime change. Complicating the picture further, the UN, with strong backing from Secretary General Kofi Annan, was seeking in 2000 to negotiate a renewal of an inspection arrangement positing an UNSCOM arrangement as an alternative to war, and coupled with some indication that sanctions could eventually be ended if the new scheme worked successfully. It became clear that Washington rejected such an approach, and viewed the inspection issue as a diversion and distraction from its obvious goal of coerced regime change. But the

United States played a double game: if Iraq resisted inspection, it would validate the need for intervention, but if it assented, then the unreliability of inspection would also validate the need for intervention — a deadly Catch-22!

In the meantime during the latter half of the 1990s, a cruel stalemate arising from the imposition of sanctions and intrusive U.S. claims persisted. It had long been apparent to objective observers that these undertakings were not succeeding in weakening the control of Baghdad over the country, but policymakers in Washington lacked the political courage to acknowledge, even indirectly, that their approach had failed to dislodge Saddam Hussein and was doing great damage to the people of Iraq, as well as to the humanitarian reputation and political autonomy of the United Nations. The Clinton administration had so committed itself to the support of sanctions, as well as the continuation of periodic bombings within the no-fly zones, that it seemed completely unable and unwilling to reevaluate this futile and immoral policy in light of the harm being done to Iraqi civilian society. Such a reluctance was consistent with the overall approach in the Clinton years to exhibit "toughness" in foreign policy, especially in the Middle East, so as to minimize criticism from the hard right that made little secret of its push all along for supporting with money and weaponry Iraqi exile movements, if not a renewal of outright war against Iraq.[7] Much as with Vietnam, leaders in Washington could not bring themselves to admit that their policy was a dreadful failure, and so it went on and on, with the goal of shifting the burden of decision to the next president. During his presidential campaign and upon arrival in Washington, George W. Bush announced that sanctions against Iraq would be continued, and even intensified, although the undisclosed escalating intention — to move from sanction to the more proactive option of intervention and war — has now been well established by insider account.

From the perspectives of international law and morality these policies directed at Iraq were of a highly dubious character, yet their continuation despite widespread criticism from most governments in the region and the world revealed the extent of American influence within the United Nations specifically, and international politics generally. The whole experience was a demonstration of the primacy of geopolitics at the expense of basic standards of law and morality. Despite the pragmatic and humanitarian misgivings of many governments, there was little disposition to challenge openly the American position.

And then came the September 11 attacks on the World Trade Center and the Pentagon, which inflicted heavy symbolic and substantive damage on the United States, and led the Bush administration to declare war on global terror. Despite some criticisms directed at the overgeneralized way this recourse to war was formulated and applied to Afghanistan, it did seem to most commentators to represent an understandable and generally acceptable effort to retaliate against the main locus of Al Qaeda operations and to diminish the prospect of future attacks.[8] In the face of these attacks, President Bush, in his address to a Joint Session of Congress on September 20, 2001, outlined the U.S. government's resolve to wage an overall war against "every terrorist group of global reach."[9] Iraq was mentioned by name in the speech only to make the point that the character of the war being launched was different than the Gulf War: "This war will not be like the war against Iraq a decade ago, with a decisive liberation of territory and a swift conclusion." True, a generalized warning declared that "[f]rom this day forward, any nation that continues to harbor or support terrorism will be regarded by the United States as a hostile regime."

But the hawks in Washington smelled Iraqi blood from the moment of the Al Qaeda attacks. There were early statements by right-wing think tank analysts urging the extension of the military response to Iraq, and we now know that war planning commenced on September 12, 2001, if not before. Leading members in Congress had sent a bipartisan letter to President Bush, coordinated by Senators Joseph Lieberman and John McCain, insisting that the war on terrorism could not succeed unless the threat posed by Saddam Hussein was confronted by military force. Israel, as well, made little secret of its wish to extend the battlefields of Afghanistan to Iraq (and Iran). Various efforts were made to encourage war against Iraq by trying to show (on the basis of conjecture and unconvincing evidence) that there were links between Baghdad and Al Qaeda agents prior to September 11, or to imply that Iraq was the source of the anthrax distributed via the U.S. Postal Service. Throughout this period there were inconsistent and inconclusive comments deriving from top members of the Bush security team. The secretary of state, Colin Powell, was seen soon after September 11 as still reluctant to endorse such a belligerent stance against Iraq, realizing that it would interfere with his diplomatic priority, which involved building up a global coalition against the Al Qaeda network and finding some way to dissipate anti-Americanism arising from the unresolved fate of the Palestinians. Such caution on Powell's part seemed to have disappeared in the wake of the successful campaign by American military forces to turn the tide of battle within Afghanistan so quickly and decisively in favor of the Northern Alliance, producing the collapse of the Taliban regime, the destruction of the Afghan nerve center of Al Qaeda, and the dispersal of its leadership. This American victory was achieved with almost no American casualties sustained during the air campaign. At first, it seemed far more dangerous to be a journalist covering the U.S. war in Afghanistan than to be a soldier on the American side. Later on, this state of affairs changed somewhat, as American forces were used on the ground to deal with enclaves of Taliban and Al Qaeda resistance and some deadly firefights occurred. A new wave of American triumphalism emerged, painted in vivid colors of geopolitical achievement in the course of President Bush's State of the Union Address on January 29, 2002.[10] This occasion was seized to expand the scope of the war against global terror by extending its goals to include a series of countries, Iraq, Iran, and North Korea, which were provocatively labeled members of "the axis of evil." Ever since that speech, the assumption has permeated media treatments and public attitudes that a U.S. decision to wage war against Iraq had been already made by the White House, and that the only uncertainty that remained was related to the adoption of specific war plans; the extent, timing, and nature of the attack; and the degree of dependence on a ground attack, the availability and relevance of Iraqi opposition forces both inside and outside of the country.

This further turning of the screw by the U.S. government moved the sanctions debate into the background, shifting world attention in 2002 and early 2003 to the avoidance of war. The UNSC continued to advocate a course of conduct that would suggest that a reliance on the inspections mechanism authorized by UNSC Resolution 1441 could avert a second Gulf war. Despite this sidelining of sanctions, it remains important to consider the reliance on sanctions for more than a decade, which continued to impose hardships on the civilian population of Iraq, from the perspective of international law and morality. The sanctions regime, whatever else, challenges our political understanding of global justice. We should perceive this regime as an inexcusable descent by the organized international community into criminality.[11]

THE SANCTIONS REGIME

Despite the superseding of sanctions by invasion and occupation, it seems important to review the experience of the sanctions imposed on Iraq after 1991. The sanctions regime is usefully separated into five distinct phases, each of which poses the question of legality and morality in a different way:

- the reliance on sanctions in the months after the Iraqi invasion of Kuwait in August 1990 and until the start of the Gulf War in January 1991;
- the immediate postwar reliance on sanctions to achieve compliance with Security Council Res. 687;
- the persistent reliance on sanctions during the UNSCOM period in the face of growing evidence of civilian suffering;
- the shift to "smart sanctions" to deflect criticism of the sanctions regime during its first several years, and to sustain a UN consensus supportive of their continued imposition;
- the maintenance of sanctions as a secondary policy, while increasingly resorting to blatant "war talk" as the primary policy, threatening a military attack unless there took place a regime change in Baghdad that satisfied the goals being set in Washington.

PREWAR SANCTIONS

It is of great importance to distinguish sharply between the imposition of comprehensive sanctions by virtue of UNSC Resolution 660 and the initiation of the Gulf War on January 15, 1991. In the months following Iraq's conquest and annexation of Kuwait in August 1990, the approach advocated publicly by the United States, and adopted by the United Nations Security Council, was to endorse Kuwait's right of self-defense and seek a resolution of the conflict via Iraq withdrawal by a combination of diplomacy and sanctions. The limited goals of this policy were to restore fully the sovereign rights of Kuwait, and to impose on Iraq the burden of defraying the economic costs of the harm inflicted. The issue of Iraq's actual and potential possession of weaponry of mass destruction was not part of the UN engagement in this phase. Such a response to the Iraqi invasion of Kuwait in 1990 was widely and genuinely supported, including by the members of the Security Council, with the sole exception of Yemen's abstention. Reliance on sanctions, even if they imposed hardships on Iraq's population, were seen as a reasonable and appropriate reinforcement of constructive diplomatic efforts to obtain Iraqi withdrawal. Sanctions also seemed the best way to fulfill the Charter goals of protecting states that have been victims of international aggression while doing everything possible to avoid recourse to war. In this fundamental sense, sanctions prior to the Gulf War were fully consistent with international law and morality, and enjoyed the almost unanimous backing of the membership of the United Nations, including most of the countries of the Middle East.

Indeed, to the extent that criticism was made, it moved in the direction of advocating a greater reliance on the mix of sanctions and diplomacy, especially providing more time to generate effective pressure on Baghdad. A related criticism was that the United States did not genuinely seek a diplomatic resolution of the dispute, and put forward the demand for withdrawal and reparations in such unconditional and rigid terms as to ensure that the Iraqi government would respond negatively, thereby building the U.S. case for war. The UN secretary general at the time, Javier Perez de Cueller, supports the view in his memoirs that a somewhat more flexible approach might well have achieved the stated UN goals without war.[12] But even in 1990 to 1991, for undisclosed reasons, Washington preferred a military solution that would eliminate Iraq as a regional power, as a threat to the Gulf oil reserves, and to Israel. Part of this preference was the possibility of connecting the aggression against Kuwait with the quite separate concerns arising from Iraq's efforts to acquire weapons of mass destruction, including biological, chemical, and nuclear weaponry. Only with war, and an imposed ceasefire, could this wider security concern be addressed, as was done in Resolution 687 establishing the mandate for destruction and inspection of such capabilities.

POSTWAR REALITIES

In contrast, the perpetuation of sanctions by way of UNSC Resolution 678, during the period after the ceasefire in 2001 and Iraqi withdrawal from Kuwait, was
initially justified as leverage needed to ensure compliance with Iraq's various
obligations to make amends for the harm inflicted, as well as to satisfy the most
serious disarmament demands imposed on a sovereign state since the end of the
Second World War. It should be noted that after World War II the defeated countries were not subject to economic sanctions, in contrast to after World War I,
when punitive reparations burdens were placed on Germany. On the contrary,
despite the terrible costs inflicted by aggressive wars in the 1930s and 1940s,
these defeated and devastated countries were immediately given major help with
economic reconstruction, and soon achieved positive economic growth.

The devastation wrought by the war in Iraq was extensive, and included severe
damage to the civilian infrastructure. The former president of Finland Martti
Ahtisaari presented a report to the UN on the basis of a fact-finding mission
shortly after the military campaign ended, which indicated the destruction of
Iraq's entire industrial and modern sectors, concluding that the country had
literally been bombed back to a preindustrial reality.[13] Declassified documents
from the U.S. Defense Intelligence Agency (DIA) confirm early complaints that
the United States deliberately and illegally targeted the civilian infrastructure of
Iraq, especially the water-treatment system, with the acknowledged purpose of
disrupting civilian life throughout the country.[14] Under these circumstances, the
imposition of comprehensive sanctions was legally and morally dubious from the
outset. It was perfectly obvious that the war had left Iraqi society in a situation
of great vulnerability to a health crisis of a major magnitude, and that increasing
pressures by sanctions in such a setting would be sure to exact a heavy toll on the
civilian society.[15] To go ahead with comprehensive sanctions under these circumstances would seem certainly to have the foreseeable effect of imposing massive
indiscriminate death and illness on the civilian population, thereby engaging the
moral, and possibly, the legal responsibility at some level of those governments
that supported postwar sanctions. The case for responsibility was aggravated by
the degree to which it was clear that the military and political leadership would
husband its resources to avoid the impact of sanctions, leaving only the civilian
population at risk. This punitive approach to implementing the agreed ceasefire also eroded the legitimacy and moral standing of the United Nations, first,
for agreeing to sanctions given its knowledge of their probable effects, and then,
extending the ceasefire to cover aspects of coercive disarmament and inspection
that were not closely connected with the claim of collective security associated
with restoring Kuwaiti sovereignty that was properly put forward as the main
justification for the 1991 war.

SUSTAINING THE SANCTIONS

As the months and years went by, evidence accumulated to confirm what should have been anticipated and publicly known: the sanctions were exacting an enormous toll among the civilian population, and were doing virtually nothing to hamper the activities and lifestyle of the Iraqi elite. The U.S. government favored the maintenance of a tough sanctions regime even in the face of the well-documented reports detailing the suffering of the Iraqi people. In the lamentable words of Madeline Albright when asked to comment on the huge loss of life among Iraqi women and children, spoken on network TV in 1996 at a time when she was serving as U.S. ambassador at the UN, not long before becoming secretary of state, "[w]e think the price is worth it."[16]

Humanitarian considerations were only part of the discontent experienced by governments when periodically asked to extend the sanctions under UN auspices. Public opinion expressed similar hostility in various ways outside of the United States. Another part of the growing antisanctions movement within the UN had to do with the degree to which the United States was seen as throwing its weight around in the UN and elsewhere, without pursuing a diplomatic path that might lead to a quick and peaceful resolution of the conflict. Closely related here was the European concern that lost business opportunities in the Middle East, especially in the field of energy development, were being sacrificed by imposing the sanctions regime on Iraq for no plausible reason of security.

Maintaining sanctions under these conditions certainly seems to run counter to international humanitarian law, as well as to the more general just war doctrine in its application to sanctions. The most basic conception embedded in the law of war at the close of the nineteenth century, in the Hague Convention, was the idea of agreements by governments that force could be legally used in warfare only if directed against military targets and the related broad injunction against the "unlimited" use of force against an enemy state. Admittedly, some conceptual and interpretative issues are raised by extending these normative principles to the Iraq-sanctions regime. International law is directed at states, not at international organizations such as the UN. The imposition of sanctions in this comprehensive form was initially authorized and periodically reaffirmed by the UN Security Council. Is the Security Council bound by the restraints of international humanitarian law? Existing international law gives no clear answers to such a question. By legal analogy and moral reasoning, it would seem that the UN as political actor should not be freed from rules of behavior seeking to protect civilians from the ravages and excesses of warfare, but can such an analogy be legally relied upon in the absence of its formal acceptance by the UN Security Council? It could, then, be cautiously concluded that the maintenance of sanctions, given the evidence of their effects, is both immoral and in violation of the just war doctrine, involving three separate aspects: sanctions as applied seem indiscriminate, disproportionate, and have little prospect of achieving the ends being pursued.[17]

THE MOVE TO SMART SANCTIONS

In response to the rising tide of antisanctions sentiment, especially in Europe, the United States took a series of backward strides from its preferred unyielding position so as to prevent the international consensus from falling apart. It had earlier agreed to an oil-for-food program that allowed Iraq to sell its oil on the world market, importing civilian goods, with the use of the revenues earned by Iraq being scrutinized by the UN Office of the Iraq Program (OIP) in such a cumbersome and restrictive way as to compromise the humanitarian rationale.[18] In May 2001, after elaborate diplomatic negotiations in which the United States did its best to maximize sanctions while retaining support of the Security Council, the UN finally approved a much-heralded move to "smart sanctions."[19] Then in November 2001, with the adoption of UNSC Resolution 1382, the sanctions regime somewhat modified this focus; all traded goods were banned that had military or dual-use applications. All Iraq overseas contracts were made subject to rigorous review, and rejection by UN administrative action. Any member of the Security Council could delay a contract almost indefinitely by seeking review if any of the challenged items appeared on the extensive Goods Review List. The OIP turned any questionable contract with Iraq over to the United Nations Monitoring, Verification and Inspection Commission (UNMOVIC) and the International Atomic Energy Agency (IAEA) to determine whether the traded goods were related to potential Iraqi military applications. The so-called 661 Committee of the Security Council had the last word on whether a contract survived this review process, and many did not.

In fact, to uphold governmental interests Iraq appears to have successfully circumvented many of the constraints associated with the early years of sanctions via internal adaptation and regional smuggling arrangements designed to sell oil outside the reach of sanctions, especially to Syria. Iraq and the UN played a lengthy cat-and-mouse game related to the renewal of inspection, which at times was made to seem a bargaining process, exchanging access by inspectors for a gradual lifting of sanctions. Also, the smuggled goods tend to reflect state priorities relating to security and regime stability, and do not emphasize the alleviation of the humanitarian tragedy. While the United States has at times seemingly endorsed this approach, it has maintained a degree of ambiguity by stressing its inability to have confidence that inspection would ever be able to determine whether Iraq is upholding its obligation to refrain from the production, development, and possession of weaponry of mass destruction. After the American presidential elections in 2000, this ambiguity was almost entirely suppressed by the unilateralist climate of opinion in Washington that expressed its determination to take whatever steps would be necessary to achieve a regime change in Baghdad. As a consequence, sanctions seemed of diminishing relevance both to advocates of a hard line on Iraq, who favored a military solution, and advocates of normalization, who favored an end to sanctions and a resumption of diplomatic relations.

It became clear long before September 11 that to the extent that sanctions sought political results beyond a punitive effect, their impact was negligible, although maintained for more than a decade in the face of strong objective evidence that massive loss of civilian life was being caused on a monthly basis over the course of many years. Consequently, it can be concluded that the indiscriminate civilian harm being caused was not "collateral," especially after the initial period when it might have been reasonable to suppose that over time the sanctions would erode internal support for Saddam Hussein's leadership, possibly stimulating internal and external Iraqi forces to achieve a change in government. Without the intervening reality of September 11, despite this assessment, and by making adjustments of the sort involved in the adoption and administration of smart or selective sanctions, U.S.-led policy toward Iraq would in all likelihood have maintained this futile and punitive course indefinitely, squeezing the people of Iraq without any realistic hope of achieving political objectives. Of course, some supporters of the U.S. approach argue that sanctions did succeed in keeping Saddam Hussein pinned down, "within his box," to use Beltway jargon.[20] Further, without sanctions, Iraq would have by the end of the 1990s, the argument went, acquired a formidable arsenal of weaponry of mass destruction. Even if this latter conjecture is accurate, there is no reason to doubt, particularly in light of the Gulf War and U.S./Israeli regional security policy, that containment and deterrence would have been fully available and likely effective in minimizing the threat of future Iraqi expansionism. A careful examination of Iraqi behavior under Saddam Hussein discloses an ambitious approach to the use of power in regional settings, often coupled with serious strategic miscalculations. At the same time, Baghdad adopted a consistently rational approach to gains and losses, and exhibited a willingness to back down rather than engage in self-destructive warfare. In effect, then, sanctions after 1991 were essentially punitive, and although supported by the UN, seemed to violate the most fundamental values embodied in international humanitarian law, and arguably raise plausible allegations of genocide, although not in its legal meaning. Most respected experts would argue that although qualifying as Crimes Against Humanity, the sanctions do not constitute genocide because of the absence of evidence establishing specific intent.[21]

FROM SANCTIONS TO WAR

Undoubtedly, September 11 created an opportunity for those seeking regime change in Iraq to acknowledge tacitly the failure of the sanctions approach, yet propose an even more aggressive approach to Iraq. Recourse to war against Al Qaeda gave the Bush administration a wide berth in foreign policy, virtually suspending domestic scrutiny, and muting international criticism for many months. There were attempts in the immediate aftermath of the attacks to insist on the existence of significant Iraqi connections to Al Qaeda.

The decisive move was made in the 2002 State of the Union address when Iraq headed the list of "axis of evil" states, and President Bush announced a new doctrine of preemption as an essential feature of the war on terror. Drawing on public anxieties about megaterrorism, Bush declared that "axis of evil" countries with the will and capability to produce weaponry of mass destruction posed severe threats to American security, not by the likelihood that such weapons would be directly used, but rather by the prospect that the weaponry would be transferred to Al Qaeda and possibly other terrorists groups with global agendas. Without explicitly indicating that an attack upon Iraq was forthcoming, what Bush and others in Washington were saying clearly implied that the United States would do what was necessary to supersede the Saddam Hussein regime, thereby achieving regime change comparable to that which took place in Afghanistan.

It is important to underscore the degree to which such war talk was at odds with the most fundamental rules and principles of international law, as well as incompatible with the just war tradition that continues to be influential in religious and humanist circles, and provides a backdrop for law talk. Throughout the twentieth century, there were a series of high-profile efforts to outlaw and criminalize nondefensive wars. The core undertaking of the UN Charter is famously expressed by the pledge of the Preamble "to save succeeding generations from the scourge of war." The Nuremberg/Tokyo prosecutions of German and Japanese leaders after World War II proceeded on the premise that aggressive war was a Crime Against Peace, and that as such it was the most serious form of international criminality encompassing all others. The Charter norms on war were drafted with the intention of minimizing the role of subjective interpretation by leading states, which are always capable of producing self-serving explanations by governments as to why their recourse to war is justifiable. The Nicaragua decision of the World Court in 1986 upheld this Charter approach as also paralleled by the norms of customary international law that is applicable under all circumstances of conflict and to all actors, including states with a veto power in the United Nations. It is arguable that the September 11 attacks by Al Qaeda cannot be addressed within this template of modern international law as the threat, or capability to inflict harm, and an appropriate response cannot be territorialized. Under these circumstances, restrictions on the use of defensive force need to be loosened to permit a threatened state to take reasonable steps to protect its people and uphold its security.[22] Such reasoning does not apply in the setting of the so-called axis of evil states as deterrence offers an adequate way to reconcile containment with the avoidance of war. The foundation of security for both sides in the Cold War for over forty years was deterrence, and they succeeded in avoiding a major war despite intense hostility and a geopolitical rivalry of global scope. In this regard, the provocative war talk that was directed at Iraq for several years was a direct challenge to the overall framework of modern international law with respect to war/peace issues. The war unleashed against Iraq was a dangerous and unacceptable undertaking that if given the status of a valid precedent would justify recourse to international force in a wide range of future circumstances. Above all, anticipatory defense and preventive war would be available as a rationale for almost any contemplated war. Furthermore, recourse to such wars of choice could be undertaken by a state without a prior mandate from the UNSC. At least in the Kosovo War of 1999 the use of force by NATO was a collective decision with the backing of states within the region. It is also disturbing to contemplate the implication of denying a state its sovereign rights by unilaterally classifying it as "a rogue state" or part of "an axis of evil," which seemed to be using political language to deny states the normal protection of international law.

CONCLUSION

The Iraq experience with sanctions is best evaluated by reference to the five distinct temporal intervals discussed above. No blanket generalizations can be applied to the sanctions regime as a whole. The imposition and maintenance of sanctions *after* the Gulf War involved a deliberate and indiscriminate program that inflicted severe harm on the civilian population of Iraq. The UN discredited itself by endorsing sanctions having this effect, although after much harm to the people of Iraq some efforts were made within the UN to mitigate the humanitarian catastrophe being caused. The initiatives taken by the secretary general and others did eventually reduce the suffering of the Iraqi people produced by the sanctions. The UN tarnished its reputation by providing the auspices for the sanctions regime. It should by appreciated, at the same time, that the UN reflects the political will of its leading members and generally is no more respectful of international law or sensitive to humanitarian consideration than are its leading members. In this regard, the United States and the United Kingdom, the most ardent proponents of sanctions and the enforcers of the no-fly zones, bear a particularly heavy political, legal, and moral responsibility for the harm inflicted on the people of Iraq, as well as for the damage done to the image of the United Nations, especially in the Middle East.

The debate about the Iraq sanctions policy was superseded after the end of the Afghanistan War by the debate about recourse to an American-led war against Iraq. President George W. Bush claimed that such a war was necessary as an integral part of the counterterrorist campaign that represented the U.S. response to September

11. Most of the world disagreed, despite generally recognizing that Saddam Hussein was an oppressive ruler guilty of serious Crimes Against Humanity and Crimes Against Peace during his period as head of state. In an attempt by the Bush administration to build greater international support for launching a war against Iraq, the United States purported to work with the UN, and rely on its procedures, supposedly to give Iraq a last chance to avoid war. The United States persuaded the Security Council to establish a very intrusive mechanism of unconditional inspection that Iraq accepted, presumably seeking to avert the threatened American attack. This inspection process was tasked with the job of ensuring the complete "disarmament" of Iraqi weapons of mass destruction, with Iraq facing the prospect of "serious consequences" if it obstructed the inspectors or was found to be in "material breach" of the operative Security Council resolution, 1441. As the process went forward a widening gap between the American-led war party and the French-led inspection party became evident. As the drama unfolded, the French approach prevailed within the UN, but the United States went ahead with its war plans supported by the United Kingdom and a reluctant small group of coalition partners.

Despite this overshadowing of sanctions by the actuality of a prolonged war, it is important to assess the sanctions imposed on Iraq that set the stage for the initiation of this failed instance of aggressive war. What we should learn from this reliance on sanctions that were first introduced to induce Iraq to withdraw from Kuwait, and then revived for twelve further years as the centerpiece of a punitive peace imposed on Iraq in the aftermath of the Gulf War, is that such a policy can be extremely devastating with respect to the civilian population. This is especially true when the sanctions are imposed on a country whose centralized electricity, water purification, and sewage systems have been destroyed during a war. Indeed, in such a setting sanctions are more indiscriminate than war itself, primarily and massively hitting the most vulnerable and poorest sectors of the civilian population. The experience of Iraq between 1991 and 2003 demonstrates precisely this set of consequences. In such circumstances, sanctions amount to a criminal continuation of war, without even the restrictions on the use of force provided by the rather vague constraints of international humanitarian law. For the United Nations to have formally endorsed such a sanctions policy when these realities were widely reported, and essentially uncontested, is a severe blight on its own mission to prevent war and raise the moral standards of the world politics, especially with regard to the protection of vulnerable peoples confronting a humanitarian disaster. Let us hope that the dismal experience associated with post-1991 sanctions will be appreciated in subsequent situations, and the suffering inflicted on the people of Iraq will not be repeated elsewhere in the future.

4

Toward Regional War

A REGIONAL PERSPECTIVE: PHASE 1

It should be recalled, and was almost forgotten, that the Iraq War has always been viewed in hard-core neoconservative thinking as a stepping stone to a much more ambitious vision of regional restructuring that included Syria, Iran, Lebanon, and possibly Saudi Arabia and Egypt. This way of thinking on a regional scale made its initial appearance in 1996 by way of a notorious study entitled "A Clean Break: A New Strategy for Securing the Realm" authored by a tightly knit group led by Richard Perle, working under the auspices of the right-wing Israeli think tank The Institute for Advanced Strategic and Political Studies. The perspective developed in the report rested on repudiating any pretension by Israel of a willingness to negotiate a political compromise with Palestinian aspirations by way of the "the peace process" then associated with the Oslo Framework of Principles agreed upon in 1993.

In contrast, "A Clean Break" advocated support for Israel's expansionist quest for establishing its sovereignty over virtually the entire territorial domain of historic Palestine, including above all Jerusalem and the West Bank. The authors of this report fully understood that to achieve such an outcome, without endangering Israeli security, it would be necessary to challenge those several regimes in the Middle East that seemed hostile to Israel and the United States, with a special emphasis on the need to engage Syria militarily, and to form a de facto alliance with Turkey and Jordan. The United States was not expected at that time before the neoconservative star had risen to be an active military partner in this quest, but it was hoped that it would lend diplomatic support and extensive financial support, and supply weapons, and in due course acknowledge Israel as no longer a costly dependency, but rather as a formidable regional actor that shared American strategic concerns throughout the Middle East. Much of this thinking had been contained in a parallel memorandum prepared by Perle and Paul Wolfowitz on behalf of the right-wing Likud political figure Binyamin Netanyahu, then an incoming prime minister who had promised his constituents a coherent anti-Oslo approach to Israeli ambitions and security embodying a regional perspective that could alone ensure Israeli long-range security. In other words, the regional strategy was devised as a new basis for Israeli foreign policy, but was written by neoconservative heavyweights who believed that its recommendations would also serve as a desirable foundation for recasting the pursuit of American strategic interests in the Middle East.

To the extent that this same cadre of neoconservatives came to supply the Republican right wing with its main worldview, this Clean Break approach is notable as an illuminating prelude, although reflective of a vastly different global setting. Long before September 11, 2001, the Republican right was privately critical of Bush Sr. and angrily dismissive of Clinton's foreign policy, due to its supposed conceptual muddles, policy priorities, and above all its failure to grasp the changed imperatives of geopolitics after the Cold War, especially as pertaining to the Middle East.

The neoconservatives attacked their mainstream adversaries then shaping foreign policy as unfocused, wimpy, insufficiently attentive to the role of dominant military power, anachronistically Eurocentric, and fecklessly distracted by their humanitarian pretensions. Enlarging the scope of concerns, most fully set forth in the report of the Project for a New American Century (PNAC) entitled "Rebuilding America's Defenses," published in September 2000, and prepared on the basis of study-group discussions in the prior two years, several revealing features are worth observing: (1) an insistence on setting forth a grand strategy as essential for a successful American foreign policy to be developed in light of the altered world conditions arising from the end of the Cold War, presenting the United States with a new series of opportunities and risks; (2) the shared conviction that Europe was no longer the main arena of geopolitics, but rather that the defining issues in world politics in the near future would involve a struggle for control over the Middle East and, secondarily, a decision as to how to manage the containment (or alternatively to provoke a confrontation) with China; (3) a reliance on a Westphalian-era assessment that risks to American supremacy arose from hostile and potentially hostile *states*, and that hostile armed political movements were hardly worth worrying about on their own, being nothing more or less than instruments of these states, making it necessary and justifiable to deal with the statist roots of armed insurgencies as well as their nonstate branches; terrorism as such was not treated as a serious threat unless linked to an otherwise hostile and dangerous state; (4) that sufficient military capabilities accompanied by an interventionary diplomacy and the correct strategic goals would alone make it possible for the United States to act forcibly and effectively to reshape the political landscape of the Middle East, and maybe additionally, to confront China in a manner that intimidated Beijing, even at the risk of provoking a war with China, hoping to blunt any Chinese regional challenge before China became too strong to defeat at an acceptable cost; (5) and disturbingly for this program, that the political mood in the United States as of the year 2000 was recognized as not being currently supportive of this approach, and unlikely to become so without the occurrence of what the PNAC infamously called "a new Pearl Harbor"; it was this phrase, combined with this then politically incorrect militarist vision of America's future, that lurks in the vicinity of the many suspicions that have surfaced about the official account of the September 11 attacks.[1]

In addition to these explicit features advocated in the PNAC a number of *implicit* features can be surmised despite not being openly avowed: (1) that such a plan depended for its formulation and implementation on a primary regional partnership with Israel, the country that stood most directly to gain if the plan became operative policy for the United States; (2) that an impending energy squeeze arising from relatively fixed and depleting oil and natural gas supplies in the face of rising demand made American control of the Middle East indispensable for both the effective maintenance of a stable world economy, and an assurance that rising Asian demands for oil would not have a negative impact on American interests; (3) that this foreign-policy blueprint could not be effectively put into practice unless the role of international law and the United Nations was *minimized*, if not repudiated; and (4) that the United States' former heavy reliance on the Atlanticist alliance during the Cold War needed now to be superseded by a far more unilateralist approach to foreign policy, supplemented as feasible on an ad hoc basis by "coalitions of the willing."[2]

After September 11 this set of rightist ideas and assessments, previously relegated to the angry margins of American policy making was instantly, yet secretly, adopted as American foreign policy with some minor adjustments and major extensions. What the September 11 atmosphere enabled, as skillfully taken advantage of by the Bush presidency and reinforced by the mainstream media with the help of the religious right, was a new patrioteering language to validate the pursuit of global ambitions in a manner that had not been previously possible. This language newly stressed the menace and the "evil" of "terrorism" and declared "a war on terror" of global dimensions that gave a green light to state actors around the world, but particularly Israel, to disguise militarist behavior contrary to international law beneath an all-embracing umbrella of exemption labeled "counterterrorism."

Israel, as should have been expected, quickly took the cue, with Ariel Sharon, leader and strong man until suffering a stroke in 2005, declaring that Yasser Arafat was their Osama Bin Laden and pushing a security agenda by harsh means that completely circumvented Palestinian claims for a just solution of the conflict, and acting as if the various UN resolutions demanding immediate withdrawal from the Palestinian Territories occupied in 1967, including East Jerusalem, had become irrelevant.

The demonstration on September 11 of American vulnerability to attack also encouraged the U.S. leadership to portray any opposition at home to its war (of unspecified dimensions in time and space) on terror as unpatriotic, thereby crippling principled criticism in either Congress or the media, weakening the constitutional checks on abusive governmental power, and confirming the refusal of the U.S. government to deal *democratically* with this new security challenge (that total war capabilities were vested in the American president was rationalized most fully by John Yoo[3]).

The elusive character of the Al Qaeda network held publicly responsible for the attacks on America also encouraged the formation of a policy consensus embracing innovations in thinking about national security that endorsed the "Clean Break"/PNAC pre–September 11 blueprints: it now seemed more reasonable to view states that were alleged to be supporting any nonstate actor engaged in armed struggle as enemies and as the main responsible parties, an attitude that was initially given a plausible basis in the American rationale for the Afghanistan War; it seemed necessary and reasonable to act in an anticipatory fashion to address these emergent threats, especially if these might at some future time manage to gain access to nuclear and other weapons of mass destruction.[4] This whole approach to alleged threats was given prominence by asserting claims to wage preemptive wars as a necessary means to avoid future devastating attacks.

This nightmare scenario of terrorists with weaponry of mass destruction was relied on, although reinforced with "cooked evidence," to justify the invasion and occupation of Iraq. The official packaging of "Clean Break" and PNAC as a statement of American thinking in the post–September 11 world took the form of the influential White House document "National Security Strategy of the United States of America," initially released in September 2002, which was followed in March 2006 by a new version that took self-serving account of intervening developments. The cruder expression of this militarist model of world order is to be found in a comprehensive neoconservative insider tract, written by David Frum and Richard Perle, *An End to Evil*, which is more explicit than U.S. official statements about the need to promote "regime change" throughout the Middle East, starting with Iraq as Act I of a multiact geopolitical drama, consisting of a series of wars in the region, which, these authors contend, is the only way to overcome successfully the challenges of global terrorism.

All versions of neoconservative thinking show this comforting reliance on a highly partisan dualism pitting the "evil" terrorists (who are lumped together as all armed political actors that are nonstate actors unless they happen to be working on behalf of the Israeli-American partnership) who visit death and destruction on the innocent, particularly Americans and Jews, and the "good" political actors who wage just wars against these criminal regimes, and their nonstate proxies, so as to have an opportunity to bring "democracy" (a parallel dualism involves "civilized" and "uncivilized"). The visionary claim underlying launching this just war on global terrorism was linked to the achievements of World War II, including the argument that what was done after the war to restore Germany and Japan would in the future be done for the countries of the Middle East that endured the experience of regime change by force of arms.[5] Bush has also linked the war on terror to the Cold War, presenting it as the great ideological struggle of the twenty-first century.

The Iraq War was intended to show skeptics that the vision was viable and legitimate, but even before the war commenced, it aroused controversy and opposition throughout the world, both on the part of traditional American allies, but even more so on the level of overseas public opinion. Never before in world history had there been such a global display of antiwar sentiments *prior* to the outbreak of war than was exhibited at the demonstrations held on February 15, 2003 in some sixty countries, involving eight hundred cities, and as many as eleven million participants. Above all, outside the United States and Israel there were deep suspicions that a war against Iraq could not be convincingly justified as a counterterrorist project, and that its initiation was definitely not about what it was claimed to be about, and subverted the core commitment of the UN memebership to renounce aggressive war as a permissible option of foreign policy. Critics of the policy insisted that evidence of Iraqi threats to the region and beyond were greatly exaggerated and manipulated, if not callously invented, and further, that the effects of such a war were likely to be harmful to regional and global security in a variety of respects, including the aggravation of extremist threats emanating from the Islamic world, as well as deepening dangerous fissures within Islam.

It was accepted in antiwar circles that Saddam Hussein was a loathsome dictator, but it was strongly believed that removing him by military force was a dangerous and unpredictable precedent that would bring death and destruction to the people of Iraq, add to regional instability, and undermine international law and the authority of the United Nations. When the United States, despite this unprecedented display of popular and governmental opposition, in collaboration with Britain went ahead with the invasion of Iraq in March 2003, and seemed initially to pull it off successfully given the low level of battlefield resistance by the Baghdad regime, there was immediate talk in Washington of moving beyond Iraq in reconfiguring the region by relying on a mixture of warnings and coercive diplomacy directed at hostile regimes backed by the threat of a military option that would be kept "on the table." If formidable Iraqi resistance had not materialized, and the American invaders had been truly welcomed by most Iraqis as liberators, the Bush/neoconservative approach would have seemed vindicated, most critics quieted, making the planned subsequent steps in the grand strategy feasible from global and domestic American political perspectives.

But as we know, the Iraq War has turned into a costly quagmire, which has increasingly suggested comparisons with Vietnam rather than with the experiences of Germany and Japan after 1945. The high cost in lives and resources has meant that the regional plan seemed temporarily suspended, and finding a face-saving solution for failure in Iraq became the obsession of the Bush presidency during its final years. In the background, the promotion of democracy remained a rhetorical motif, exhibited both in the Greater Middle East Initiative and American pressures throughout the region to hold free elections. But just as American military superiority failed to produce a political victory in Iraq, so has the electoral path failed to result in the sort of leadership in the region that the U.S. government expected to emerge, and hoped for: secular moderates who looked to Washington and the World Bank/IMF for security, assistance, development policy, and overall guidance. In Iraq itself, Iraqis strongly repudiated these American preferences as to political orientation, despite an occupying army and an ongoing insurgency, and those candidates overwhelmingly favored by the voters were religiously oriented Shia with strong ties to Iran.

An even more emphatic repudiation of "made in the USA" democracy than this experience in Iraq occurred when Hamas scored a clear victory in the January 2006 elections in Palestine. It was these elections that finally drove home the unwelcome message that should have been obvious all along: namely, the stark incompatibility between "democracy" as conceived in Washington and "counterterror" as the operational vector for American foreign policy. As late as June 2005, Condoleezza Rice, speaking at the American University in Cairo, lauded the reversal in American security thinking from a privileging of "stability" over "freedom" to a new stress on trusting the citizenry through the establishment of genuine democracy, with elections as the centerpiece of the policy. Surprisingly, the PNAC issued an over-the-top statement that compared her banal remarks in Cairo to George C. Marshall's historic Harvard Commencement Address of 1945 proposing massive American economic assistance in the reconstruction of Europe, what became known as the Marshall Plan, one of the great triumphs in American diplomacy after World War II. The PNAC praise was accompanied by the even more surprising claim that the Rice speech could only live up to this hyped potential if and when its pro-democracy sentiments were reinforced by concrete steps. It is something of a mystery as to why these close observers of the region did not seem to realize that the more democratic Arab countries became, the more intense would be the opposition of their elected leaders to the goals and practices of the U.S./Israel regional partnership.

But underneath the continuation of the Iraq project of democratization, and this high-profile pressure on the Arab governments to embrace genuine democracy, was a rising crescendo of doubts as to whether American policy was on the right path either with respect to its interests in the region or its counterterrorist efforts. It did appear that the Bush presidency in the early part of 2006 was edging toward the more standard realist approach to American foreign policy. This would have meant a drastic downgrading of interventionary ambitions as set forth in the "Clean Break"/PNAC proposals, as endorsed by NSS 2002, 2006. This seeming shift led to rumblings of discontent from neoconservatives who privately, and even publicly, expressed their disappointment with this apparent unwillingness of the Bush presidency to move forward, despite difficulties, along the lines earlier prescribed. A growing discontent was beginning to fracture an earlier neoconservative united front. There was grumbling in the influential right-wing think tanks in Washington that the White House was no longer committed to the grand strategy associated with the forcible restructuring of political life in the Middle East. Richard Perle, often a weathervane of the neoconservative mood, chastised the Bush administration, contending that it was guilty of an "ignominious retreat" with respect to confronting Iran about its nuclear energy program.

The Israeli leadership was particularly agitated by evidence of a growing arsenal of weaponry under the control of Hezbollah, by Iran's suspected nuclear weapons ambitions combined with the inflammatory anti-Israeli rhetoric of the new Iranian president, Mahmoud Ahmadinejad, and by the Hamas political victory in the Palestinian Territories. The neoconservative/Israeli collaboration seemed desperate to find a way to revive support for the earlier *regional* strategy of comprehensive restructuring that Washington seemed to be on the verge of abandoning. In effect, just as the original embrace of the strategy depended on a new Pearl Harbor, this renewal of support for the strategy depended on a new, new Pearl Harbor — that is, a further shock administered to the political system that would renew patriotic fervor in the United States for striking at supposed enemies.

This time instead of the Al Qaeda attacks on the World Trade Center and the Pentagon, the impetus for the revival of American embrace of belligerency was supplied by routine border incidents in which a single Israeli soldier was abducted by Hamas militants in Gaza and some days later on July 12, 2006, two others by a cross-border Hezbollah operation in northern Israel. The Israeli response by way of war, rather than by measured retaliation and diplomacy, created a similar, although less dramatic effect to September 11 in Washington — an occasion for the display of unconditional, unwavering bipartisan domestic and governmental U.S. support for Israel, which could only be made fully credible by an American governmental re-embrace of the regional scenario, but in a new more militarist form of a single war rather than the prior primary reliance on diplomacy, to be sure, backed by the threat of serial wars.

So in place of the September 11 hyperbolic declaration of a global war on terror, the border incidents generated a reaffirmation of a regional strategy directed against all those elements in the Middle East that seem to threaten Israeli security or American grand strategy, which currently meant, above all, Syria and Iran. This shift also seemed politically beneficial given Bush's low popularity among Americans, the upcoming November Congressional elections, the need to divert attention from bad news coming out of Iraq, and the unwillingness of the entire U.S. establishment to question, whatever the circumstances, Israel's motives and behavior. As we shall note, the shock-and-awe tactics Israel used in Lebanon initiated a new phase of the earlier plan for regional domination. This later version was more overtly dependent on war as the instrument of control, and largely abandoned the promises of benign democratization and a patient implementation scenario of one country at a time. It also overtly relies on a diplomatic/military partnership between Washington and Tel Aviv. Which of the partners is actually calling the tune, however, remains in the realm of conjecture. (Recall Cheney's public statement months earlier about Israel taking matters with Iran into its own hands, and Israeli defense leaders saying they could not live with a potential Iranian nuclear weapons program.) Of course, it is only possible to speculate at this point as to why Israel went so far in its military campaign beyond its supposed objectives of destroying Hezbollah. One possibility is that Israel may have actually wished to engender an anti-Israeli backlash in Tehran and the Arab street so as to produce a retaliatory response by Iran that would, in turn, give the United States the excuse it needed to widen its own battlefield by taking on Iran and Syria.

ATTACKING GAZA AND LEBANON

Israeli launched its wars in Gaza and Lebanon in a highly provocative manner that seems linked to widening a regional war with severe global consequences. Addressing these wider dangers is not meant to minimize the human suffering and regressive political effects of the carnage that has already taken a severe toll in these two long-tormented war zones. Looking at this bigger picture is crucial for its own sake, but also to help us understand the various dimensions of the specific crises more fully than if as officially presented by Israel, and unfortunately echoed by many governments around the world, as dealing only with Hamas and Hezbollah.

Whatever else, this outbreak of major two-front violence is not about Israel's right to defend itself against an enemy that is seriously threatening its territorial integrity or political independence, the only acceptable grounds in international law for justifiable war. To treat border incidents, involving initially a few military casualties and the abduction of a single Israeli soldier by a Gazan militia and two by Hezbollah near the Lebanon border, as an occasion justifying war is a gross distortion of well-accepted rules of international law and patterns of state practice. A huge chasm in law and morality separates the contested claim that Israel enjoys "the right of self-defense" and Israel's indubitable "right to defend itself." The latter right is narrow in scope and duration, and is essentially an accepted option of proportionate retaliation, while the former right gives a state the option of engaging its adversary as a totality in a defensive war. To legally justify a claim of self-defense requires a full-scale armed attack across Israeli borders. If every violent border incident or terrorist provocation were to be treated as an act of war, the world would be aflame. If India had responded to the July 11, 2006, Mumbai train explosions that killed some two hundred Indian civilians as a Pakistani act of war, the result would undoubtedly have been a devastating regional war, quite possibly fought with nuclear weapons. Many other flashpoints around the world might justify police methods in reaction to provocations, and in extreme instances, specific military responses across borders, but certainly not recourse to war. Recent Hamas/Hezbollah provocations, even if interpreted through a self-serving Israeli lens, were not of a scale or posing a threat that warranted large-scale military actions directed at a wide array of targets unrelated to the particular incidents and causing severe damage to civilians and the entire civilian infrastructure of highly vulnerable societies (water, electricity, roads, bridges).[6]

The wildly disproportionate and excessive Israeli response, together with circumstantial evidence, shows persuasively that Israel used the Hamas/Hezbollah incidents as pretexts to pursue a much wider and long-planned security agenda directed at Palestine and Lebanon, and beyond this, as an opportunity for reinvigorating the plan for the political restructuring of the entire region in partnership with the United States. In this regard, George W. Bush quickly obliged with his comments in mid-July 2006 at the St. Petersburg G-8 summit attributing the *real* responsibility for the anti-Israeli incidents to Syria and Iran due to their support of Hamas and Hezbollah. What made this Bush line so startling in this context was that it was Israel that had been provoking these relatively passive nonstate adversaries in the weeks before these incidents, and it was Washington that had supplied the funds and weapons enabling Israel to embark on such major military operations. In effect, the United States was the sponsor of the state that ruptured the delicate structure of stability in the region, and Iran and Syria, even if linked closely to Hamas and Hezbollah, that were acting cautiously, and mainly in defensive modes.

Israel was apparently undertaking a major change of tactics with respect to the pursuit of this regional vision, or put differently, it was trying to rescue this vision from abandonment due to earlier miscalculations. The initial plan for regional restructuring seems to have been based on a decisive military and *political* victory by the American-led forces in Iraq followed by an essentially *diplomatic* campaign to exert major pressure sequentially on other problematic governments in the region, relying on the Greater Middle East Project of "democratization" to do the heavy lifting, possibly without requiring further military action. The decisive victory in Iraq was to signal the self-destructive futility of resisting American diplomatic pressures — that it was better to comply than face devastation and occupation. Instead of this expected scenario, what has occurred has been failure and frustration in Iraq, which is slowly becoming an American nightmare, but even more seriously for the wider plan, a consistent set of electoral outcomes throughout the region that have discredited a tough-love *political* approach to the regional vision embraced by Washington and Tel Aviv.

That paragon of conventional wisdom, Thomas Friedman, without the slightest expression of remorse for his earlier advocacy of the Iraq War for the sake of democracy rather than in light of the alleged threat emphasized by the Bush/ Cheney administration, adopted a new line. Back in 2003 Friedman felicitously championed an attack on Iraq as "a war of choice" (rather than necessity); now with an equally dogmatic tone he audaciously declares that the outcome of recent elections shows that promoting democracy is a misguided project because it brings to power Islamists who do not pursue lines of policy that are pleasing to the United States and Israel, and therefore do not deserve to be treated as legitimate political leaders.[7] Friedman is not a neoconservative, and so he now reverses course, counseling a measured withdrawal from Iraq rather than "staying the course," and does not seem to favor upping the ante in Iraq by extending the boundaries of the battlefield to include Iran.[8]

The contrasting neoconservative position was clearly depicted by William Kristol in the early stages of the Lebanon War, when he called for an even closer identification by the Bush presidency with the Israeli war effort in Lebanon, and most revealingly, vigorously advocated an attack on Iran's nuclear facilities without bothering to go through the motions of pretending to seek a diplomatic solution. In language softer in tone but more inflammatory than that of Ahmadinejad in substance, Kristol writes in support of striking Iran as soon as possible:

> Why wait? Does anyone think that a nuclear Iran can be contained? That the current regime will negotiate in good faith? It would be easier to act sooner than later. Yes, there would be repercussions — and they would be healthy ones, showing a strong America that has rejected further appeasement.[9]

It is a rather stunning rhetorical flourish to describe unprovoked aggression against Iran as a rejection of "*further* appeasement," especially when the U.S./ Israeli political maneuvers of recent months have been an exercise in threat diplomacy warning Iran of dire consequences if they assert their legal rights with respect to peaceful nuclear technology. Indeed, Kristol shamelessly portrays Iran as fighting Israel in a proxy war fought on Lebanese territory, avoiding the far more plausible interpretation that it is a proxy war by Israel/the United States against Iran at the expense of Lebanon.

But rather than abandoning geopolitical ambitions, it appears from recent developments that Israel is testing the waters for all-out regional war, with strong encouragement by the U.S. government taking a variety of overt forms: a public buildup of deployed air-strike forces backed by war plans for the destruction of up to ten thousand targets in Iran;[10] unconditional diplomatic support for Israel's responses, including blocking for several weeks in the UN Security Council and elsewhere widely favored calls for an immediate ceasefire in Lebanon, and the undisguised provision to Israel in the midst of the war of large quantities of aviation fuel and a rushed shipment of additional bombs. At the same time, with an arrogant embrace of inconsistency, the United States and Israel continue to insist that Syrian and Iranian funding and arms transfers to Hezbollah make them responsible for the war, not even just the provoking incidents. And further, that Israel's responses are being misleadingly treated by Washington as appropriate contributions to the overall global war on terror, as if Hezbollah and Hamas are without legitimate grievances that must be fairly addressed at some point if peace and security are to be ever achieved in the region.

Of course, other factors are at work. Such profound commitments underlying recourse to war are always overdetermined, with many contributing, overlapping causes. The Israeli leadership, especially its military commanders, never accepted being pushed out of southern Lebanon by Hezbollah in 2000, and Israeli politicians and public opinion appear to hold the Palestinian people responsible, and subject to collective punishment, for daring to elect a "terrorist" leadership. Furthermore, the anti-Syrian Lebanese response to the assassination of Rafiq Hariri on February 14, 2005 was hoped to result in a more congenial Lebanese political leadership that would effectively disarm and constrain Hezbollah in accordance with Security Council Resolution 1559 (2004), and thereby enhance the security of Israel's northern border. When this did not happen, but rather Hezbollah acquired more potent weaponry and was given two ministries in the Lebanese cabinet, it was obvious that the relatively soft Israeli option to reorient the governing process in Lebanon had failed. Even such a prominent mainstream supporter of Israeli policy as Shlomo Aveneri was quoted as believing the real objective of the Israeli attacks on Lebanon was to install a Quisling government in Beirut, which was after all a main objective of the 1982 Sharon-led invasion of the country, along with the destruction of the PLO. It turns out neither goal was then achieved, and now in some respects this represents a second try some twenty-four years later with even more disastrous results for Israel. Some also speculate that Ehud Olmert was trying to get out from under the shadow of his mentor, Sharon, by showing a comparable boldness with respect to military solutions but also to produce an outcome in Lebanon in 2006 that Israelis would hail as a major triumph in contrast with the 1982 war, which came eventually to be regarded as an Israeli setback. The first Lebanon War had also cast a dark shadow of illegitimacy due to Israel's distasteful involvement in the Sabra and Shatila massacres associated with their occupation of Beirut.

In relation to the Palestinian conflict, Israel has set for itself a unilateralist course ever since the collapse of the Camp David process in 2000, and possibly earlier. The Sharon approach, based on Gaza disengagement, the illegal security wall, and the annexation of substantial Palestinian territories to incorporate the main Israeli settlements was premised on moving toward a "solution" without obtaining the agreement of the Palestinian leadership, over the heads of the Palestinian people, and without regard for Palestinian rights under international law. But to move in such a direction in an internationally palatable manner required the absence of a credible Palestinian negotiating partner. Several steps were taken. First, Arafat was humiliated by direct military attacks on his headquarters; he was almost killed, and made subject to a harsh form of house arrest; then his successor, Mahmoud Abbas, despite being a moderate Palestinian voice to the point of virtual cooption, was quickly marginalized by Tel Aviv, being declared too weak to exert political weight; and now Hamas has been repudiated as unfit to govern the Palestinians or represent their interests, and warranting their destruction and the arrest of their elected leadership. Given such a construction of alternative Palestinian realities, Sharon/Olmert unilateralism appears to be the only remaining option, a worrisome conclusion on its own as it is sure to keep the conflict at boiling point for the indefinite future, as well as to prolong and intensify the Palestinian ordeal still further.

Another piece in the regional puzzle is the Israel/U.S. confrontation with Iran centered on its nuclear program. Here again Israel and the United States are at the forefront of an insistence that Iran not pursue its legal right under Article IV of the Nonproliferation Treaty to possess a complete nuclear-fuel cycle under its sovereign control, although subject to inspection by the International Atomic Energy Agency to ensure that highly enriched uranium and plutonium are not being diverted for military purposes. Whether this unfolding crisis, conveniently yet dangerously abetted from Tehran by the extremist anti-Zionist populism of Ahmadinejad, is part of a deliberate strategy of regional tension devised by Washington and Tel Aviv cannot be determined at this point. What is clear is the selective and discriminatory enforcement of the nonproliferation regime. Several parties to the nonproliferation treaty (Germany, Japan) have complete nuclear-fuel cycles under national control; India in violation of the NPT is being assisted in further developing its nuclear technology despite its nuclear weapons program and refusal to become a party to the treaty; Israel itself disallows a nuclear weapons option to other states in the region while maintaining and developing its own arsenal of these weapons; and, of course, the United States flexes its nuclear muscles as it wishes, including developing new categories of nuclear weapons ("bunker-busters" and "mini-nukes") that are apparently being integrated into battle plans for possible future use.

This adds up to an alarming picture, but with a clear risk of a regional war emerging from the present situation, given the shared Israeli/American vision of sustainable security, and the degree to which the control of this region is vital for the energy future of the world, decisive in the struggle by the West to withstand the challenge of political Islam, and central to satisfying Israeli underlying concerns and ambitions for U.S./Israel hegemonic control over the Middle East.

Some factors are working against this dismal future: the political/military failure in Iraq (and now Lebanon) inhibits recourse to further warfare, conveying the lesson that military superiority often cannot be translated into victory in the face of determined *political* resistance; the probable devastating economic and political effects of engaging Iran in war; the rising oil prices; the growing opposition of European and Arab countries to Israeli/American militancy. But can we be reassured at this point? I think not. Israel tends to view its security fears and ambitions in unconditional terms that seem almost oblivious to wider detrimental consequences or to adverse world public attitudes. The current United States leadership seems perversely to be in the process of reaffirming its grand strategy of regional restructuring, and is not yet encountering politically meaningful opposition at home or even serious media criticism as a result of either its support of the Israeli offensives in Gaza and Lebanon or of its efforts to widen the arc of conflict by doing its diplomatic best to pull Syria and Iran into the fray.

I fear that we are witnessing a potentially disastrous set of moves to shift the joint Israeli/American regional game plan in an even more menacing and overtly militarist direction. Although it always had a military centerpiece associated with the Iraq War, the earlier basic strategy was expected to be a decisive and successful show of force against a weakened Iraq that was ruled by a hated tyrant, followed by falling political dominoes elsewhere in the Middle East. Neither the UN, world public opinion, other centers of state power, nor opposition by Arab countries seem to have the will or capacity to halt this slide toward regional war. We can only hope that the neoconservative revival of ideological hegemony in Washington is temporary, and that this cabal is not again calling all the shots. The hope must be that common sense and prudence can somehow mysteriously regain the upper hand to act as a restraining force, at least in Washington. Already there are signs of blowback, with Hezbollah emerging as the political winner in Lebanon, with Iran not far behind. The central cleavage in the Middle East that is now gaining media attention is the supposed contest between Iranian-led Shias and Saudi-led Sunnis for regional supremacy among contesting Islamic elites. It seems clear that such a cleavage is partly constructed and manipulated by outside forces, but to the extent that it expresses authentic tensions it makes Iran a regional force in ways that did not exist prior to the American failure in Iraq. But it should also be noted that among the peoples of the Islamic Middle East there exists considerable solidarity that appears almost oblivious to the Shia/Sunni split. Undoubtedly, this split is operative to varying degrees at governmental levels, and explains the slowness of Arab governments to give support to Hezbollah in the early stages of the Israeli attacks on Lebanon, but as popular pressure mounted, even Sunni governments felt compelled to side with the Shia Hezbollah. After the war Sheik Nasrallah became a major hero throughout the Arab world, including in the Sunni countries.

A CONCLUDING REFLECTION

The argument above rests on the conviction that Israel with at least tacit support by the United States generated a global crisis by launching its 2006 war against Lebanon that deeply threatens regional peace and security in the Middle East. The original rationale for embarking on this path can be found in the "Clean Break" and PNAC reports discussed earlier, but under altered conditions created by the unanticipated failure of American policy in Iraq coupled with the renewed challenge of a resurgent Iran. These developments were beginning to erode neoconservative/Israeli influence in the White House, raising concerns in neoconservative circles of a quiet abandonment of the grand strategy for coercing a series of regime changes in the Middle East. The Lebanon War, in particular, can be seen as a bold gamble to revive the commitments of the grand strategy, but on a basis that risks, even invites, a single definitive, regional war. The earlier hopes for legitimizing the grand strategy by emphasizing democratization are being discarded, and replaced by an undisguised reliance on military dominance and the geopolitical determination to engage hostile forces and governments by means of major military attacks and all-out war, as necessary.

It is obvious that there are additional implications for other countries in the region, especially those faced with ethnic conflict and transnational armed struggle. As tempting as it might be for Turkey to follow Israel's lead by intervening in northern Iraq to deal with the PKK insurgent elements operating from there, following such a course would magnify present dangers. It is rather revealing that Turkish leaders simultaneously condemned Israel for its indiscriminate use of force in Lebanon and invoked the attacks as "an international law precedent" to justify its own possible future cross-border military operations. The U.S. government seemingly worried about an expanding war zone beyond its control has reassured Ankara that it would take care of Turkish concerns in northern Iraq, making an incursion unnecessary.

The U.S./Israel partnership threatens to ignite what could easily morph into a world war causing death and destruction throughout the Middle East and beyond, perhaps setting loose a tsunami of suicide bombings engulfing the entire world. (Newton Gingrich argues that we are already in the midst of World War III, and that the "global war on terrorism" is too modest a conception.[11] Such a war, with adversaries that believe in pursuing their goals on a global battlefield, could only end in defeat for both sides and tragedy for the peoples of the world. It is impossible to imagine victory and peace if the full fury of regional war fought on the basis of civilizational antagonism becomes a reality instead of, as is presently the case, just a troublesome danger that governments and public action must act with utmost urgency to prevent.

But even if these dark forebodings never materialize, the negative impacts of the Lebanon War of 2006, together with the Gaza Offensive, have further undermined the quality of world order in at least four respects: (1) further weakening the prohibition on discretionary war; (2) further weakening respect for the UN Security Council in relation to its primary role of protecting victims of aggression; (3) further weakening the authority of international humanitarian law as a respected restraint on war making; (4) further demonstrating the subordination of international law and global justice to geopolitics as the foundation of world order, as well as the cruelty and dysfunctionality of present geopolitical leadership.

At this stage, the regional picture is clouded. It could be clarified in various ways by later developments. The Lebanon War could be followed by attacks on Iran and confrontation with Syria, with many bad repercussions likely to follow, including a possible worldwide economic recession, or even collapse. But there is another possibility, namely, that the failure in Iraq and Lebanon will lead to a quiet reappraisal of a war-driven grand strategy for the Middle East, inducing finally a clean break from clean break advocacy. If this were to happen it could lead to withdrawal from Iraq, reconstruction of Lebanon, renewed negotiation with the Palestinians along the newly revived lines of the 2002 Arab League initiative, normalization of relations with Iran and Syria, the prohibition of any possession of nuclear weapons in the region, establishing a nuclear weapons–free zone throughout the Middle East, and finally, a regional security framework based on mutual recognition, respect for international law and the United Nations Charter, and assurances of the resolution of all disputes by peaceful means.

5

What Future for the UN Charter System of War Prevention?
Reflections on the Iraq War

The impact of the Iraq War on the future role of the United Nations is a highly speculative matter at this stage. Even the combat phases of the war were far from over despite President George W. Bush's ill-conceived, and retrospectively ridiculous, proclamation of victory in May 2003. The war later assumed the form of an escalating and multifaceted resistance to foreign occupation, and then further evolved into a multilayered armed struggle that combined resistance with civil war. It remains unclear whether, as Washington officially contends, the main perpetrators of the initial insurgency were mainly remnants of the Baathist regime, or something more complex. At the start of the occupation of Iraq, the American leadership was inclined to minimize the UN participation in the restoration of normalcy in Iraq, but as early as July 2003, the U.S. government began to encourage a much-expanded set of UN responsibilities, and to call on a wide range of countries to supply troops and share the peacekeeping burdens and risks in Iraq. This never happened, but the degree of UN response to this American call for assistance did implicate the UN in the occupation, as was dramatically exhibited by the bombing of UN Headquarters in Baghdad some months later. Although much has changed over the course of the American occupation of Iraq and in the world more generally, the impact of the early role of the UN in the Iraq War remains relevant as we consider the future for the UN Charter conception of war and security.

FRAMING AN INQUIRY

President Bush historically challenged the United Nation Security Council when he uttered some memorable words in the course of his September 12, 2002, speech to the General Assembly: "Will the UN serve the purpose of its founding, or will it be irrelevant?"[1] In the aftermath of the Iraq War there are at least two answers to this question. The U.S. government's immediate answer was to insist that the UN turned out to be irrelevant due to its failure to endorse recourse to war against the Iraq of Saddam Hussein. The answer of those who opposed the war is that the UNSC served the purpose of its founding by its refusal to endorse recourse to a war that could not be convincingly reconciled with the UN Charter and international law. This difference of assessment is not just on such factual matters as to whether Iraq possessed weapons of mass destruction, whether it was a threat to peace and security, and whether the inspection process was effective in detecting Iraqi compliance with UN resolutions. The issues at stake were also conceptual, even jurisprudential. The long-term outcome of this assessment is likely to exert a major influence on the future role of the United Nations, as well as affect the attitude of the most powerful sovereign state as to the relationship between international law generally and the use of force as an instrument of foreign policy.

These underlying concerns antedate the recent preoccupations provoked by debate on Iraq. Similar issues were vigorously debated during the Cold War era, especially during the latter stages of the Vietnam War.[2] But the context of recent discussions of the Iraq War with respect to the interplay between sovereign discretion as to the use of force and UN authority was earlier framed in the late 1990s around the topic of humanitarian intervention, especially in relation to the Kosovo War. The burning issue in the Kosovo setting was whether "a coalition of the willing" acting under the umbrella of NATO was legally entitled to act as a residual option given the perceived UNSC unwillingness to mandate a use of force despite the urgent humanitarian dangers facing the Albanian Kosovars. In that instance, a formal mandate was sought and provided by NATO, but without achieving the sort of legal foundation that seemed textually required by Article 53(1) of the UN Charter — that is, a formal expression of explicit authorization by the UN Security Council. Legal apologists for the Kosovo initiative argued that such authorization could be derived from prior UN Security Council resolutions, as well as from the willingness of the UN to manage the postconflict civil reconstruction of Kosovo without ever censuring NATO's recourse to war. It would seem that such actions amounted to a tacit assent on the part of the UN, providing the undertaking with a retroactive certification of at least quasi legality. To similar effect were arguments suggesting that the defeat in the Security Council of a resolution of censure introduced by those members opposed to the Kosovo War amounted to an implied acknowledgement of legality, or at the very least a refusal to categorize the war as "illegal" or in violation of the Charter. But whether such a failure should be deemed of *legal* relevance or only an indication of the primacy of geopolitics within the operations of the Security Council was never really considered.

The tension between the Kosovo War and the Charter rules on the use of force was so clear that these efforts at legalization seemed highly artificial and even evasive. The Independent International Commission on Kosovo adopted a more candid approach. It concluded that the intervention in Kosovo was "illegal, but legitimate."[3] The troublesome elasticity of such a legal conclusion was qualified in two ways: by suggesting the need for the intervening side to bear a heavy burden of persuasion as to the necessity of intervention to avoid an impending or ongoing humanitarian catastrophe; and by a checklist of duties that need to be fulfilled by the intervenors to achieve legitimacy, emphasizing the protection of the civilian population, adherence to the international laws of war, and a convincing focus on humanitarian goals, as distinct from economic and strategic aims that would appear to benefit the intervening side. In Kosovo the moral and political case for intervention seemed strong: a vulnerable and long-abused majority population facing an imminent prospect of ethnic cleansing by Serb rulers; a scenario for effective intervention with minimal risks of unforeseen negative effects or extensive collateral damage; and the absence of significant nonhumanitarian motivations on the intervening side. As such, the foundation for a principled departure under exceptional circumstances from a strict rendering of Charter rules on the use of force seemed present. The legality/legitimacy gap, however, was acknowledged as unhealthy, eroding the authority of international law over time, and the Commission recommended strongly that it be closed at the earliest possible time by UN initiative. Its report urged, for example, that the permanent members of the Security Council consider informally agreeing to refrain from casting adverse votes in the setting of impending humanitarian catastrophes, and thus suspend the operation of the veto despite disagreeing with the initiative under consideration.[4] The adoption of such a practice would have enabled the Kosovo intervention to win approval in the Security Council despite Russian and Chinese opposition, which would have been registered in the debate, but not in the form of a veto that would preclude UN authorization of NATO's recourse to war.

More ambitiously, the Commission proposed a three-step process designed to implant within the United Nations Charter System the enforcement role of the Organization in contexts of severe human rights violations. The first step consists of a framework of principles designed to limit claims of humanitarian intervention to a narrow set of circumstances, and to assure that the dynamics of implementation adhere to international humanitarian law and promote the well being of the people being protected. The second step is to draft a resolution for adoption by the General Assembly in the form of a Declaration on the Right and Responsibility of Humanitarian Intervention that seeks to reconcile respect for sovereign rights, the duty to implement human rights, and the responsibility to prevent humanitarian catastrophes. The third step would be to amend the Charter to incorporate these changes as they pertain to the role and responsibility of the UN Security Council, and other multilateral frameworks and coalitions that undertake humanitarian interventions.[5] It should be noted that no progress toward closing this legitimacy/legality gap by formal or informal action within the United Nations has occurred, or can be anticipated in the near future. There exists substantial opposition on issues of principle as well as policy, especially among Asian countries, to any expansion of the interventionary mandate of the United Nations and other political actors in the setting of human rights. This opposition has deepened since Kosovo because of the controversial uses of force claimed by the United States in its antiterrorism campaign that have combined security and human rights arguments in settings where widespread suspicion existed with respect to the true geopolitical motives of Washington.

Iraq tested the UN Charter system in a way complementary to that associated with the Kosovo controversy, but much more fundamentally. The Iraq test was associated with the overall impact of the September 11 attacks and the challenge of megaterrorism to the viability of the Charter framework governing the use of international force.[6] The initial American military response to the Al Qaeda attack and continuing threat was directed at Afghanistan, a convenient territorial target because it both seemed to be the nerve center of the terrorist organization and a country ruled by the Taliban, a regime enjoying the most minimal diplomatic stature, and complicit in the attacks on American targets, at least passively, by allowing Al Qaeda to operate extensive terrorist training bases within its territory. As such, Afghanistan, as represented by the Taliban, lacked some crucial attributes needed for full membership in international society, including the failure to obtain widespread diplomatic recognition. The reasonableness of waging war to supplant the Taliban regime and destroy the Al Qaeda base of operations in Afghanistan was widely accepted by the entire spectrum of countries active in world politics, although there was only the most minimal effort by the U.S. government to demonstrate that it was acting within the UN framework. The Al Qaeda responsibility for September 11 was demonstrated to the satisfaction of most, although controversy and skepticism persist as to whether the attacks could and should have been prevented. Beyond this assurance about responsibility for September 11, the prospect of future attacks seemed great and possibly imminent in the immediate aftermath. As well, the American capability to win a war in Afghanistan at a proportional cost seemed convincing. For these reasons, there was no significant international opposition to the American initiation and conduct of the Afghanistan War, and varying levels of support from all of America's traditional allies. International law was successfully stretched in these novel circumstances to provide a major state with the practical option of responding with force to one important territorial source of megaterrorist warfare, thereby upholding the White House claim that a government that knowingly harbors such transnational terrorists shares in responsibility for the political violence that ensues. Such a precedent was established, although without the benefit of UN endorsement. The U.S. government devoted no attention to obtaining UN approval for its Afghan policy, because back in 2001 it wanted to demonstrate that its unilateralist approach to world order was effective.

But when American leaders began to discuss the Iraq phase of the September 11 response beyond Afghanistan, most reactions around the world were deeply opposed, generating a worldwide peace movement dedicated to avoiding the war and a variety of efforts by governments normally allied with the United States to urge an alternative to war. The main American justification for proceeding immediately against Iraq was articulated in the form of a claimed right of preemptive warfare, abstractly explained as necessary, given the alleged interface between weaponry of mass destruction and the extremist tactics and suicidal mentality of the megaterrorists.[7] It was argued that it was unacceptable in these circumstances for the United States to wait to be attacked, and that preemptive warfare was an essential and reasonable response, to the extent required to uphold the security of the "civilized" portion of the world. Bush in his speech at the United Nations said, "We cannot stand by and do nothing while dangers gather."[8] It was the application of this reasoning that was rejected by the UN Security Council refusal in early 2003 to go along with U.S./UK demands for an enforcement mandate against Iraq. The precise American contention was more narrowly and multiply framed in relation to the failures of Iraq to cooperate fully with the UN inspectors, the years of nonimplementation of earlier Security Council resolutions imposing stringent disarmament obligations on Iraq after the Gulf War, and, above all, by the supposedly heightened threat posed by Iraq's alleged arsenal of nonnuclear weapons of mass destruction.[9]

The Iraq War was initiated on March 20, 2003, and the battlefield phase of military operations led to an early euphoria about victory. President Bush so declared, "In the battle of Iraq, the United States and our allies have prevailed. And now our coalition is engaged in securing and reconstructing that country."[10] The president carefully described the military operations as "a battle" rather than as "a war," subsuming the attack on Iraq within the wider, ongoing war against global terrorism, and implying that the undertaking should be seen as one element in the counterterrorism campaign launched in response to the September 11 attacks. Again, as in relation to Kosovo, the UNSC refrained from censuring the United States and its allies, and the UN has seemed at first fully willing, even eager, to play whatever part was entrusted to it by Washington during the ensuing period of military occupation and political, economic, and social reconstruction. Such acquiescence by the UN was particularly impressive given the failure of the victorious coalition in the Iraq War to find any evidence of weapons of mass destruction, or to be attacked by such weaponry despite launching a war designed to destroy precisely these supposed capabilities of the regime of Saddam Hussein. It now seems more reasonable than ever to conclude that such weaponry did not exist, or that even if it did, it had no operational relevance and that a strategy of deterrence would have been fully able to discourage any future aggressive moves by Iraq.

But let us indulge the unlikely fantasy that Iraq possessed such weapons, but they were removed from the country, never found, or destroyed before the invasion. That is, if such weapons were not used by Iraq to defend the survival of the regime in extremis, then it is highly unlikely that they would ever have been used in circumstances where an annihilating retaliation could be anticipated. If Iraq refrained when it had nothing to lose, why would Iraq use such weaponry when the assured response would be the certain destruction of country and regime? There has never existed any basis for supposing the Baghdad regime to be suicidal, and what evidence exists suggest the opposite — a strong willingness to subordinate other goals to the survival of the Baathist governing process. Even in this current occupation phase of the war, the impulse to survive as an independent and sovereign political entity seems to be the primary foundation of fierce Iraqi resistance, and one of the few elements of unity at the grassroots level in the country.

How should such a pattern of circumvention of Charter rules combined with the reluctance of the UNSC to seek censure for such violations be construed from the perspective of the future of international law? There are several overlapping modes of interpretation, each of which illuminates the issue to some extent, but none seems to provide a satisfactory account from the perspective of international law:

- The United States as the dominant state in a unipolar world order enjoys an exemption from legal accountability with respect to uses of force irreconcilable with the UN Charter System; most other states, unless close friends of the United States, would be generally held to account;
- The pattern of behavior confirms a skeptical trend that suggests the Charter System no longer corresponds, or never did correspond, with the realities of world politics, and is not authoritative in relation to the behavior of states;[11]
- The American pattern of behavior is in some tension with the Charter System, but it is a creative tension that suggests respect for the underlying values of the world community, viewing legality as a matter of degree, not either/or, and as requiring continuing adjustment to changing circumstances; as such, the claims of preemption in relation to megaterrorism provide a reasonable doctrinal explanation for an expanded right of self-defense even if the application to Iraq was unreasonable;
- Acknowledging the behavioral pressures of the world on the Charter guidlelines with respect to force, the possibility exists that contested uses of force under the Charter are "illegal, yet legitimate" either by reference to the rationale for initiating action without UNSC approval

or on the basis of the beneficial impact of the intervention.[12] From this perspective, the failure to find weapons of mass destruction does not definitively undermine the residual American claim that the intervention is "legitimate." It still could be judged as legitimate due to a series of effects: the emancipation of the Iraqi people from an oppressive regime, reinforced by the overwhelming evidence that the Baghdad rulers were guilty of systematic, widespread, massive, and crucially, *imminent* Crimes Against Humanity, and an occupation that prepares the Iraqi people for political democracy and economic success.[13]

Even now it remains impossible to predict how the Iraq War will affect the Charter system with respect to the international regulation of force. It will depend on how principal states treat the issue, especially the United States, but also such countries as France, China, India. International law, in this crucial sense, is neither more nor less than what the powerful actors in the system, and to a lesser extent the global community of international jurists, as well as the global jury of public opinion, say it is. International law in the area of the use of force cannot by itself induce consistent compliance because of sovereignty-oriented political attitudes combined with the gross disparities in power that prevent the logic of reciprocity and the benefits of mutuality operating with respect to the security agenda of states. The "realist" school has dominated the foreign-policy process of major countries throughout the existence of the modern state system, being only marginally challenged by a Wilsonian approach that is more reliant on legalism and moralism.[14] Restraints with respect to the use of force will be supported by realists only to the extent that adherence to legal norms is consistent with cost–benefit assessments. These assessments can be quite sophisticated, incorporating the diplomatic virtue of prudence and emphasizing the avoidance of overextension that realists throughout history have blamed for the decline of major states and empires.[15] A more normative perspective would argue on behalf of the intrinsic benefits arising from an acceptance of the constraining limitations of the rule of law as the only acceptable framework for the practice of geopolitics in the twenty-first century.

There are grounds for supposing that the approach of the Bush administration may not fit comfortably within the realist paradigm, but rather represents a militant and reactionary version of Wilsonian idealism.[16] President Bush has consistently described the war against terrorism in terms of good and evil, or for the sake of a democratized world, which refuses to accept constraints on force even when based on calculations of self-interest and prudence.[17] To the extent that such an orientation shapes the near future of American conduct, the UN Charter system will be disregarded by policymakers in Washington, except in those circumstances where the Security Council would support an American claim to use force.[18]

THE IRAQ WAR AND THE FUTURE OF THE CHARTER SYSTEM

Against the jurisprudential background described in the previous section, an interpretation of the Iraq precedent is necessarily tentative. It depends, in the first analysis, on whether the American battlefield victory in the Iraq War would be converted by reasonable means in a short time period into what might be generally interpreted as a political victory. Such an outcome would be best measured in Iraq by such factors as stability and security, democratization, recovery of Iraqi sovereignty, economic development, and public perceptions. If the American occupation had been viewed as successful, then the intervention was likely to be treated as "legitimate," despite being generally regarded as "illegal." If such a perception had materialized, which it has not, then the Iraq invasion would have encouraged even greater flexibility in the application of the Charter system. Against a background of a possible interplay between megaterrorist tactics and weaponry of mass destruction, claims of anticipatory self-defense would likely be granted a wide range of interpretative freedom. At the same time, some analysts will object to any effort to rewrite the Charter on the basis of such an opportunistic and retroactively rationalized repudiation of legal restraints by the world's sole superpower. Of course, the failure to convert battlefield success into political victory has undermined the formation of any precedent supporting a less textually grounded view of the right of self-defense, and undoubtedly bolsters the case for as narrow a conception of self-defense as possible.

There are two main conceptual explanations for this likely divergence of opinion. The first relates to issues of *factual plausibility*. The doctrine of preemption, as such, is less troublesome than its unilateral application in circumstances where the burden of persuasion as to the imminence and severity of the threat is not sustained. The diplomatic repudiation of the United States in the Security Council resulted mainly from the factual unpersuasiveness of the U.S. arguments about the threats associated with Iraqi retention of weaponry of mass destruction and the always flimsily supported claims of a supposed linkage between the Baghdad regime and the Al Qaeda network, thereby making reliance on deterrence and containment unacceptable in relation to Iraq. The brutality of Saddam Hussein's rule was never doubted, but there was little support for recourse to an international war with the avowed objective of achieving regime change. This skepticism has been heightened by the failure to uncover weaponry of mass destruction in the aftermath of the war, despite unimpeded access to suspicious sites, the cooperation of Iraqi scientists and weapons personnel, a massive intelligence effort, and the American insistence that the Baghdad government possessed large quantities of such weaponry.

The second ground of divergence arises from arguments about how to treat a *retroactive justification* for behavior that at the time seemed legally unacceptable. Here the focus is on whether a war opposed because its side effects seemed potentially dangerous, and its advance rationale was not convincing enough to justify stretching the Charter System of restraint, could be properly justified after the fact. The justifications combine the quick military victory on the battlefield with relatively low casualty figures, as reinforced by the documentation of the magnitude of Saddam Hussein's criminality as an Iraqi leader. Such an argument would seem more convincing if the American-led coalition forces had been clearly welcomed as "liberators" rather than mainly viewed as "occupiers," and if the postcombat American presence in Iraq was less marred by a continuous and escalating violent movement of resistance that produced a steady stream of American and Iraqi casualties. It remains still premature to reach any definitive judgment as to the political effects of the war and its wider ramifications regionally and globally. The American occupation has not succeeded and is by now widely perceived to have brought greater harmer to the Iraqi people than to their American occupiers, making arguments based on retroactive justification unlikely to gain support. The more prevalent pattern of argument relies on retroactive invalidation — that is, maintaining that the failure of the occupation confirms critics and skeptics who had issued stern warnings prior to the war. If the Iraq War had been a success within its own terms it would likely have been seen as reinforcing the then emerging enlargement of the role of the international community to protect societies vulnerable to abusive governments.[19] But as a failure the opposite effects seem the most probable.

Of course, the issue of process is important, as well as the substantive outcome. The Iraq War represented a circumvention of the collective procedures of the Charter System with respect to uses of force in contexts not covered by the Article 51 conception of self-defense. To some extent, a favorable view of the effects of such a use of force weakens objections to unilateralism, but a negative view of these effects leads to a much more restrictive view of what is allowable under the Charter. Adopting a constructivist view of international law makes "legality" depend significantly on the future conduct and attitudes of the United States government. Constructivism is an assessment of political and legal reality that places decisive emphasis on dominant mental perceptions as to a given set of conditions, whether or not such perceptions are accurate as evaluated from other standpoints.[20] Will the U.S. government in the future generally exhibit respect for the role of the Security Council or will it feel vindicated by its decision to act unilaterally in conjunction with cooperative allies, and continue to rely on such a model for conflict resolution? If the latter interpretation shapes future American foreign policy, then the Charter System will be seriously eroded, and marginalized, at least with respect to the United States. Since the United States sets the rules of the game, the overall acceptance of the prohibition on recourse to nondefensive force is likely to seem almost irrelevant so long as neoconservative attitudes hold sway in Washington.

Can the Charter System work without adherence to its procedures and restraining rules by the dominant state in the world? The constructivist answer is clarifying to a degree. To the extent that other states continue to take the Charter System as authoritative it will certainly heavily influence international responses to challenged uses of force by states other than the United States, and might deeply affect global attitudes toward American leadership. There will be complaints about the degree to which geopolitical realities trump international-law restraints and about double standards, but these complaints have been made since the United Nations came into being, and arguably were embedded in the Charter by granting a veto to the permanent members.

The approach taken in 2003 after the collapse of the Baghdad regime by the Security Council in its Resolution 1483 is indicative of a tension between acquiescence and opposition to the United States/United Kingdom recourse to war against Iraq. The resolution divides responsibility and authority between the occupying powers and the United Nations, granting the U.S./UK predominant control over the most vital concerns of security, economic and political reconstruction, and governance. At the same time, the resolution stops far short of retroactively endorsing recourse to force by the U.S./UK under the factual circumstances that existed at the time of the invasion. It dodges the issue of legality/legitimacy by avoiding any formal pronouncement, while accepting as a decisive political given the realities of the apparent outcome of the war. As a result, a high degree of ambiguity surrounded the Iraq War as an international legal event. Undoubtedly, this ambiguity has been reduced, and possibly eliminated, by a clearer consensus as to the unacceptable political outcome of the war. Future patterns of UNSC practice in peace and security contexts will be illuminating with respect to the general understanding of Charter constraints on recourse to international force.

THE CHARTER SYSTEM, MEGATERRORISM, AND HUMANITARIAN INTERVENTION

The 1990s saw a definite trend toward accepting a more interventionary role for the United Nations with respect to the prevention of ethnic cleansing and genocide. The Security Council, as supported by the last three secretaries general, reflected a greater prominence for the *international* protection of human rights and less anxiety about risks of escalation that were operative during the Cold War, thereby narrowing the degree of deference owed to the territorial supremacy of sovereign governments. As such, the domestic jurisdiction exclusion of UN intervention expressed in Article 2(7) was definitely under challenge from the widespread grassroots and governmental advocacy of humanitarian intervention in the years following the Cold War, especially in relation to the conflicts in the Balkans. These interventionary patterns of claims and practice remained hotly contested, and were resisted especially by China and other Asian countries. There was at the same time strong intergovernmental and grassroots support for humanitarian intervention. The UN was more often and more sharply attacked for doing too little to mitigate human suffering, particularly in Bosnia and Rwanda, than criticized for doing too much.[21]

A variant on this debate is connected with the instances of uses of force under American leadership in the post–September 11 world. In both Afghanistan and Iraq recourse to force rested on defensive claims against the alleged new threats of megaterrorism, but the effect in both instances was to liberate captive populations from extremely oppressive regimes, establishing patterns of governance and potential self-determination that seemed virtually impossible for the oppressed citizenry to achieve by normal modes of resistance. Even though the humanitarian *motivations* of the United States are suspect in both instances, due to a past record of collaboration with these regimes while their abusive conduct was at its worst, the effect of the interventions seemed emancipatory, and the declared intention of the occupation to support human rights and democratization, had it been implemented, would have strengthened the humanitarian justification. Undoubtedly, such forcible liberations would not have taken place without the pressures mounted and the climate created by the September 11 attacks. Nevertheless, to the extent that megaterrorism is associated with criminal forms of governmental authority, would it not have been reasonable to construe uses of force that accomplished "regime change" as part of an enlarged doctrine of humanitarian intervention had these test cases turned out favorably? As it is, the chaos and disorder that has brought suffering without end to both of these countries has undercut the humanitarian rationalizations, and given humanitarian intervention, unless authorized *in advance* by the UN, an extremely bad name.

Even without these discrediting outcomes there were many grounds for questioning retroactive humanitarian justifications for what appears from the perspective of international law to have been "aggressive war." Recourse to war is too serious a matter to allow decisions to be made by governments acting on their own. For this reason also, prudential considerations alone would seem to rule out humanitarian intervention in all but the most extreme and flagrant instances, and even in most of these due to the magnitude of the undertaking and the uncertainty of the consequences, the viability as well as the legality of humanitarian intervention would be seldom realized. Who would be so crazy as to advocate humanitarian intervention by military means on behalf of the Chechens, Tibetans, Kashmiris? Of course, many options not involving the use of force that could range from expressions of disapproval to the imposition of comprehensive sanctions are open to the international community and its member states. The case for humanitarian intervention relying on force should be treated as a principled, and even then, a rare exception to the generalized prohibition of the Charter with respect to the use of force embodied in Article 2(4).[22] If the Security Council does not mandate the intervention, and a coalition of the willing proceeds, the undertaking could still be substantially vindicated, as in Kosovo, if some sort of collective process was involved, the facts confirmed the imminence of a humanitarian emergency, and the victimized population manifested support for the intervention. The Kosovo Commission tackled this issue of principled humanitarian intervention, as have scholars, seeking to provide guidance that preserves the balance between the prohibition on uses of force contained in international law and the moral/political imperatives to mitigate impending or ongoing humanitarian catastrophes by stretching the legal restraints.[23]

A prointervention argument should not be treated as acceptable in circumstances where the use of force is associated with alleged security threats posed by the menace of megaterrorism, but the justification tendered after the fact emphasizes the case for humanitarian intervention. In Afghanistan the security argument was sufficiently convincing to make the humanitarian benefits of the war a political and moral bonus, but without bearing the burden of the legal case for recourse to force, which was sufficiently convincing on the defensive grounds claimed to satisfy most international law experts. In Iraq, by contrast, the security and related anti–Al Qaeda arguments were unconvincing before, during, and after the invasion of Iraq. The claimed humanitarian benefits that were supposed to result from the war seemed emphasized by American officials as a way to circumvent the illegality and unpopularity of the American-led recourse to force. Such post hoc efforts at legalization do not deserve much respect, especially in the context of a major war in which prior efforts to obtain a mandate for the use of force were not endorsed by the Security Council despite major diplomatic pressures mounted by Washington in the several months preceding the Iraq War, and where subsequently released evidence suggests that the supposed Iraqi threat associated with weapons of mass destruction was deliberately exaggerated, if not altogether contrived.[24]

A CONSTRUCTIVIST FUTURE FOR THE UN CHARTER SYSTEM

The position favored here is that the United States would be best served by adhering to the UN Charter System, and to international law generally.[25] This system is flexible enough to accommodate new and genuine security imperatives as well as changing values, including a shifting balance between sovereign rights and world-community responsibilities.[26] In both settings of humanitarian intervention and responses against megaterrorism the Charter System can be *legally* vindicated *in appropriate factual circumstances.*

From this perspective recourse to war against Iraq should not have been undertaken without an explicit authorization by the Security Council. The refusal of the UNSC to give a green light to war should never have been regarded as "a failure" of the United Nations. Such a refusal to bend the rules in response to geopolitical pressures represented a responsible exercise of its institutional responsibility to administer an intergovernmental system of constitutional restraints.[27] The facts did not support the case for preemption, as there was neither *imminence* nor *necessity*. As a result, the Iraq War seemed, at best, to qualify as an instance of *preventive war*, but there are strong legal, moral, and political reasons to deny both legality and legitimacy to such a contemplated use of force, and even the more remote threat being countered by "prevention" was not factually credible with respect to Iraq, given the weakness of the country after a devastating war followed by twelve years of sanctions. Preventive war was not an acceptable exception to the Charter System, even if the rationale could have been made in a convincing manner. In fact, the U.S. government claim, phrased in the abstract and vague phrasing of the preemptive war doctrine as set forth in the National Security Strategy of the United States, would have been more accurately formulated and explained if described as "a preventive war doctrine." Yet even such an unacceptable doctrinal claim could not have been convincingly used to justify recourse to war against Iraq, as insufficient evidence existed that Iraq would in the future possess the sort of capabilities that would pose an unmanageable threat to neighboring countries, much less to the United States.

My legal constructivist position is that the United States (and the world) would benefit from a self-imposed discipline of adherence to international law as embodied in the UN Charter System governing the use of force. Such a voluntary discipline would overcome the absence of geopolitical limits associated with countervailing power in a unipolar world.[28] It would also work against tendencies by the United States and others to rely too much on military superiority, which encourages the formation of defensive alliances, and possibly generates expensive and dangerous arms races. International law is flexible enough to allow the United States, and other countries, to meet novel security needs that pose genuine threats. Beyond this, neither American values, nor strategic goals, should be construed to validate uses of force that cannot win support in the UN Security Council. If one considers the course of American foreign policy over the course of the last half-century, adherence to the Charter System with respect to the use of force would have avoided the worst foreign policy failures, including that of Vietnam. Deviations from the Charter System of prohibitions on the use of force can be credited with no clear successes.

It is not the Charter System that is in disarray, providing sensible grounds for declaring the project of regulating recourse to war by states a failed experiment that should now be abandoned. It is, rather, leading states, and above all the United States, that need to be persuaded that their interests are served and their values realized by a commitment to pursue a law-oriented foreign policy. The Charter System is not a legal prison that presents states with the dilemma of adherence (and defeat) and violation or disregard (and victory). Rather, adherence is the best policy, if understood against a jurisprudential background that is neither slavishly legalistic nor cynically nihilistic. The law can be stretched as new necessities arise, but the stretching must to the extent possible be in accord with procedures and norms contained in the Charter System, with a factually and doctrinally persuasive explanation of why a particular instance of stretching is justified.

Such positive constructivist attitudes will renew confidence in the Charter System. It is also true that constructivism can work negatively, and so if the sorts of disregard of the legal framework, public opposition, and governmental resistance present in the Iraq case are repeated in the future, then indeed the Charter System will be in a shambles before much longer.

Undoubtedly, the Iraq War and the disastrous American occupation that has ensued represent a serious setback for advocates of a law-governed approach to world order, as well as to the procedural effort to give the United Nations Security Council primary authority to mandate exceptions to the Charter prohibition on the nondefensive use of force to resolve international conflicts or to protect vulnerable peoples. But history can be cunning. Some possibility exists that the burdens of occupation in Iraq, as well as the discrediting of the rationale advanced to justify the American recourse to war, will cause a political swing in the United States and elsewhere in the direction of greater respect for the cardinal rules and principles of international law, for the United Nations, and for a peace-oriented public opinion at home and abroad.

6

Engaging Normative Consciousness

The lingering of Hobbesian assumptions of international anarchy beyond their natural life cycle threatens the world with empire, chaos, and catastrophe. Worldviews premised on realism have a limited and increasingly dysfunctional purchase on the reality of peace and security given the world-order challenges posed by globalization from above, unipolarity, and nonstate actors. Realism as historically associated with the interplay of sovereign territorial states and nationalist ideologies remains deeply entrenched in the consciousness of political elites and their publics around the world. Despite the mismatch with an increasingly post-Westphalian set of defining circumstances, realism is still to be preferred, as an orientation toward action on the global stage, over nihilistic and regressive visionary outlooks of the sort that translate prospects of global political unification into various scenarios of domination, exploitation, and collapse. Against this background of tension between organizing and mobilizing ideas and actual conditions, the most frequently proposed escapes from realism appear to be the radical imaginaries being proposed from the right and left ends of the political spectrum. Short of utopianism, only a disciplined adherence to norms and collective procedures of restraint at the level of governmental behavior can sustain a tolerable level of world order, especially those norms and procedures associated with international law and the United Nations. Respect for these modernist limits, never fully realized or entirely ethically satisfactory, nevertheless have the potential to lengthen the interval of and decrease the anguish of transition between the familiar parameters of an essentially statist world and the still-fuzzy features of a world-order sequel to the Westphalian solution.[1]

The Bush presidency departed abruptly from the familiar consensus outlook of realist geopolitics as soon as it came to Washington. Very quickly in early 2001 a series of its foreign-policy initiatives alarmed much of the world, and more than a few Americans. The new American leadership appeared to be embarking upon an ambitious and grandiose form of imperialism, establishing global security under Washington's unconditional authority for the entire world by aggressive projections of military power.[2] That plan to impose drastic global reform was temporarily shattered by the pictures of abuse at Abu Ghraib prison and the ordeal of the American invaders that has resulted from Iraqi resistance to occupation, and related patterns of civil strife in the country. The left-utopian dream of a peaceful and just world remains just that, a misty dream "without legs" — that is, presently lacking the necessary launching resources or a political base. As such, despite the seeming plausibility and ethical attractiveness of a democratic global government and an ethos of human solidarity in responding to the ecological fragility, political violence, transnational crime, and acute injustices of present world order, this left vision lacks any political prospect of enactment, or even serious advocacy, in a world of gross economic unevenness, developmental preoccupations, and fiercely diverse ethnoreligious identities. Given such a skeptical assessment, I would pin current hopes for a sustainable human future more modestly on the recovery and extension of "normative consciousness" as a necessary prelude to the sort of dramatic restructuring required to achieve an acceptable form of global governance.[3]

To the extent that political legitimacy is now tied to constitutional democracy and human rights, it is also dependent on respect for the rule of law. Given the dynamics of American military dominance and global force projection (foreign military bases, navies, militarization of oceans and space; interventionary diplomacy), the incorporation of the discipline of international law into the foreign policy process of this hegemonic actor would amount to little more than a political commitment to self-deterrence, given specific content by a consistent adherence to the norms of international law. Such a commitment will never be forthcoming at official levels of government unless this goal becomes politically activated as a central demand of societal forces associated with "globalization from below," a widespread recognition at the grassroots, especially in the United States, that such a legal framing of foreign policy is necessary for human well being, prudent for society, and expressive of the values and interests of the state. It is a difficult public pedagogy, as the Hobbesian mentality, fearful of chaos and striving for order, remains deeply embedded in societal, as well as elite, consciousness, and will not be easily dislodged. This is especially so in light of the greater disaster offered by rejecting realism in favor of global authoritarianism, the clear implication of the neoconservative worldview that has controlled American policy since George W. Bush became president in 2001.

Perhaps the foreign policy debacles associated with the Vietnam War and the Iraq War, the two most notable and costly instances of an American repudiation of international law in the last fifty years, can be converted into geopolitical learning experiences. It is not reasonable to have high hopes for any quick adjustments. Slow learning is characteristic behavior for hegemonic actors throughout history, helping us understand better the connection between short political memories by dominant political actors when it comes to their failures, and the various narratives depicting over the centuries the decline and fall of great powers. If not doomed by memory lapses, then the collapse of empires is often caused, or at least accelerated, by a refusal to recognize and respect limits on financial and material capabilities, producing the recurrent self-destructive dynamic of "overreach." Such pre-decline indicators as falling currency values, trade and fiscal deficits, and overinvestment in military capabilities are warning signals in the United States that have so far been largely ignored by competing political tendencies and the maintenance of an economic comfort zone.

I have no doubt that any undertaking dedicated to normative recovery is subject to criticism, and even dismissal, as a species of utopianism. Immediately the question arises, "Recovery to what?" As is explained in Note 1, recovery is purged of sentimentality by being confined to the sort of encouraging developments evident in the course of the 1990s.[4] Such recovery does not, at present, seem politically feasible, and thus at best can be recommended and explained as a political project only from a self-consciously radical perspective of "a politics of impossibility." A credible formulation of impossibility depends on a willingness to suspend disbelief by enlarging the conception of reason beyond its typical means/ends instrumental usages. This would allow reason to encompass the pursuit of goals that are validated by their intrinsic worth and practical potentialities, and not merely as a matter of testing the receptivity of existing governmental capabilities to absorb expansive goals.

The affirmation of a prospect of normative recovery is not posited out of thin air. Hopeful Hegelian omens exist, including a noticeable turn by exemplary intellectuals from preoccupations with esoteric cultural theory in its various neomodern modes to a candidly exoteric embrace of political and ethical responsibility. This turn is partly notable for its serious engagement with current issues of global policy. It includes a stress on the positive contributions that law, legal consciousness, and legal limits could make to the exercise of power by the governments of sovereign states, especially those states that project their power beyond territorial boundaries. Such concerns are unprecedented at this level of discourse, and they reflect a sense of cultural emergency and political hazard by previously rather aloof intellectual figures who exclusively inhabited ultra-abstract domains of thought without attention to practice. Various expressions of this interpretation of the historical situation can be found in the recent work of several of the most radiant and influential intellectual presences of our time, including Jacques Derrida, Jürgen Habermas, and Homi Bhabha.[5] Principal factors in shaping this mood include anxieties about weaponry of mass destruction, about violence emanating from extremist political and religious circles, about global warming and planetary sustainability, about an incipient threat of global fascism, and about the loss of limits in the turmoil of transition to a postmodern future.

It is against this background of an assumption of human responsibility and renewed political seriousness by public intellectuals that it is useful to explore the prospects for normative recovery in the post-9/11 world, giving particular emphasis to linkages between the United States and global destiny. This inquiry is not meant to be a detached assessment, but rather to provide persuasive grounds for assigning a high priority to the disciplining of hegemonic state power through compliance with international law, especially in the context of war and peace. Europe has been moving in this direction, although the neoconservative author Robert Kagan derisively argues that such moves are not in his view a trend to be celebrated, but rather reflect European geopolitical decline and weakness relative to the United States.[6] I would insist, in contrast, that rather than weakness, it is a sign of the revival of European creativity with respect to the design of a viable future world order. After all, it is Europe that fashioned modernity on the basis of the interplay of sovereign territorial states, and it is now Europe that is offering the postmodern world a work in progress — constitutional regionalism — that remains impressive despite recent setbacks and obstacles.

Some intellectual and political space also now seems available for the depiction and enactment of a post-Westphalian system of global governance in which international law is a far more integral aspect of world politics than has been the case hitherto in international relations. Recent books by authors as different as Zbigniew Brzezinski, Amitai Etzioni, and Anne-Marie Slaughter show a shared disposition to advocate two adjustments: repudiate the unilateralist and imperial geopolitics of the Bush presidency and move prudently beyond the conceptual and behavioral confines of statism, which based world-order design predominantly on the application of realist suppositions that only states counted as significant political actors and international relations consisted of only their interaction.[7]

My purpose in this chapter is mainly to identify "normative recovery" as a promising strategic site of struggle within the United States. The intention is also to point to a far wider quest for a postrealist way of thinking about and acting in the global lifeworld. The rationale for such a selective emphasis on the United States is a reflection of the historical situation as it has evolved in the period since the end of the Cold War. Obviously, if other periods were selected, a different focus would be chosen, as would be the case with Britain in the nineteenth century.

To build such an argument it is first necessary to clarify the contours of normative recovery by referring to the historical ebb and flow of the complex and contradictory American response to the law-oriented dimensions of world order. Some discussion will also be devoted to the issue of normative agency, with the most attention given to international law governing the use of force, and to an exploration of the particular roles, responsibilities, and potentialities of three sets of actors: Europe, global civil society, and issue-oriented coalitions between transnational social forces and sovereign states. These perspectives will not be explored here, but their relevance is noted for any adequate treatment of this theme of normative recovery.

CONCEIVING OF NORMATIVE DECLINE AND ASCENT ON A GLOBAL LEVEL

"Normative" in relation to world order refers to reliance on norms of behavior derived from law, morality, and religion in the conduct of international relations. "Decline" refers to the diminished reliance on such norms, or the invocation of norms on the basis of very parochial, unilateralist, and self-serving lines of interpretation that undermines their universalist claims to serve as guides to behavior and judgment. "Ascent" refers to an evolving reliance on such norms, being interpreted and acted upon in accordance with widely shared sentiments within global society. Ascent also involves taking steps toward the implementation of norms and deference to regional and global procedures and institutional arrangements on a basis that generates transcivilizational approval, and is respectful of regional and global community attitudes and procedures.

A full investigation of these issues is unmanageably broad for a short essay. Attention here is given primarily to how international law relative to war and international uses of force has experienced decline and ascent over the course of the last century. Even here the assessment is made at high levels of generality intended only to identify principal trends and developments, but at the admittedly serious cost of neglecting nuances, contradictory subtendencies, and conceptual and interpretative controversies.

As indicated, the focus of substantive concern will be upon the American relationship to the legal dimensions of the global normative order. Such emphasis is an obvious reaction to a world-order crisis associated with the September 11 attacks and the immediate American recourse to a "war on terrorism," not *declared* in accordance with the U.S. Constitution, but *announced* to the nation and the world by an imperial president. This preoccupation with United States behavior is also responsive to the predominant influence exerted by the United States over the course of the last century in raising and then dashing hopes with respect to normative constraints on the exercise of power, especially through the use of force.[8]

THREE PHASES OF NORMATIVE DECLINE

Appeasement Backlash

In the aftermath of World War I, Wilsonian idealism converged with a populist revulsion associated with a particular, large-scale, long-lasting war that was costly in human terms and morally and politically dubious, if not pointless. Such a political mood, although complex and variable in its totality, did have as a primary consequence a somewhat pacifist diplomacy of appeasement in response to the rise of Hitler's Germany. The failure of the liberal democracies to be prepared militarily and psychopolitically to confront Nazi expansionism at an early stage was widely interpreted as a failure by leading states to discharge their managerial functions in a world of sovereign states. Particularly influential were realist criticisms of appeasement, and associated views supportive of the League of Nations, disarmament, and legal constraints on the use of force. The onset of World War II was a confirmation of the failure of "legalism" as the foundation of world order, and provided an example of a *necessary* and *just* war that successfully, if expensively, confronted and defeated the challenge of fascism and Japanese militarism.

Writers such as E. H. Carr, George Kennan, Hans Morgenthau, Raymond Aron, and Hedley Bull shifted the balance of opinion in the liberal democracies, including the United States, in the direction of believing that countervailing power, not normative restraint or international institutions, was the basis of stability and moderation in world politics. In this regard, despite the establishment of the United Nations, this time with American participation and strong support, there was an overwhelming consensus in the United States and elsewhere that the force of arms, not the rules of international law, provided the indispensable basis of peace. Doctrines of deterrence and containment, embodiments of realist thinking, were seen as far more relevant than the UN and international law for the prevention of future aggression *and* an avoidance of the onset of World War III. The advent of nuclear weapons, as well as the memories of the human costs of the two world wars, raised the stakes of realist thinking to the level where *both* the prevention of aggression and the avoidance of war were regarded as possible, desirable, and necessary goals.

The British school of international relations was more subtle and sophisticated than its counterparts elsewhere, especially in the United States, counseling a generalized adherence to international law and a prudent management of international power. The American view tended to treat law and morality as either the basis of or an obstacle to the intelligent use of power rather than as the British believed, a modest, although indispensable, complement in the maintenance of a stable world order.

Cold War Geopolitics

This ideological triumph of realism was reinforced by the bipolar pattern of world order, and by the cynical internationalist outlook of the Soviet Union. It was also reinforced by the high stakes of geopolitical rivalry in which the entire world was converted into a potential battleground in which force and other forms of coercive influence were relied upon in struggles by bipolar rivals for influence. At the same time, the dangers of nuclear war encouraged mutual restraint and the management of crises, not out of respect for any norms of prohibition, but due to the realization that the consequences of such a war meant long-term catastrophe for both sides. The logic of conflict and restraint, then, operated by reference to realist considerations, which included an appreciation of prudence in the conduct of foreign policy and such expressions of shared interests as the pursuit of "arms control" and "crisis management."

With the fall of the Berlin Wall in 1989, followed by the Soviet collapse, a triumphalist belief emerged, especially among the American foreign policy elite, that a realist geopolitics had been fully vindicated, and that there was no need to take additional steps to strengthen the global normative order in relation to war/peace issues. And indeed, the perception of "a unipolar moment" encouraged neoconservative opinion in the United States to shift toward a geopolitics of dominance based on ideological vindication, military superiority, technological momentum, and private sector economics as the most stabilizing and beneficial sequel to the Cold War. The absence of any significant strategic rivalry in the relations among leading sovereign states made such goals seem attainable.

September 11 and the Bush II Presidency

The election of George W. Bush as president accelerated this dynamic of normative decline, as the rejection of treaties and institutional authority became an immediate signature expression of a new turn in American foreign policy starting in January 2001. Important multilateral treaty and institutional initiatives were repudiated in ways that signaled to the world a determined American unilateralism that seemed perversely insensitive to the opportunities for and benefits of international cooperation. In this sense, a peripheral feature of reliance on international law was the recognition that complex global problems, including those bearing on global security, depended on establishing overlapping layers of international cooperation among states and on regional and global regimes that could impart a measure of order upon a particular domain of global policy (e.g., a treaty regime establishing the public order of the oceans, or of Antarctica). The Bush presidency immediately and unmistakably adopted a unilateralist stance by refusing to seek ratification of the Kyoto Protocol on global warming, by terminating its participation in the Anti-Ballistic Missile Treaty, and by its unprecedented step of withdrawing an earlier American signature (made in the closing days of the Clinton presidency) from the Rome Treaty establishing the International Criminal Court.

The Bush foreign policy posture went well beyond what realism had previously been understood to entail in the foreign policy of a leading state. The realism of the Cold War involved rejecting a supposedly naive reliance on legal and institutional restraints to curb the political ambitions of geopolitical rivals, but even realists were generally receptive to conditioning conflictual behavior by concluding mutually beneficial international agreements and by a sophisticated reliance on international institutions for certain marginal security roles. Such traditional realism was also very positive about the usefulness of alliances among states with similar agendas in world affairs. The American leadership of the Atlantic Alliance was a defining motif of the Cold War era that rested on a fundamental agreement about the character of common security threats, and although the alliance frayed at the edges from time to time, it was held firm over the course of four decades by a sense of essential unity vis-à-vis the Soviet bloc and the challenge to capitalist forms of political economy posed by Marxist–Leninist alternatives. This extraordinary legacy of unity and political effectiveness seemed to be given only an insultingly nominal endorsement by U.S. foreign policy initiatives taken in the early months of the Bush presidency. This turn away from realism exhibited geopolitical hubris by demonstrating contempt for normative constraints and by its refusal to show respect for the views of even its closest allies in Europe.

Then came September 11, and with it rationales and pretexts for a further weakening of normative constraints on the American approach to world order. This was accompanied by an insistence that the rest of the world follow the American lead by joining in all-out war against global terrorism. The nature and severity of the threat posed by transnational megaterrorism was relied on to move explicitly away from the sort of limits on war associated with international law. Such a return to a more discretionary view of war was coupled with a shrill insistence on a global effort under American leadership that explicitly threatened those who preferred to remain neutral and uninvolved. ("You are either with us or with the terrorists" were words often quoted and frequently repeated by Bush in various formulations.) The Bush Doctrine of preemptive war, first publicly articulated in June 2002, claimed the right to wage nondefensive wars of choice in response to unsubstantiated apprehensions of threats. War was no longer limited to defensive reactions to prior attacks by states as was prescribed by the UN Charter and international law.[9] The Iraq War of 2003 was initially justified by reliance on this innovative post–September 11 neoconservative reasoning. It was buttressed by contentions that Iraq was in illicit possession of weaponry of mass destruction that might cause harm in the future. It was claimed that the prospect that such weaponry might be transferred with lethal effect to undeterrable jihadist groups around the world accentuated this danger. This instance of war making, in effect, repudiated the prohibition on aggressive (or nondefensive) use of force, or so unilaterally reinterpreted the constraint as to make it almost useless as a means to minimize the legitimacy of war as a policy instrument. This repudiation was coupled with a virtual American ultimatum to the United Nations Security Council that insisted on receiving legitimating support for the decision by the U.S. government to embark on a regime-changing war against

Iraq. President Bush advised the Security Council that its failure to mandate the invasion of Iraq would render the UN "irrelevant." Such a call for adherence to geopolitical priorities rather than Charter norms represented the climax of this phase of normative decline. The apparent military success of coalition forces in conquering Iraq was celebrated in the immediate aftermath of the combat phase of the Iraq War. For instance, Richard Perle, a leading exponent of neoconservative foreign policy, argued that the United Nations had been revealed to be a dead body when it came to establishing global security, and that this demonstration should be seen a positive side effect of the Iraq victory.

The unanticipated failure of the Iraq occupation policy led to a shift in the official mood and policy of the U.S. government. In an abrupt about-face, the Bush administration came back to the Security Council to plead for the maximum participation of the United Nations in Iraq, both to defuse the tensions stemming from the occupation and to manage the economic and social reconstruction of the country. This move seemed tactical in response to the extreme situation that arose in occupied Iraq. It did not signal a broader neoconservative reevaluation of the importance of multilateralism, and it certainly did not imply a rejection of normative unilateralism. The Bush leadership remains as dedicated as ever to denigrating the relevance of international law to the conduct of American foreign policy. Of course, the broader normative picture remains confused, as the Bush presidency, far more than its realist predecessors, claimed guidance from religious and ethical norms, which has added fuel to the previously burning fires of transcivilizational relations. The non-Western world was now seemingly threatened with a new religiously grounded crusade that was more troubling than the familiar fears of Western material and political encroachment that had surfaced in the late 1990s in reaction to globalization. The radical vision depicted by the Bush neoconservatives was supposedly one of a benign global domination, even "benevolent empire," that would serve the well being of all states, but its benign rationale (global security and prosperity for all) was viewed as an absurdly unconvincing masking of bellicose imperial ambition.[10]

THREE PHASES OF NORMATIVE ASCENT

Overcoming War

Woodrow Wilson's vision of collective security was an alternative to war-prone international relations based on the balance of power. This vision responded to a widespread popular revulsion against war in general that followed the experience of World War I. The keystone of this ambitious program of global reform was the League of Nations, an international institution that was supposed to represent international society as a whole, although, due to colonialism and Eurocentricism, most of the peoples of the world were not represented within the new structure, and so contradictions and hypocrisy undermined the foundations of this supposedly idealistic effort. In addition, states failed to agree on any real transfer of sovereignty, meaning that the whole scheme dubiously rested on the good faith of League members to renounce aggression and serve the global public good by coming to the rescue of states that were in the future victims of aggressive war. Even this level of voluntary commitment, although not coupled with any transfer of capabilities, was threatening to sovereignty-oriented states, which helps to explain why Wilson's vision of global security could not even be sold to the United States Senate and meant that the League of Nations was decively weakened and discredited at its inception by the refusal of its most ardent champion to participate as a state.

Nevertheless, despite the disappointments associated with this first wave of attempts to convert Wilson's vision into concrete forms of implementation, the globalizing impulse has provided a continuing normative inspiration for future generations. This inspiration was expressed through commitments to collective security, to a comprehensive organization soliciting the participation of the governmental representatives of all the peoples in the entire world, to enact a prohibition on nondefensive war making, to an obligation to pursue the peaceful settlement of international disputes, to human rights, and to disarmament. These ambitious undertakings were all prefigured in Wilson's peace diplomacy, and are still part of the agenda of global reform.

Nuremberg: Overriding Sovereignty

After World War II there was a second notable impulse to build on Woodrow Wilson's failed legacy, although from an avowedly more realist perspective. The United Nations was established to fulfill more or less the same goals as had been set for the League, but with significant differences of being located in the new geopolitical center of world power, of giving the five leading states in 1945 a veto power and permanent membership in the Security Council, and of aspiring to achieve universal membership by all independent states. Of even greater normative weight than the UN, however, was the Nuremberg experience associated with imposing criminal accountability on German (and Japanese) leaders for their failures to pursue national policies that conformed to international law. From the perspective of normative discipline this represented a major step forward, subordinating sovereign conceptions of authority to the fundamental limits on state behavior based on international law. Perhaps as important as the punishment of civilian and military leaders on the basis of the failures of responsibility on their part to uphold international law was the articulation of prohibited categories of behavior associated with "Crimes Against Peace" and "Crimes Against Humanity." To set forth these categorical prohibitions, which have attained the status of *peremptory norms* (also known as *jus cogens*) — that is, not subject to exception or revision by state action — is to impose unconditional normative limitations on governmental discretion with respect to war both internally and internationally.[11] In one sense, giving these peremptory norms operational relevance in the conduct of American foreign policy would be the decisive sign of normative recovery. Perhaps "recovery" is a misleading word to use, as such a move by the United States would be welcomed as a spectacular advance over any posture previously held by dominant state actors.

Conceived historically, of course, the Nuremberg experience was rather flawed. The indictments and the scope of the prosecutions were specified according to the dictates of "victors' justice," which should not be confused with justice. Only defeated leaders were subject to accountability. The use of atomic bombs against Hiroshima and Nagasaki was not considered, nor was the extensive strategic bombing of German and Japanese cities that evaded the core prohibition of the law of war with respect to indiscriminate uses of force. The rhetorical commitment by the victors to condition their *future* behavior by reference to the Nuremberg Principles was in subsequent years honored only in the breach.[12]

The 1990s: A Global Justice Movement

Unlike the initiatives for global reform associated with the aftermath of the two world wars, the end of the Cold War produced a mood of normative passivity on the part of major states. The United States interpreted the end of its rivalry with the Soviet Union as an opportunity for unprecedented national economic and ideological expansion yet seemed oblivious to the need for and potentiality receptivity to global reform. The locus of reformist energy of the 1990s was the new social movements in the domains of human rights and environment that exerted ethical and political pressures on the intergovernmental system, making especially good use of global policy arenas provided by the United Nations official conferences on world issues. Additionally, the economistic priorities of globalization during this period created a moral vacuum that was filled by a variety of normative initiatives: a human rights diplomacy, humanitarian interventions, diverse initiatives seeking redress for historic grievances, and the renewal of the Nuremberg impulse (via the establishment of tribunals at The Hague to deal with crimes associated with the breakup of the former Yugoslavia, at Arusha to deal with genocide and Crimes Against Humanity in Rwanda, the detention of the former Chilean dictator Augusto Pinochet, and the successful push for the establishment of a permanent international criminal court). The cumulative momentum of these initiatives provided grounds for hope that normative constraints would influence the practice of realist geopolitics, as well as give some preliminary content and relevant institutionalization to an ethically benevolent form of global governance.[13]

The American response to September 11, as well as Washington's thinly disguised pursuit of global dominance by militarist means, disrupted the normative momentum of the 1990s, and induced a series of regressions with respect to the construction of an equitable architecture of global governance.[14]

TOWARD NORMATIVE RECOVERY

The Bush presidency has highlighted the risks associated with the use of military power in flagrant defiance of the boundaries of international law. These risks antedated Bush and September 11, but they were intensified by several developments: the collapse of the Soviet deterrent, the emergence of a nonstate actor with extremist methods, formidable capabilities and antagonistic goals, and the rise of neoconservative influence within American governmental arenas.

Progressive intellectuals up through the Cold War tended to view international law through a realist lens equipped with a Marxist optic — that is, as essentially marginal to the deployment of power by antagonists, and as at best an instrument of propaganda useful to capitalist elites for the rationalization of their recourse to war. In this regard, the pretension of providing a normative grounding for world order was treated as partly a legalistic diversion from the pursuit of crass interests of business and finance. Marxists attacked normativity as a feckless idealistic venture of ruling classes that lacked any secure footing on the terrain of politics.

Such a critique of the roles played by international law were quite persuasive if the concern was with uses of force, but they always overlooked the niche contributions of legally formulated resistance to the excesses of realist geopolitics.[15] Resistance to the Vietnam War was definitely associated with the perception of the war by increasing segments of public opinion as incompatible with international law and the UN Charter, and as well as in violation of the international humanitarian law and the Nuremberg Principles.

Recall that the cultural shift of marquee intellectuals in the direction of normative restraint signals a new popular and progressive receptivity to international law as a mode of resistance and reconstruction within the parameters of the present global setting. In the specifically American context, this signaling has relevance for the refiguring of such seminal notions of identity and participation as "patriotism" and "citizenship." A disturbing feature of the post–September 11 orchestration of public opinion in the United States was its highly successful mobilizing emphasis on flag-waving nationalism, and a celebration of national unity as synonymous with the suspension of any criticism of governmental policies or action. Such closures of debate were exhibited in the mainstream media in two relevant ways: first, by presenting debate on proposed official policies as confined to the means being chosen to pursue belligerent ends, inviting an endless stream of military experts to discuss issues of feasibility and costs with think tank apologists who never strayed more than a degree or two from the general line of governmental policy; and second, by excluding any discussion of proposed foreign-policy initiatives that raised serious concerns about whether such initiatives were permissible under international law.[16]

Of course, the controversy surrounding the Iraq War has given these issues renewed salience, above all, by the contradictory effects of the American claim to act preventively and unilaterally (without "a permission slip") as a precedent for the future and as providing a confirmation that the neglect of international-law guidelines in the context of contested foreign-policy initiatives involving uses of force produces disastrous practical outcomes. On this latter point, it was not always the case that illegal wars usually turned out badly for the aggressor. The history of the colonial era supports the opposite conclusion, namely, the efficacy of war, superior military skills, and conquest as means of enhancing the relative wealth and power of a state. My argument is that social change occurs when strong public sentiments converge with practical considerations. In this sense, the case for repudiating "illegal wars" (that is, wars of aggression, nondefensive wars, so-called "wars of choice") seems stronger than at any point in international history.

Another key element here is the hegemonic or imperial claim to be entitled to claim a "geopolitical exception," extending to the global arena the jurisprudential notions associated with arguments articulated in the Germany of the 1930s by Carl Schmitt. It applies very much to the approach the United States has taken to international law, especially in recent years. The essence of the geopolitical exception is to suspend the operation of a norm of global application in relation to the behavior of a hegemonic actor, treating the exception as behavior not subject to the scrutiny of law. The veto power given to the permanent members of the UNSC is a paradigmatic instance of a geopolitical exception inscribed in the UN Charter itself, the constitutional foundation of world order. Another important context involves the nonproliferation treaty regime, and its implementation; the exemption is extended to nuclear weapons states, with the United States assuming the role of enforcer to the extent of disallowing certain states (Iran, North Korea) to exercise their right of withdrawal from the obligation although that right is formally conferred in Article X. The most troublesome reliance on a geopolitical exception is associated with uses of force and, especially, recourse to wars of choice. Here the exception risks becoming so prominent as to endanger swallowing the rule itself, and the exception claimed can be seen from another perspective as a political effort to sanitize crime.

What I am describing as normative recovery also implies the adoption of a critical stance toward traditional thinking about patriotism and citizenship. Instead of an ethos of submission to the national will, the first duty of the patriot and citizen is one of conscience, including the essential denial of governmental authority to engage in illegal wars — that is, wars of choice that cannot be reconciled with international law and do not have the benefit of a clear mandate from the UN Security Council. This reorientation of perspective is of special urgency in the United States due to its global reach and military dominance. In effect, as global political authority is now organized, the U.S. government imposes its policies on many foreign countries whose people have no means of participating in the American political process. Territorial democracy no longer correlates with patterns of de facto global governance, with a consequent effective massive disenfranchisement of most of the peoples of the world. Even those enfranchised have strong grounds to doubt whether their vote is of consequence when opposing political parties are both beholden to the dictates of the Pentagon and Wall Street, meaning that neither security policy nor basic economic policy can be transformed for the sake of global peace and justice.

A process of normative recovery is not presented here as a panacea, but only as a means of gaining time to allow forces favorable to genuine global democracy to exert greater influence during the transition to a reframing of global governance. The broader overall objective is to realize the values of global or cosmopolitan democracy as the basis for what might be described as "humane global governance" — that is, governance that is consistent with the religious, ethical, and legal norms enshrined in a global culture of individual and collective human rights and responsibilities. The ethics of engagement with this project at the present time places heavy burdens on the rational intellect because no transition path seems plausible. Only the hazardous embrace of "the politics of impossibility" can avoid succumbing to despair about the human future.

7

Demystifying Iraq

"If you demystify something, you make it easier to understand."
— *Collins Cobuild English Language Dictionary* (London: Harper Collins, 1993)

WHY DEMYSTIFICATION?

Mystification as a description of behavior should be distinguished from the degree of uncertainty, confusion, and bias that inevitably accompanies any decision associated with contested facts, differing opinions, and choosing a course of action.[1] Mystification implies some serious degree of deliberate or knowing deception with specific goals in mind, or at least a strong suspicion to that effect. In relation to the limited inquiry of this essay it refers to government explanations of official policies in the setting of war/peace concerns, a process that should be sharply distinguished from "the fog of war" that is endemic to the phenomenon of war itself. To the extent that mystification is present, especially in a society premised on constitutional government, concerns about the legitimacy of policies and leaders should follow. This perception should alert the citizenry that governmental checks and balances on the abuse of power are not functioning as intended and the time for popular resistance is at hand. Mystification is necessarily never innocent, and on matters of vital public safety, the realization of its presence undermines trust that binds citizens to government and is inconsistent with the qualities of integrity that enable representative government to uphold the values of democracy, never more so than in time of war when killing and dying are involved.[2]

"Politics" will always involve favoritism, and corruption, but even with cynical attitudes toward the behavior of leaders, there is normally a widely shared belief that elected leaders will not knowingly jeopardize the national security of the state for the sake of private gain or an undisclosed strategic project. Of course, leaders may believe, falsely yet sincerely, that such a project enhances security and can only be made politically palatable by way of mystification. This observation may explain, but hardly excuses, the behavior of some or even all of members of the inner circle of the Bush presidency with respect to recourse to the Iraq War, as will be argued below.

Mystification also, by concealing or deliberately lying about the true bases of policy, necessarily subverts both the role of law and informed citizen participation via electoral policy, and to the extent perceived, creates fear and anger in public space. A vigilant citizenry should treat perceived mystification, particularly on matters that affect the life and death of citizens and others and bear upon the security of the society and world, as such a serious abuse of governing authority as engaging procedures of accountability, including at the very least electoral repudiation but possibly such extraordinary remedies as impeachment and the imposition of individual criminal accountability. The refusal of the majority of citizens, and cognate branches of government, to respond vigorously to such instances of perceived or demonstrated mystification by the presidency is a sure sign of political decline, even decadence; if this acquiescence is persistent and pervasive enough, it is likely to cause the discrediting and weakening, and even the collapse, of a democracy, especially on the part of the minority enraged by its belief that a war has been publicly validated by reliance on a mystifying rationale. Currently, this belief is so embedded in anti-Bush constituencies in the American electorate that it has given rise to fears that the government is embarked on an illegal and imprudent course of perpetual war and that a police state is imminent in the country, leading such individuals to contemplate abandoning the country and taking up residence elsewhere. Of course, such reactions are likely to be treated by the leadership as tantamount to treason, leading to further alienation and a vicious cycle of repression and resistance.

Sophisticated arguments abroad in the land at this time look on mystification as a necessary and natural prerogative of all political leaders in a democracy, including the wisest and most virtuous among them. These *ideological* arguments are often associated with political theories of leadership that draw sharp distinctions between the masses supposedly unable to comprehend the subtleties and hidden nuances of benevolent governance and elites entrusted with the awesome responsibility of rulership, which can only be fulfilled by reliance on special qualities of understanding and insight that concern truths and policy objectives too inflammatory to acknowledge and too complex to be understood by ordinary persons. In short, "the people," for their own sake, must be led. Especially in a democratically constituted society, mobilization of support often will depend on finding a rationale for a preferred course of policy that the citizenry will accept, whether true or false. Another approach is to create the conditions via inculcated misperception that make what was previously unacceptable as a public rationale become acceptable. I believe that such a pattern of mystification bears centrally on all aspects of the American approach to the Iraq War, including the prewar buildup of support and the postbattlefield occupation of that tormented country, and that, somewhat paradoxically, the dynamic of this war will remain incomprehensible if we do not grasp the role of the oddly clarifying impact of mystification. It should be evident that mystification is something deeper and more sinister than putting the best face on a course of action, which any government does to the extent possible, or hiring spin doctors to give a controversial and unsuccessful official policy the maximum possible public appeal.

There are good reasons to believe that some of the most influential advisers to the Bush presidency are ardent proponents and consistent practitioners of such profoundly antidemocratic views, although, as might be expected, none has acknowledged this directly, as it would severely undermine their viability as public servants. The proclaimed ethos of public service is radically inconsistent with any acknowledged reliance on mystification.[3] It is this apparent presence of such perspectives in the high echelons of political power that makes the consideration of mystification an urgent matter at this historical moment. More pointedly, it is the coherence of this outlook and its preoccupation with gaining influence in government, generally described beneath the label "neoconservative," that has made the world-imperial project of the Bush presidency a profound and unprecedented threat to democracy in America. Democracy is generally understood, in the first instance, as responsiveness to the will of the citizenry (with the caveat of protecting minorities against "the tyranny of the majority"). The sublime irony associated with this particular phenomenon of mystification is the degree to which the foundational neoconservative belief is the *overseas* promotion of "democracy" as the cardinal undertaking of American foreign policy, a goal explicitly linked to the achievement of security for the country and the world, particularly in the Middle East. Such a normative line of advocacy has led observers to identify the neoconservative worldview as an antirealist visionary outlook superficially reminiscent of Woodrow Wilson's interventionary diplomacy on behalf of democracy.[4] Arguably, there are such crucial differences, especially Wilson's antiwar dedication to the establishment of international institutions capable of keeping the peace versus neoconservative unilateralism and militarism, as to cast doubt on the asserted lineage. Nevertheless, in both instances of visionary outlook the realist consensus based on the prudent pursuit of national interests is repudiated in favor of a normative geopolitics that is value-driven, and only partly disclosed to the citizenry. Both Wilson and Bush could not carry forward their distinct projects without relying on degrees of mystification to embark on a war that the majority of the American citizenry did not initially favor.[5] In both instances, mystification succeeded, and once the war was undertaken, it appealed to the majority and even some awareness of the deception did not shake the political foundations of support, although military failure in Iraq has led to popular disenchantment with the war.

Additionally, neoconservative mystification is especially potent in the political climate that emerged after September 11, allowing an imperial geopolitics to be pursued without disclosure and justification, carefully disguised and misrepresented as a vital phase in prosecuting the war against terrorism, for which there was fervent national support in the years following the attacks. This wider undertaking exceeding a response to the Al Qaeda threat has proved to be seriously destructive of world order based on respect for the core norms of international law and the United Nations Charter with respect to the use of force in world politics. It has also greatly diminished respect for the United States as a global leader. Such a path of indefinite nondefensive warfare of global scope seems likely to afflict many peoples in the world with an escalating, unpredictable, and unending cycle of unconditional political violence. In this regard, neoconservative mystification in the present geopolitical context is *substantively* extremely dangerous, as well as *procedurally* incompatible with an ethos of democratic governance to such an extent that it threatens the survival of democracy. Such incompatibility goes far beyond the dangers to democracy that emerged during the Cold War through an excessive reliance on governmental secrecy as justified by national security.

Beyond this, in two senses the Bush presidency's reliance on a legitimating embrace of democracy is extremely misleading. First, neoconservative advocates lose no sleep over the abridgement of traditional rights at home, and they lend their unqualified support to the authoritarian tendencies of the Justice Department and such gratuitous deformations of the American way of life and belief as are embedded in the Patriot Act and the Military Commissions Act and have surfaced in the course of the latter's implementation, especially in the widespread torture of detainees and terror suspects. "Democracy" as slogan generates increasing fear of a police state, or even fascism, as reality. Second, the trumpeting of democracy as the key goal of American foreign policy, especially in the setting of Iraq and throughout the rest of the Middle East, should raise eyebrows. If democracy is understood to refer to a governing process that is responsive to the will of the citizenry, then it is inconceivable that the White House strategists are opting for political leadership that is almost certain to exhibit the anti-American, anti-Israeli sentiments of the people. Democracy as a goal for the Middle East can only be understood as a euphemism for authoritarianism, qualified to some degree by periodic elections that present the citizenry with limited choices that are by their nature "antidemocratic." It seems likely that "democracy" for the Middle East resembles for strategic planners in Washington what Moscow bureaucrats had in mind by "socialism" in East Europe during the Soviet era. Recall that if there were political moves toward real socialism, as with "the Prague Spring" in 1968, it was virtually certain to trigger a Soviet intervention to restore Moscow's deformed sense of socialism. One of the costs of mystification is the loss of language as a means of conveying reality, and nothing better illustrates this loss than this double sacrifice of democracy on the altar of ideological expediency in the period since September 11. As the war in Iraq has gone from bad to worse, the assessments from Washington include expressions of doubt about the capacities of the elected leadership of the country, with intimations that their views on how to restore normalcy can be cast aside by American political and military commanders.

Of course, there are *bureaucratic* explanations for the general phenomenon of mystification that have been illuminating in other contexts but seem of minor relevance in the Iraq context. The so-called credibility gap that existed during the latter stages of the Vietnam War seemed to flow from the unwillingness of the government — that is, its top officials — to face the political consequences of a failing policy that were feared likely to result from a candid disclosure. Elements of ideological closure also arose from the dogmatic anticommunism of the political and military leadership at the time that facilitated the entry into and maintenance of the war and the national security state more generally, but seemed always secondary to the bureaucratic refusal of elected leaders and their advisers to accept responsibility for a failed policy. Undoubtedly, the governmental insistence that the Vietnam War was being "won" in the late 1960s was a form of mystification that generated wide and deep anger on the part of the public as soon as the dynamics of demystification were unleashed.

The Tet Offensive traumatically initiated this process in February 1968. The impact of this dramatic tactic was far greater because the unanticipated show of North Vietnamese and National Liberation Front power had seemed impossible given the way progress in the war was being claimed by American leaders and conveyed by a passive media. At the time, Vietnam hawks (by 1968, diehard supporters of the war) counterattacked, contending that the surge of skepticism about the course of the war resulted from a gross misinterpretation of the Tet experience. These pro-war advocates insisted that in view of the heavy casualties sustained by the DRV/NLF attackers, the U.S. government should have been claiming victory instead of caving in to the antiwar, media-induced public mood. Instead of succumbing as it did to the spectacle of massive opposition, which resulted in seizing "defeat out of the mouth of victory," the government should have been celebrating. It was undoubtedly a great political victory for the attackers and vividly illustrated the vulnerability to reversal of a course of action that depended on mystification in the event that enough of the target audience became convinced that it had been knowingly misled by previously trusted leaders.

Despite these notable failings of substantive mystification associated with Cold War geopolitics, which reached their climax during the latter stages of the Vietnam War, these were only marginally connected with procedural mystification, as the leaders never repudiated accountability, and, indeed, Nixon resigned the presidency under threat of impeachment. Daniel Ellsberg's role in releasing the Pentagon Papers in 1971 provided ample evidence to support allegations of governmental mystification and offered a rare documented illustration of the workings of the whistle-blowing politics of demystification. Ellsberg believed at the time that the exposure of the mystifying arguments for the war would produce a decisive antiwar backlash. Such a backlash attributable to the Pentagon Papers did not materialize in the short term, although this whistle-blowing revelation has remained an epic event in the struggle for demystification during a time of war in the United States, making the citizenry much readier to be suspicious of war talk issuing from the government.

Robust reasons and ample evidence support the belief that a massive campaign of mystification had been relied on with respect to the Iraq policy as it evolved during the Bush presidency. Above all, there exists at all points a glaring mismatch between the stated goals of a policy of antiterrorism based on the September 11 attacks and recourse to war against Iraq. Such a mismatch can to some extent be explained away as one more instance of policy misperception, governmental incompetence, turf battles, inertia, and the slow learning curve of governments. Taking such elements into account does not overcome doubts arising from the extent and character of the American war on global terror, especially when it comes to the momentously misguided decision to invade and occupy Iraq as a supposed response to the Al Qaeda threat in the absence of notable international support or a UN mandate. The mismatch would be less manifest if a geopolitical rationale for the war had been relied on, but it would have seemed impossible to achieve political mobilization or to claim legitimacy without this reliance on massive mystification. In effect, the only way to gain sufficient political backing for the war at its inception was to confuse as much of the citizenry as possible about the rationale, misleadingly presenting Saddam Hussein's Iraq as connected with the September 11 attacks, as a menacing potential ally of Al Qaeda, and as an attractive target for attack that would yield a quick, vindicating victory.

There are additional reasons to believe that the avowedly ideological leadership surrounding the Bush presidency engaged in mystification. A reading of the neoconservative blueprint for grand strategy, "Repairing American Defenses," prepared in the late 1990s under the auspices of the Project for a New American Century (PNAC), and issued shortly before George W. Bush "prevailed" at the polls (arguably by nefarious means in the state of Florida and as a result of a constitutionally sanitized instance of mystification on the part of the majority of justices in the United States Supreme Court) in the contested November 2000 elections.[6] This report contained a recognition by its prominent neoconservative signatories that the American people needed to be awakened by "a new Pearl Harbor" if the country was to seize the opportunities and control the threats presented by the emergence of a unipolar world order after the Soviet collapse. To take geopolitical advantage of this historical circumstance of undeterred American military power depended on the existence of a political climate that would enable the Bush presidency to push successfully for the militarization of American foreign policy being proposed in the report, including the provocative call for force to achieve "regime change" in Iraq, a priority in the initial phase of a far-wider grand strategy of global domination. Iraq was presented in this revealing text as a prelude to the overall adoption of a more interventionary diplomacy, justified by claims of "security" and an American mission to spread "democracy" relying on coercion to the extent necessary. These words are in quotes to underline their Orwellian content, as the result of such a grandiose approach is to induce "insecurity" and to diminish prospects for "democracy," at least as such terms should be properly understood.[7] The PNAC report prefigures the seminal official document issued by the Bush administration in 2002 under the title of "National Security Strategy of the United States of America," and updated in early 2006.[8]

To a certain extent the PNAC advocacy of aggression against Iraq had been already endorsed in 1998 by a bipartisan consensus in the Senate in the form of a nonbinding resolution positing Iraqi regime change as a goal of American foreign policy. This interventionary posture, although provocative and arguably itself a threat of force prohibited by Article 2(4) of the UN Charter, was widely interpreted as a meaningless political gesture at the time, and was not seriously regarded as a step toward war. It occurred in a pre-neoconservative, pre–September 11 atmosphere of government that viewed such expressions of political engagement as exercises in "rhetoric" and at most a mainstream mandate for encouraging the U.S. government to accelerate its existing programs of indirect and covert harassment of the Baghdad government by way of sanctions, support for exiles, propaganda, and episodic bombings, but this hostility was distinctly not meant or understood by the general public or by foreign governments as a mandate for or prelude to launching a major war. Of course, the neoconservative pressure to obtain the earlier resolution was an integral part of their campaign to tilt American foreign policy in an overtly militarist and hegemonic direction, especially in the setting of the Middle East, regarded as the vital center of post–Cold War geopolitics, as well as the regional setting of Israeli security. The PNAC report remains an important text, because it so clearly demonstrates that the Bush foreign policy team was advocating the Iraq War before the Al Qaeda threat was on its radar screen, and was sharply criticizing the Clinton foreign policy for its unwillingness to invest sufficiently in military power and to undertake *strategic* (as opposed to *humanitarian*, as in Kosovo, or *counterterror*) interventions allegedly made feasible in a unipolar world order, which lacked any countervailing force to check American ambitions. As the 9/11 Commission makes clear in what is generally an unsatisfactory report as far as the explanation of the attacks is concerned, "terrorism" was not given policy priority by any American presidency, including that of Bush II until the attacks, suggesting that the advocacy of regime change and war against Iraq was motivated by other considerations of foreign policy and world order.[9]

The September 11 attacks generated an intense nationalist backlash in the United States that was skillfully used to pursue these previously articulated foreign-policy goals, now repackaged as preemptive defense against megaterrorism. Secretary of Defense Donald Rumsfeld, speaking on national TV on the second anniversary of September 11, intriguingly referred to the tragedy of the attacks as "a blessing in disguise."[10] The only plausible way to interpret such an odd phrasing is as an unconscious acknowledgement by one of the key policymakers that the agenda being pursued by the Bush presidency was causally enabled by the attacks, and that this helpful role of the September 11 made the attacks not an occasion for regret, but an event of sufficient magnitude to provide the necessary political basis for undertaking a course of action that the neoconservative cabal and their allies (especially the religious right) had long believed to be highly desirable, allegedly necessary, but previously impractical. The dynamic of mystification organically informs the political process of generating such a mandate from the citizenry, and explains the various steps taken by the Bush leadership to convince the public that an invasion of Iraq was justified and essential from the perspective of national security. Perceived mystification was generated during this process by the manipulation of intelligence estimates of the Iraqi threat and surrounding facts, as well as by an orchestrated effort to adopt abstract doctrinal formulations of altered security requirements in light of the September 11 attacks.

The domestic mood was kept on edge by what appeared to be a complementary manipulation of the color-alert coding of prospects for further attacks. A counterterrorist *ideology* was proclaimed to effectively obscure at home an *imperial* geopolitics that the Bush administration was according operational priority ever since it came to Washington. In fact, with respect to Iraq the remarkable fact is that the counterterrorist campaign was apparently *subordinated,* quite possibly deliberately *sacrificed,* to enable the contradictory pursuit of geopolitical goals. That is, it was widely anticipated by informed observers that to attack Iraq would likely intensify and spread the terrorist threat associated with Islamic extremism. It is difficult to believe that intelligent and honest government officials could overlook or disagree with this consensus to the extent of actually believing that attacking Iraq was a contribution to counterterrorism. Admittedly, sincere neoconservatives undoubtedly did believe that dominating the Middle East and securing its oil reserves was an indispensable geopolitical priority, and that without such control American (and Israeli) security would be severely jeapordized in the near future. As both Richard Clarke and Anonymous, probably the most authoritative anti–Al Qaeda experts within the U.S. government, have convincingly contended, it is a no-brainer to understand that embarking on the Iraq War would increase the threat posed by Islamic extremism by fanning the already intense flames of anti-Americanism throughout the Islamic world.[11]

There are additional reasons to suspect mystification. The invasion of Iraq seemed to most objective observers as most likely to make post–September 11 security in the United States and the world more, not less, difficult to restore. It seems impossible for American leaders to be oblivious to these warning alarms sounded inside and outside of government about the consequences of initiating a senseless war in a country weakened by defeat in a prior war and by twelve years of crippling sanctions. Sober warnings coming from generally cautious mainstream voices went unheeded or were angrily cast aside. Normally supportive allies, which had earlier fully supported the United States in the anti–Al Qaeda undertaking directed at Afghanistan, opposed the invasion of Iraq, in large part for these reasons of anticipated dysfunction with respect to counterterrorism, but also because such a course of action seemed to be an example of aggressive war making contrary to international law and making world order less stable.[12] For the United States to proceed with the Iraq War in the face of extremely widespread opposition in civil society and on the part of long-friendly governments strongly adds to suspicions that unacceptable (and undisclosed) views were driving the policy.

The plausibility of recourse to mystification also arises from a casual consideration of past governmental efforts by the United States government to avoid an honest disclosure of its foreign-policy posture. Whether dealing with the Japanese attack on Pearl Harbor, the assassination of John F. Kennedy, the reliance on the Gulf of Tonkin incident to justify an extension of the Vietnam War to North Vietnam, and most of all, the September 11 events, the heavy footprints of official mystification are present for almost all to discern. David Ray Griffin, a distinguished philosopher of religion, has rendered a great national service by detailing the multiple grounds and abundant evidence for doubting the official accounts of what happened on September 11 in his book *The New Pearl Harbor*.[13] There is an important difference between contending that mystification exists, and demonstrating the presence of a conspiracy to depict an alternative account of the occurrence of the attacks.[14] The essence of a conspiracy is the conspiring together by a group to achieve an undisclosed and criminal result. Available evidence does not now support inferences of conspiracy to arrange the September 11 attacks, nor, it must be admitted, does available evidence support their denial. The evidence of deception and avoidance does establish the rather pervasive reliance on mystification at crucial past instances of American foreign policy, especially during periods of national crisis.

The politics of mystification have also been relied on to hide the driving force of American grand strategy by pretending that contested foreign-policy initiatives were chosen to achieve defensive goals, or aims strongly endorsed by the citizenry. President Bush has shifted the goalposts several times to sustain political support for the Iraq policy, arguing before the invasion that Iraq's possession of weaponry of mass destruction, together with links to Al Qaeda, justified a preemptive attack. In the aftermath, given the failure to find a single weapon of mass destruction in Iraq, the Bush argument shifted to a stress on the liberation of the Iraqi people from an oppressive dictator, and a vague claim that this result, despite the continuing turmoil in Iraq, meant that the American people were safer than if Saddam Hussein were in power. Bush even made the ludicrous claim that fighting and dying in Iraq is somehow better than the alleged alternative, fighting and dying in the United States, as if the latter would have been more likely to result if Iraq were still ruled by Saddam Hussein, an assertion that cannot withstand even a modest degree of neutral scrutiny. Indeed, the opposite conclusion seems far more plausible, that the upsurge of support for extreme anti-Americanism would in due course bring more, not less, violence to territorial America.

It should be understood that mystification as a tactic of policymaking depends on certain political factors. It worked for a long time with the American people in relation to the Iraq War because of the aftermath of anger, fear, and confusion and the low level of political literacy with respect to September 11 among the American people, and because of George W. Bush's credibility as a tough leader and his related effectiveness as a proponent of an assertive American foreign policy. Bush's leadership was essentially uncontested until the Iraq War lost centrist support in America. The mainstream media failed to fulfill its critical role, Congress and the Democratic Party leadership remained entirely passive for several years, and because it accepted a large part of the official American rationale for the war, the international community seemed helpless to oppose it. The political mood in the United States was overwhelmingly one of acquiescence, not vigilance. It seemed to produce in vast sections of the population a refusal to allow facts and evidence to shake their support for the neoconservative global agenda, a phenomenon of populist complicity with mystification, a process that can be best described as self-mystification. This is a serious condition that tempts leaders, so disposed in any event to mislead, to disguise the failures of their approach by exaggerating dangers and instituting even harsher measures of control in the name of "security." Even in mid-2007, faced with declining popularity, President Bush still warns the country that "failure" in Iraq is unacceptable, as if it has not already occurred.

The international dimensions of this phenomenon are often overlooked, yet important. Contrary to most perceptions, American hegemony produced a considerable degree of acquiescence on the part of foreign governments, including those that refused in the end to be stampeded into supporting the Iraq War at the United Nations and elsewhere. Undue credibility was given to American prewar arguments, including by France and Germany, as indicated by the acceptance on the part of all members, of UN Security Council Resolution 1441. The unanimous view expressed in this resolution adopted the unexamined premise that if Iraq did possess *any* weapons of mass destruction, then an American-led, UN-mandated recourse to war against Iraq should be validated and supported. What was inexcusably unexamined by an international organization, with its central mission being the prevention of war, was why such possession would constitute such a threat as to validate a nondefensive war against Iraq, seemingly in violation of the Charter, and certainly of international law as generally understood. If the Security Council had properly fulfilled its role under the UN Charter, it would first have examined this issue of whether Iraq posed a threat to its neighbors and beyond, and probably would have reached the conclusion that even if Iraq did possess some weapons of mass destruction it was not a sufficient threat to the peace to validate war. Even if Iraq posed potential and hypothetical dangers to its neighbors, there was no reason to believe that the Iraqi government could not be effectively deterred. The case for preemptive war fell far short of satisfying the burden of persuasion legally required to sustain a decision to initiate war. If the concern was whether Al Qaeda could obtain these weapons, then Iraq was the wrong source of worry, as the greatest danger by far was Pakistan, as well as other states holding large arsenals of such weaponry without ample safeguards, above all, Russia. Fairly considered, the role of the UNSC given the priorities associated with war prevention written into the UN Charter should have been to view Iraq, despite its distasteful leadership, as a country whose security, including its territorial integrity and political independence, was being improperly and illegally threatened by American diplomacy and military deployments and behavior. From the perspective of international law and the UN, Iraq deserved to be protected, and certainly not attacked. The UN did not allow its authority to be used as a geopolitical instrument in support of an aggressive war, but it also deferred to geopolitical pressures by its failure to consider the rights of Iraq as a member sovereign state faced with the likely prospect of being attacked by the strongest military power in the world.

This essay reflects the conviction that it is the proper role of a public intellectual and citizen to be engaged in a critical politics of demystification, a responsibility that is heightened in times of national crisis.[15] This role assumes a particular urgency in the present national and global setting, which presents radical and unprecedented challenges relating to world order. The inability of current leaders to meet these challenges successfully has been underscored by what appears to be a disastrous failure of American foreign policy in Iraq that has only recently been partially acknowledged in mainstream American politics, although it has long been abundantly discussed elsewhere in the world. The failure is both retrospective and prospective, threatening a new layer of mystification, with strong

Orwellian undertones, designed to present the continuing Iraqi failure to the American people as still capable of achieving success, and to provide a political basis for possibly repeating the failure in other settings, particularly Iran and possibly Syria, relying on a rationale that combines counterterrorism with counterproliferation. The geopolitics of unipolarity and empire are here being pursued less by mystification than by the unilaterally construed theory of "exception" that allows the United States to decide who shall be prevented from acquiring nuclear weapons, claiming a right to wage a preventive war to carry out this policy, and who is breaking the rules of the international power game so seriously as to warrant attack. At the same time, the Bush leadership is pushing for the development of new types of nuclear weapons with possible future battlefield applications ("bunker busters" and "mini-nukes") for integration in the U.S. nuclear arsenal, and dangerously proposing to enlarge the war zone in the Middle East beyond Iraq.

Demystification, as with mystification, is a process that is itself beset by inconclusiveness due to the inability to achieve interpretative closure and report with assurance on a course of events.[16] The ethos of demystification involves a dedicated search for truth and transparency, and a willingness to acknowledge evidence even when it undermines preferred policy positions. Demystification is the opposite of the ethos of mystification, which depends on intentional disinformation and concealment. It is a truth-seeking endeavor, acknowledging fallibility and the limits of knowledge but dedicated to portraying "realities" being concealed and manipulated by the great mystifiers of the day.

"INNOCENT" MYSTIFICATION

The possibility exists, at least in principle, that what has been depicted here as mystification is nothing more serious than an honest difference of opinion, and is thus an example of misperception. Such a conclusion would imply that in the setting of the Iraq War the neoconservative advocates, and their collaborators, disclosed their real reasons for favoring war, and did not attempt to manipulate facts and perceptions in a deceptive manner. In the end, it is usually not possible to "prove" mystification, short of confessions or the release of confidential documents, but an inference of mystification seems appropriate if the available circumstantial evidence indicates beyond a reasonable doubt that the official line of explanation is incoherent and implausible, and there exists no other coherent explanation of the course of action taken.[17] Such a demonstration, even if not airtight, helps us understand better a contested course of action, such as the Iraq War, and allows us to address more knowingly the real challenge posed by the policies being pursued. Demystification, even if incapable of providing an alternative account, is an essential foundation for meaningful citizenship and the attempt expresses a hope, often seemingly forlorn, that an ethos of vigilance can be again generated on the part of the United States citizenry, the Congress, the official opposition, and the mainstream media.

From a logical perspective there are several alternative explanations for the Iraq War that treat the official explanation as deserving respect despite the considerations discussed above that give rise to suspicions of mystification. None of these seems to withstand even modest scrutiny, although it is entirely consistent with the inference of mystification to conclude that there was some degree of sincere adherence to the official explanation by some of those engaged in the mystification process.

The most obvious innocent explanation is the suggestion that Iraq was perceived to pose a credible threat given the intelligence assessments provided to American leaders, combined with a misconstruction of past Iraqi behavior and probable future intentions. In this regard there did exist a widely shared belief on the part of leading intelligence agencies in a variety of countries, including France and Germany, that in 2003 Iraq possessed some quantity of chemical and biological weapons, and had previously used chemical weapons in the Iran/Iraq War and in subsequent operations against Kurdish villages in the late 1980s. But there was never any evidence that Iraq could not be contained within its borders, especially as its past behavior in relation to both Iran and the Gulf War of 1991 indicated a strong impulse by the Baghdad regime to reduce the damage from foreign policy miscalculations and, above all, survive as a political entity. Additionally, the weakness of Iraq due to twelve years of sanctions, repeated bombing attacks in the no-fly zones, and the lingering devastating effects of the 1991 war meant that it was not credible to view Iraq as threatening aggression beyond its borders at any point after 2001, and indeed as far ahead as it was possible to anticipate.

Some accusations were also made that Iraqi officials had provided encouragement, if not assistance, to Al Qaeda in mounting the September 11 attacks, and that in the aftermath it was an unacceptable danger to allow a hostile regime with a stockpile of WMD to survive. The argument contended that there was some serious risk that the Baghdad regime could in the future allow Al Qaeda to acquire such capabilities. Again, the factual basis to endow such an allegation with credibility never did exist. Despite a large effort, the Bush administration could only come up with some minor circumstantial contacts between individuals associated with the two political actors. This flimsy evidence of a connection is not persuasive on its own that something more substantial did not exist, but when set off against the long record of hostility between the secular Baathists and the forces of political Islam it seems highly implausible. This impression of implausibility is further reinforced in light of Iraq's apparent unwillingness to risk its survival by challenging the United States directly, which would be a consequence of such a provocative collaboration. There has been no evidence forthcoming that Saddam Hussein was ever prepared to take such risks, and the main indications are that the Baghdad regime was determined to regain a state of normalcy by doing all it could to reach an accommodation with the United States.

The American case for war also emphasized the ease of the military operation combined with the prospect of a welcome by a liberated Iraqi population. Belief in this scenario of quick victory reflected the accurate intelligence assessments of the weakness of the Iraqi battlefield capabilities, which were politically reinforced by the highly inflammatory, partisan, and unreliable information provided by Iraqi exiles, most notably by Ahmet Chalabi. These exile groups understandably had their own political agenda that was centered on inducing an American military intervention. It was this uncritical attitude toward a nondefensive war that led the United States into a quagmire that became in these respects increasingly reminiscent of Vietnam, but in a context where the strategic stakes and risks are far higher, and the prospects of an expanding war zone are becoming stronger.

There is no reasonable way to discount the conclusion of mystification by giving credence to these various interpretations based on acknowledging the theoretical possibilities of innocent mistake. Contrary voices and evidence were systematically ignored or repudiated so as to proceed with the Iraq War. This governmental resolve to wage war against Iraq was not susceptible to arguments based on prudence or law, because the advocates were motivated by grand strategy and their own version of nonnegotiable values.

TOWARD DEMYSTIFICATION

The struggle for demystification is difficult and complex, and will necessarily remain partial and incomplete. In the setting of challenging the official rationale for the Iraq War, demystification has been a multidimensional process that has so far had only modest success in delegitimizing the Bush presidency with the majority of American citizens, leading to the wresting of control from the Republicans after the congressional elections of November 2006. What is surprising is that the grip of mystification on the American body politic remained firm enough to earlier lead to the reelection of Bush in 2004, and despite the failure to find weapons of mass destruction in Iraq, despite the alienation of world public opinion, particularly in the liberal democracies of Western Europe; despite the gross miscalculations associated with the politics of forcible regime change in Iraq, including casualties that have crossed the threshold of one thousand American combat deaths (and several times that number wounded or traumatized); and despite the inability to capture or kill the top leadership of al Qaeda, especially Osama bin Laden. Aside from these factors, a growing number of Americans doubt the veracity of the official accounts of September 11 and are critical of the evasive reassurances offered by the 9/11 Commission Report. In addition, a series of high-level defectors from the Bush administration have confirmed the failure by the Bush White House to accord protection against terrorism a high priority in American policymaking and have given authoritative testimony on the obsessive resolve of the Bush inner circle to mobilize the country for the Iraq War in the face of efforts by high civil servants to oppose the invasion on grounds that it badly hurt the antiterrorist effort.

The post–September 11 aura of mystification has been sustained by public fears, heightened by government manipulation, and bolstered by a sense of utter confusion about how to defeat such an enemy that is everywhere and nowhere and cannot be associated with a territorial sovereign state. In this circumstance, bold language of resolve, combined with a clear action plan that tends to blunt criticism, especially given the passivity of Congress and the media, carried the day with the American public. Centrist commentators on world affairs still do not question this mystifying web of disinformation, but confine their carping to the details of tactics and implementation, thereby indirectly validating the principal falsehoods. It was a shocking disappointment that the Democratic candidate in the 2004 presidential elections refused to challenge the Bush administration on its disastrous and tragic decision to make war in Iraq and then bungle the occupation. In this respect, the neoconservative mystification is reinforced by acquiescence by its political opponents, and there is present the double failure of avoiding a serious discussion of how to address the challenge of Islamic extremism and why the pursuit of the global empire project is both a prescription for worldwide anti-Americanism and entails a self-destructive process of overreach that imperils American democracy, financial stability, and the safety of the citizenry.

Revealingly, the realities associated with the Iraq War and the American project of global empire are rather clearly perceived in most parts of the world. Demystification of the American doctrinal and policy stance, especially in light of the Iraq War, has taken place overseas to an impressive degree, overcoming the inhibiting impacts of American hegemonic authority. If the peoples of the world had voted in the 2004 elections there seems little doubt that George W. Bush would have been resoundingly defeated. Unfortunately, demystification outside of the United States has only a limited impact on the struggle within the country, and possibly, at least in some circles, the criticism from abroad stiffens the nationalist will of citizens to follow the Bush hard line at home.

Initiatives associated with government or media are not likely to further to any great degree prospects for demystification in the United States. It is possible that an Iraqi "Tet Offensive" could have had the same shock effect on the Iraq policies as it did on the Vietnam War–prone consensus back in 1968. Just as the neoconservatives needed a new Pearl Harbor to launch their plan effectively, so the anti-Bush demystifiers may need a new Tet Offensive to break through the complacency of the public mood.

In the background is a many-sided global process of restructuring world order in some sort of post-Westphalian mode.[18] At present, it is a matter of whether the American project of global empire will encounter sufficient resistance to produce viable alternatives. The most promising alternative, currently being incubated in civil society, and embodied in grassroots activism as on display at the World Social Forum, involves the establishment of global democracy. Some institutional initiatives have already been taken, most dramatically the establishment of an International Criminal Court. Others are in the advocacy stage, including moves to establish some sort of Global Peoples Parliament.

The broader goals of demystification need to include the fundamental historical task of promoting and achieving a peaceful transition to a post-Westphalian structure of human security that preserves the autonomy of particular national and regional communities while encouraging the development of the rule of law on a global basis in an atmosphere dedicated to democracy and the realization of human rights, including economic and social rights. The future of the sovereign state as central political actor will inevitably be drawn into question during this process of transition, as has already occurred to a significant degree, but is masked by the persisting attitudes and frameworks of the superseded state-centric world. At least three subversive processes are under way: the dilution of sovereignty in the course of reconstituting economic, political, and cultural life in regional frameworks, especially in Europe; the extension of sovereignty by the United States in its claims to be a global state that deploys its interventionary capabilities on a planetary scale, including oceans and space; the challenges to the cruelties of artificial sovereignty as exemplified by a new questioning of those forms of African statehood that are legacies of colonial misrule.[19] The politics of demystification needs to address these broad historical trends that are shifting the tectonic realities of world order, as well as respond critically to the thralldom of mystification that is inclining a disintegrating state-centric world order toward perpetual war.

8

Democratizing the Middle East

The affirmation of "democracy" is almost universal at this point, but the meaning of that affirmation remains very much in doubt. That doubt is most acute in the Middle East and North Africa, because the promotion of democracy has become linked to the practice of controversial geopolitics in the region. The debate surrounding democracy centers on an assessment of the American role and methods, especially the distinction between its professed intentions and actual behavior. Turkey is to some extent caught in the middle, engaged in its own process of democratizing reform, as well as being an ally of the United States while at the same time seeking to move closer to Europe and eventually to be accepted as a member of the European Union. For these reasons and others, the promises and concerns provoked by the unveiling of the Greater Middle East Initiative and North Africa Project (GMI) make it a natural focus for discussion, heated controversy, and evaluation.

There is little dissent from the broad goals of regional reform as articulated by the Greater Middle East Initiative, to some extent complementary to and superseded by their formulation at the G-8 Meeting in Sea Island, Georgia, on June 9, 2004, as the Partnership for Progress and a Common Future. These goals for development in the political, social and cultural, and economic spheres are widely endorsed pieties in international society, and echo objectives set forth for the world in an array of UN documents, including the *Millennium Report* of 2000. The important uncertainties relate to the degree of resources that might be made available to help with implementation, the extent to which progress should be promoted by nonregional actors, and the evaluation of whether these goals are congruent with the realities present in the region and in accordance with the state-by-state circumstances of each country. My focus is on whether the United States is able at this stage to exert a positive influence with respect to these challenges of regional reform, which also bear on how Turkey can best participate in a constructive process for the future. Two issues that cannot be discussed fully relate centrally to this inquiry: the future of Iraq in light of the persisting American occupation, and the resolution of the Israel/Palestine conflict.

I. THE STRATEGIC, IDEOLOGICAL, AND
DIPLOMATIC BACKGROUND OF THE GMI

Perhaps the most notable development in the grand strategy of the United States in the aftermath of the Cold War was to shift its understanding of the geographic locus of world history from Europe to the Middle East, and more generally to the Islamic world. The site of both world wars of the twentieth century, as well as the central confrontation of the Cold War, had been in Europe. It thus represented a sea change in thinking about the future to regard the Middle East as having become the decisive history-making region with respect to world politics. In each of these earlier wars the Middle East had been deeply affected, despite being geographically peripheral to the main war zone. The reverberations of the European outcomes of these wars led to fundamental developments in the Middle East: the collapse of the Ottoman Empire and the emergence of modern Turkey after World War I, the erosion of the French and British colonial capacity after World War II, and the termination of the Soviet/American rivalry after the Cold War. The present situation remains in flux at the edge of dangerous forms of conflict and turmoil. There exists uncertainty as to how the region will unfold in response to a variety of internal tensions, but also serious questions about the character of United States and European participation. Turkey has an opportunity to become a central player in determining whether these nonregional actors relate to the Middle East and North Africa primarily as constructive partners or as manipulative exploiters.

Any useful assessment of regional prospects needs to address several factors: the rising and indefinite challenge of political Islam and the varying responses that might yet produce "a clash of civilizations," the presence of a large proportion of the world's proven oil reserves, the continued turbulence generated by the unresolved Israel/Palestine conflict, several governments in the region that act oppressively toward their own citizenry, and the degree to which American priorities in the Middle East are at odds with both regional security and stability and with the healthy economic and political development of the various countries.

These concerns surfaced dramatically in the Gulf War of 1991, leading the United States to organize a coalition of countries, backed by a UN Security Council mandate, that led Iraq to relinquish control over Kuwait and find itself subject to a punitive peace that included a lethal sanctions regime and intrusive inspection arrangements that lasted twelve years. With the election of George W. Bush as president in 2000, the United States' military engagement with the region escalated in its intensity. This neoconservative perspective, which dominated the worldview of the Bush presidency from its inception, favored forcible regime change in Iraq and a generally aggressive American foreign policy throughout the Middle East region, with a thinly disguised plan for a reconfiguration of the politics of the entire region. An integral element of this neoconservative agenda was to be proactive in support of the spread of democracy under the aegis of American power throughout the region. Neoconservatives had also been very critical of what they viewed as the unwillingness of the U.S. government during the Clinton years to invest more heavily in its military capabilities so as to be able to take proper advantage of its overall dominance after the Soviet collapse to establish a global security system administered from Washington. The September 11 attacks created a political atmosphere that allowed the Bush presidency to change this neoconservative agenda of goals into an operational program. It should be remembered that until the Al Qaeda attacks the Bush presidency had been very weak, having barely survived an electoral challenge that made Bush the first American president in more than one hundred years who was elected despiting losing the popular vote. The Bush victory in 2000 became possible only when a hotly contested Florida vote was decided in favor of the Republicans. After September 11 all these doubts about the legitimacy of the Bush presidency were put aside, and a tidal wave of patriotic enthusiasm allowed the White House almost unlimited room for maneuver in foreign policy. A compliant media and Congress reinforced this passive mood. In such a political atmosphere there was a total abandonment of the sort of critical oversight that is needed if a democracy is to function successfully. This abandonment of debate was especially serious because the neoconservative outlook was extremist, exposing the country, the region, and the world to grave risks through its commitment to a radical set of foreign-policy objectives, especially in the Middle East. The Iraq War was the most direct consequence of this neoconservative ascendancy in American policymaking circles.

In effect, to understand where the Greater Middle East Initiative came from, it is necessary to take account of this background of strategic thinking but also to grasp the sort of ideological climate that emerged after the fall of the Berlin Wall and the collapse of the Soviet Union. It was a triumphalist atmosphere in which the West, under American leadership, was convinced that it had prevailed over Soviet power because it had the better ideas, superior values, and a more efficient economy and government. These conclusions were encapsulated in such words as "democracy," "freedom," "liberty," and of course, "market." During the Clinton presidency from 1993 to 2001, this general outlook prevailed, often described under the banner of "democratic peace," suggesting that since democratically organized states do not wage war against one another, the spread of democratic governance to additional countries would enlarge the zone of peace in the world. This kind of pro-democracy worldview led President Clinton to formulate a doctrine of "enlargement" — namely, making it a foreign-policy goal to encourage by persuasion the adoption of democratic forms of government by other countries.

Almost covertly, an emphasis on private-sector economic policy was insinuated into the discourse on democracy, as if "market" and "democracy" were Siamese twins rather than contingent partners.

Part of the ideological preparation occurred in the 1980s when strong conservative leaders in Britain and the United States, Margaret Thatcher and Ronald Reagan, unabashedly embraced a business-first view of government that celebrated the virtues of minimally regulated capitalism. During this period an additional element of great importance emerged: the rise of an integrated and elaborately networked world economy underpinned by information technologies and ideologically associated with a neoliberal version of how the market should operate. This neoliberal ideology was quietly imported into the affirmation of democracy, creating as of 1990 a widely endorsed conviction that the only legitimate form of government was what became known as "market-oriented constitutionalism." That is, one of the fruits of victory in the Cold War was to discredit socialism as a potentially acceptable alternative to capitalism, as well as further link the successes of capitalism to the creative energies so impressively generated by democratically organized societies that reward private-sector initiatives. In an important sense, this economistic extremism preceded the political extremism of the Bush presidency, and set the stage for neoconservative thinking.

This line of thinking has been canonized in the twenty-first century. President Bush in the covering letter written in September 2002 to introduce the most important official document of his presidency, *National Security Strategy of the United States of America,* declares: "The great struggles of the twentieth century between liberty and totalitarianism ended with a decisive victory for the forces of freedom — and *a single sustainable model for national success: freedom, democracy, and free enterprise.* In the twenty-first century only nations that share a commitment to protecting basic human rights and guaranteeing political and economic freedom will be able to unleash the potential of their people and assure their future prosperity" (emphasis added). In effect, political stability and globalization were both unconditionally associated with the promotion of private-sector democracy. The electoral results in Latin America disclose a partial revival of socialist politics within the framework of constitutional democracy, and cast some doubt on whether this linkage between the market and democracy will remain as influential in political thought and practice.

From the beginning of its independent existence, the United States portrayed itself as possessing an exemplary form of government that could serve as a model for others to emulate. Even when weak and colonized, early Americans spoke glowingly of their society in exceptionalist language as "the new Jerusalem," 'the city on the hill," "a light unto nations." Later this pride in the uniqueness of the country provided a major justification for an increasingly interventionary diplomacy throughout the Western Hemisphere. The Monroe Doctrine, first enunciated in 1823, was initially designed to keep the colonizing states of Europe from intruding on the political independence of Latin American countries. Later in the nineteenth century it was used in more coercive ways to protect the interests of foreign investors and impose American will on neighbors throughout the hemisphere. Such interventionary practice was prominent during the presidency of Woodrow Wilson, who believed that U.S. interventions in Mexico and the Caribbean were paving the way for the emergence of democratic forms of governance throughout Latin America. Wilson definitely had this belief that spreading democracy around the world would be beneficial for world peace, as well as for private capital. This diplomatic background is important for an understanding of the current promotion of democracy in the Middle East, commentators suggesting that what Bush has declared and favors is, in effect, "a Monroe Doctrine for the world," as well as noting the kinship between Bush's visionary foreign policy and that of Wilson almost a century earlier.[1] It now seems that this grandiose plan to democratize the world has been stillborn in the still-unresolved urban battlegrounds of Iraq.

All along there were also strong contradictory antidemocratic elements shaping the American approach to its relations with other countries that reflected the frequent convergence of American entrenched political and economic interests with the persistence of authoritarian rule. One of the clearest expressions of this countertendency is found in an internal memo, labeled "top secret" at the time, written by the eminent scholar/diplomat George Kennan while he was director of the Policy Planning Staff of the U.S. State Department. The document was later declassified. Kennan's carefully chosen words written in 1948 are often quoted: "We [Americans] have 50% of the world's wealth but only 6.3% of the population. This disparity is particularly great between ourselves and the peoples of Asia. In this situation, we cannot fail to be the object of envy and resentment. Our real task in the coming period is to devise a pattern of relationships which will permit us to maintain this position of disparity without positive detriment to our national security. To do so we will have *to dispense with all sentimentality and daydreaming. We should cease to talk about vague . . . and unreal objectives, such as human rights, the raising of living standards, and democratization.* The day is not far off when we are going to have to deal in straight power concepts. The less we are hampered by idealistic slogans, the better" (emphasis added). These views were not at all deviant in this period, but characterized the dominant approach of "realist" thinking that shaped American foreign policy throughout the Cold War era. There were notorious antidemocratic interventions by the United States in Iran in 1953, and in Guatemala in 1954, that went to the other extreme of negating moves toward democracy in foreign countries throughout the Third World so as to ensure the protection of economic, political, and ideological interests. Henry Kissinger's strong influence in foreign policy was based on a particularly forceful and consistent version of this line of thinking. Quite characteristically, Kissinger welcomed the antidemocratic coup against the Allende government of Chile in 1973 that brought to power the Pinochet military dictatorship that committed many Crimes Against Humanity, victimizing its own citizens.

The question posed, then, is whether the language of democratization as embodied in the Greater Middle East Initiative represents a genuine shift in American foreign policy, or alternatively, is misleading, disguising the persistence of realist underpinnings by proclaiming support for social and economic development, human rights, and democracy while in actuality pursuing a grand strategy dictated by a logic of control and economic advantage. Perhaps there are also some intermediate positions between these poles of sincerity and deception that are relevant for an interpretation of current American intentions and goals in the Middle East. It may be that American leaders *hope* that the region moves toward a moderate form of constitutionalism that is not antagonistic to its strategic priorities, but such an outlook seems naive given the attitudes on the ground that seem dominant in the societies located throughout the Middle East and North Africa.

THE PROBLEMATIC RATIONALE FOR THE GREATER MIDDLE EAST INITIATIVE: REGIONAL AND GLOBAL SETTING

There is no way to separate the proposed promotion of democracy in the Middle East from its connections with the wider global and regional setting as it has unfolded in the period since the September 11 Al Qaeda attacks on the World Trade Center and the Pentagon. In addition to the factors mentioned above, three other dimensions of this advocacy of democracy and modernization for the Middle East help us to understand the timing, depth, and substance of the initiative.

The Global Struggle against Terrorism

The United States government, unable to get UN support for the Iraq War and failing to find weapons of mass destruction in Iraq, has tried to emphasize its commitment to the democratization of Iraq as integral to its struggle against the menace of global terrorism. In President Bush's words to the National Endowment for Democracy of November 2003, "The failure of Iraqi democracy would embolden terrorists around the world, increase dangers to the American people, and extinguish the hopes of millions in the region. The establishment of a free Iraq at the heart of the Middle East will be a watershed event in the global democratic revolution." On this basis, the kind of thinking that underpins the Greater Middle East Initiative is set forth as a matter of American foreign policy: ". . . the United States has adopted a new policy, a forward strategy of freedom in the Middle East. This strategy requires the same persistence and energy and idealism we have shown before. And it will yield the same results. As in Europe, as in Asia, as in every region of the world, the advance of freedom leads to peace."

Was this ever convincing, or feasible? For most of the world the Iraq War stirred up terrorist activities where none had previously existed, and diverted attention from the main sources of extremist threat. Such an understanding was so widespread outside the United States that in most of the world it is widely believed that the goal of the Iraq War could not possibly be antiterrorism. It was too obvious that such a goal could not be reached by such means. Instead, the Iraq War must have been motivated by undisclosed goals that might make some strategic sense. There is considerable evidence that oil, military bases, security in the region, and America's broader conception of world order provide the true explanation of recourse to war against Iraq.

Beyond this, the Iraq War as a model of forcible democratization has abjectly failed at this point, and has been politically repudiated by the American electorate. It did succeed in removing from power a brutal tyrant, but at the cost of extensive bloodshed, a continuing armed resistance to the American occupation, and a severe agitation of sectarian strife not only in the country but throughout the region. The idea of importing "democracy" on the backs of an invading army was not perceived by most of the Iraqi population as "liberation," but rather as hostile and unwelcome foreign occupation. This imposed a governing process that has not been able to function efficiently or to gain legitimacy from most of the Iraqi people. The elected Iraqi leadership is perceived as operating under the protection and subject to the authority of the occupying forces, while at the same time acting to consolidate sectarian control under a Shiite aegis.

Engaging in reform of the political and economic institutions in the region, as encouraged by the widely quoted *Arab Human Development Report* (AHDR) of 2002, relies exclusively on an endorsement of indigenous initiatives that satisfy the preconditions for democratization, such as the education and emancipation of women. Such moves toward democratization need to be perceived as consistent with an Iraqi right of self-determination, which is impossible to reconcile convincingly with an intervention undertaken on largely false pretenses relating to an alleged WMD threat, and without the support of either countries in the region or the United Nations. But even if it had managed to have such support a pro-democracy intervention would still be directly at odds with AHDR as it would involve reliance on external pressures rather than indigenous initiatives.

The character of "democracy" in the context of American foreign policy, or its seeming temporary embodiment in the political life of Iraq, also has a disturbing ambiguity. There is every reason to suppose that a governing process genuinely responsive to the priorities and perspectives of the Iraqi masses would be both hostile to Israel and opposed to the continuation of any American national or regional presence, especially its military dimensions. Such an assessment is applicable throughout the region, making it extremely unlikely that Washington policymakers seek to promote political outcomes that challenge principal U.S. foreign policy goals. Therefore, the only way to reconcile democracy with U.S. foreign policy would be to construct a "guided democracy" for Iraq and the Middle East that is hardly more democratic than to suppose that the sort of socialism imposed by Moscow on the countries of Eastern Europe could be considered "socialist." If the red lines of Iraqi democracy end up being established in Washington rather than Baghdad, it will be virtually impossible for Iraqis and others in the region to perceive the process as one of democratization. Without being responsive to the realities and perceptions of self-determination, it is totally unrealistic to expect that political outcomes even if preceded by elections will be regarded as democratic by the citizenry. The efforts to bring democracy to Iraq by way of elections has produced a mandate for Shia rule of the country, which has exacerbated the sectarian rivalry and led to an expansion of the Sunni insurgency, especially given the early occupation policies of the United States, which disbanded the Iraqi army and instituted a wide-ranging program of de-Baathification. The failure of these policies has by now been widely admitted, and new initiatives considered, including ironically, the possibility of re-Baathification.

Much of the inspiration for this proactive approach to democracy in the Middle East came from the happy American experience with the Helsinki process, which was understood to have contributed to the great movements for democracy in Eastern Europe during the 1980s. The Helsinki Accords, signed in 1975, were based on negotiations between Washington and Moscow in which the main concern at the time was the Soviet interest in stabilizing the disputed boundaries of the countries in Eastern Europe on the basis of the temporary agreements reached at the end of World War II. The provisions for monitoring compliance with international human rights standards were regarded at the time as a rather insignificant propaganda concession by the Soviet Union. The right wing in the United States sharply attacked the Helsinki Accords as a major and unwelcome gift to Moscow, effectively legitimating its claims to exert imperial control over Eastern Europe. It was appreciated that civil society in these countries was already strongly mobilized to engage in nonviolent oppositional politics. What the Helsinki process did was to create some new political spaces that enabled these popular movements in Eastern Europe to press their case against the legitimacy of the Soviet-bloc governments based on their poor human rights records. When Gorbachev came to power in the mid-1980s, these movements were then able to achieve a democratizing momentum *in accordance with the dynamics of self-determination* as Soviet hegemonic control and ambition dramatically weakened. This democratic outcome, promoted by the United States, posed no threat of a backlash, as the popular sentiments of these countries, unlike those in the Middle East and North Africa, were ardently and overwhelmingly pro-American at the level of civil society.

Global Economic Integration

There is another line of reasoning that is influential in Washington, and reached the same kind of conclusions. Here the argument is more avowedly geopolitical, less normative (that is, related to human rights and democracy), emphasizing the establishment of a global security system, insisting that the threats faced by the West arise almost exclusively from countries not fully integrated into the world economy. This is a strategic perspective that substitutes an insistence on connectedness for that of the establishment of democracy and is an aspect of a sweeping and recent geopolitical vision. Thomas P. M. Barnett has comprehensively set forth this outlook in his book *The Pentagon's New Map: War and Peace in the Twenty-First Century*.[2] It builds indirectly on the sort of advocacy associated with the writings of Bernard Lewis and Thomas Friedman, both of whom in somewhat different ways contend that the turbulence and failures of the Middle East and North Africa are mainly a result of countries unable to make the transition to modernity and therefore cut off from the economic and political benefits of globalization. Barnett divides the world between "the functioning core," which is essentially the OECD countries plus a scattering of others that have been successfully globalized, and "the non-integrating gap," where conditions within these countries give rise to "failed states" that, in turn, generate violent backlash actions directed at the core, of which the September 11 attacks are the most prominent example. Barnett urges developing the sort of doctrine and military technologies with the intent and capabilities to shrink by aggressive uses of force the nonintegrating gap, and to do so in ways that somehow manage simultaneously to promote "justice" as well as establish "order". What this means concretely is not made clear. What is clear is that Barnett supports the Iraq War from this perspective of coercive integration into the world economy, rather than by reference to either terrorism or weapons of mass destruction. If this had been the guiding motivation, then it would have been of cardinal importance to be sure that the Iraqi economy would be reconstructed during the American occupation so that it would become available for foreign investment and as open as possible to foreign trade.

Global Security System

If the Middle East is seen as the touchstone, then control over its evolution provides the key to the future. The Greater Middle East Initiative is a diversionary ideological move that attempted to disguise a geopolitical intention to establish strategic control. The American effort to build long-range military bases in Iraq, together with its alliance relations with Israel and Turkey, provides the real foundation of its rather traditional hegemonic policies. The rhetoric of democracy and development is invoked as a way of legitimating presence and discrediting resistance, but it is not seriously meant to pose challenges to stable, Western-oriented authoritarian rule in the region. In fact, the views Kennan expressed as to the general incompatibility between American geopolitical and economistic goals and human rights/democracy seem to remain pertinent at this point of history as well, notwithstanding the temporary abandonment of a realist approach to foreign policy by the United States government. If this analysis is even partially correct, then it would be sensible to approach the announced intentions of the Greater Middle East Initiative with a healthy dose of skepticism and suspicion.

A CONCLUDING NOTE

As suggested, the historical moment raises many questions about the relationship between the Middle East and external actors, especially the United States and Europe. Will these two major actors, with deep historical and strategic involvements in the region, define their roles in a cooperative manner as at the Sea Island G-8 or in a more competitive fashion as seems implicit in the Greater Middle East Initiative? Will the United States eventually succeed in bringing something called "democracy" to Iraq, and will this outcome be perceived elsewhere as a positive or negative development? Are there ways to overcome the obstructive persistence of the Israel/Palestine conflict by establishing a successful peace process in the near future? Will Turkey move closer to Europe, and in the process adopt a diplomacy of equidistance with respect to Europe and the United States? Or will Turkey, as seems more likely at present, reposition itself as between the United States and the Arab world? And finally, will the political emergence of Islam work to achieve or inhibit the realization of the American program of regional democratization, and will the current Turkish experience provide an encouraging demonstration of the possibility of achieving an effective intermixture of political, cultural, and economic goals, with wider regional implications?

These questions have no obvious or immediate answers. We will have to await the impact of developments in the next several years. At this point, then, we need to admit that we have far more questions than answers when it comes to assessing the likely benefits and detriments of this project to use military force and coercive diplomacy to bring democracy to the region. What is clear even now is that Turkey has the opportunity to play a significant role in the Middle East, above all, by continuing with the deepening of its own democracy, thereby highlighting the contrast between pretensions of democracy as in Iraq and its reality. Whatever else emerges from the long occupation and accompanying civil strife in Iraq, the idea that democracy can be effectively spread by military intervention seems to have been decisively discredited.

9

Executing Saddam Hussein

Given the harsh brutality of Saddam Hussein's political career I could never have anticipated a certain measure of sympathy for the man at the end of his life. It was not only the unseemliness of executing a Muslim leader in the midst of the annual hajj pilgrimages, but the perverse insensitivity of hanging Saddam Hussein at the start of Eid al-Adha for those of Sunni persuasion. The Eid holiday, the holiest of Islamic sacred observances, is revered by devout Muslims as a solemn moment of sacrifice and forgiveness, as well as the end of the Muslim pilgrimage at Mecca. The toxic sectarian element was injected by the fact that for Sunnis Eid began at dawn on the morning that Saddam Hussein was executed, while for Shia the four-day holiday does not begin until the following day. It was on this basis that the Iraqi leadership in Baghdad secured the approval of the Shiite clerics in Najaf to go ahead with the execution, after which the prime minister, Nuri al-Maliki, signed the final execution order only six hours before the hanging took place.

A respected Iraqi political analyst, Nazem Jassour, was quoted as saying, "[t]here was no good reason why the execution could not be delayed until after Eid. . . . It's going to be perceived by Iraqi Sunnis as one more example of how the Shia government is trying to humiliate them." There may not have been good reasons for such unseemly haste, but several bad reasons seemed powerfully present. First was the thinly disguised thirst for vengeance. Second seems to have been an effort to demonstrate that the Shia were now firmly in control of the Iraqi government. And third was the totally inappropriate, raucous, and disturbing display of tasteless allegiance to Muqtada al-Sadr in the execution chamber. It was Muqtada's militia, the Mahdi Army, which was widely believed to control death squads responsible for killing many Sunni civilians in Baghdad and elsewhere in the country, setting a partisan sectarian tone that was extended even to the mechanics surrounding the execution itself.

But why would Shiite religious leaders themselves not want to defer this vindictive moment until after this period of intense religious devotion by all those of Islamic faith? It is true that Saddam Hussein was responsible for years of severe criminality against the Shia, undoubtedly explaining why some religious leaders in Najaf viewed the execution at this sacred time as "a gift of God."

Another line of possible explanation gives attention to the American angle. Reme Allaf, a specialist on Iraq associated with the British expert body on international relations, Chatham House, noting that the Iraqi government lacks independence, explains the strangeness of the overall legal approach of the trial by reference to the Iraqi leadership's need "to follow an American agenda." This makes a bit more sense of the overall timing of the trial and conviction, although not the specifics surrounding the execution itself, which seems to have been completely an Iraqi operation. After all, the Iraq policy pursued by the Bush presidency is increasingly unpopular with the American people, enjoying real support from only about 20 percent of the public. Despite this stark political fact, reinforced by the escalating violence and rising body counts in Iraq, the Bush White House gives no sign of changing course on Iraq, even to the limited extent recommended recently by the bipartisan Baker–Hamilton Iraq Study Group, and mandated by the outcome of the American midterm elections in November 2006. Bush's response to this wave of criticism has been to escalate the American military presence by adding a troop "surge" of 21,500 to be deployed in Baghdad and Anbar province, and chillingly to remind the American people that he is the "decision maker" when it comes to Iraq policy.

It is against this background that the general timing of the execution can be best understood, although probably not the rush to the gallows. Bush seems as determined as ever to carry on with the war, and defer to his successor the job of acknowledging failure in Iraq. During this interval until the presidential elections of 2008, Bush will be facing an increasingly hostile American public opinion and a Congress now controlled by the Democratic Party that would seem to have much to gain by opposing the president on Iraq so long as it is not seen as undermining the security of troops in the combat area. To cope with this likely firestorm of opposition, the execution of Saddam Hussein at the end of 2006, and no later, accomplished two important goals: it allowed Bush to claim as he did in the immediacy of the event that putting the former Iraqi leader to death is yet another "milestone" on the road to Iraqi democracy. Further, that despite the appearances of failure, the Iraqi policy of the White House is actually succeeding. All that is required for "victory" is more American troops, some tactical adjustments, and more American patience. It might have been true that the execution would distract some media attention away from the awkward statistic that the number of American soldiers killed in Iraq was about to cross the 3,000 threshold, which is truly a milestone that President Bush wanted to ignore as it was a signpost pointing directly to "defeat," and his own responsibility for causing so many personal tragedies for American families, without even mentioning the enormous and mounting Iraqi casualties. Unfortunately for Bush, the unseemly spectacle of the hanging prevented the effective diversionary use of the execution.

I think when the full story of the trial, sentencing, and execution of Saddam Hussein is told it will have a simple story line, "made in the U.S.A." At each stage of this flawed judicial process until the very end, it seemed to be the American intention to use the criminal prosecution of Saddam Hussein for propaganda purposes. It represented what has turned out to be a futile attempt to rebuild American support for the Iraq policy. To pursue such a goal required and accounts for the terrible distortions of the rule of law during the trial in the name of rendering justice. President Bush's reaction to the execution, as reported from his ranch in Crawford, Texas, where he was spending the Christmas holidays, is supremely ironic, actually a caricature of Orwellian rhetoric. Bush praised Saddam's execution as ". . . the kind of justice he denied victims of his brutal regime. Fair trials were unimaginable under Saddam Hussein's tyrannical rule. It is a testament to the Iraqi people's resolve to move forward after decades of oppression that, despite his terrible crimes, Saddam Hussein received a fair trial. This would not have been possible without the Iraqi people's determination to create a society governed by the rule of law." What the world saw was precisely the kind of "justice" attributed to Saddam Hussein by his harshest critics! More ironically, the videotaped proceedings provided the kind of imagery that had never been available to visually document Saddam Hussein's many criminal acts.

The American role in orchestrating the trial process apparently did not extend to the final phase. American military commanders and diplomats reportedly anticipated the bad effects of executing Saddam Hussein on a Sunni religious holiday, although not the antics in the execution chamber, and reportedly did their best to delay the execution by a few days. At the same time, having spun the illusion that the prosecution and conviction were done under the sovereign authority of the Iraqi government, it was obviously awkward for the United States to interpose objections as to the timing and manner of execution. It is not surprising that American officials, despite their justifiable concerns, decided in the end to give in to the Iraqi insistence that the convicted dictator be executed at a time and in a manner of their choosing. After some bickering back and forth, in the end all that American military commanders demanded was that the Iraqi government comply with their own law with respect to authorizing the execution before obtaining physical custody of Saddam Hussein who had been held since his capture in an American military prison at a base called Camp Cropper. It was when high Iraqi officials, including the Iraqi president, Jalal Talabani, refused to sign off on the execution order, that Maliki, determined to go ahead with the execution on the Sunni Eid, sought and obtained approval for his desired timing of the execution from top Shiite religious leaders in Najaf. The American military officers in charge of the transfer of Saddam Hussein, when asked for an opinion, were only willing to mutter defensively, "We would have done it differently."

In retrospect, there is no doubt that the United States suffered its worst public relations disaster since the Abu Ghraib torture pictures were spread around the world a couple of years ago. As mentioned, they did their best at the very end to avoid an anticipated hostile reaction to the execution, realizing that hanging

Saddam Hussein on a Muslim holiday would be seen as outrageous, not only in Sunni Iraq, but throughout the Islamic world. But the actual event was far worse than what was feared. Not only the timing of the execution but the grisly enactment of the hanging captured on a video leaked to the media made Saddam Hussein's death into an occasion of his instant martyrdom, as well as heaped blame somewhat unfairly on the United States for its presumed role. And despite the frantic American efforts to show the world that they did not have any control over the execution, and even tried to delay it, the general impression remained throughout the world that this was a show trial arranged by Washington with the grand purpose of vindicating a very unpopular, unsuccessful, and illegal war.

As might be expected, the worldwide reaction to the execution, especially after the video was shown on TV, was universally negative. Some commentators referred to the hanging death as a "lynching." Prime Minister Maliki angrily defended the manner with which the execution was handled, insisting that it was Iraq's right to deal with Saddam Hussein in whatever way they chose. Maliki's response to international criticism was expressed in words of biting sarcasm: "We're wondering where these organizations were during the crimes of Anfal and Halabja. Where were they during the mass graves and executions and the massacres that killed hundreds of thousands of Iraqis?" In fact, major human rights organizations were very vocal about calling attention to these crimes against the Kurdish minority during the 1980s. It was not these civil society actors, but rather the U.S. government that was mostly silent about these abuses, then valued and protected Hussein's Iraq as a Cold War ally. Of course, Maliki was in no position to remind the United States government of its complicity with these Crimes Against Humanity properly attributed to Saddam Hussein, and so had to vent his anger in directions that were essentially uninvolved in the criminality of the Baghdad regime.

The trial of Saddam Hussein on charges of Crimes Against Humanity could have been and should have been a positive experience for both Iraq and the world, but to reach such a result would have required turning the case over to independent and international judicial auspices from start to finish. It would also have required avoiding the imposition of the death penalty, a form of punishment not available under the statute of the International Criminal Court, and increasingly abandoned by democratic countries as morally unacceptable. The unacceptability of imposing capital punishment was aggravated in this instance by the awful spectacle of death by hanging, projecting an ugly imagery around the world that could appeal only to the most bloodthirsty of instincts. The opportunity to establish a reliable public record of the oppressive dictatorship of Saddam Hussein was completely lost. The fearless journalist Robert Fisk conveyed the perverse impact of the trial with compelling vividness: "Saddam died a 'martyr' to the will of the new 'Crusaders.'" But in the longer run, more seriously, the people of Iraq were deprived of the cathartic effects that would have been achieved if the trial had been organized more independently, and in a suitable setting.

Beyond this, the trial and punishment should certainly have addressed the full panoply of Saddam Hussein's crimes, dwelling on those crimes that were most serious, rather than conducting a separate trial dealing with an obscure incident back in 1982 when 148 Iraqis were killed in the town of Dujail as a collective punishment imposed in response to a failed coup attempt against the Baghdad regime. Hussein's far more extensive and consequential crimes associated with the infamous Anfal campaign in the late 1980s, when as many as 180,000 Kurds were killed in northern Iraq, many by chemical weapons, the genocidal policies directed at the "marsh Arabs" of the south after the Gulf War of 1991, the aggressive war waged against Iran in the 1980s that took over a million lives on both sides, the attack on and conquest of Kuwait, and the widespread torture and killing of political opponents during the course of his entire reign were never addressed. It is likely that the adjourned separate trial on the allegations concerning the Kurds will be continued, but without the presence of Saddam Hussein as the principal defendant: it will be Hamlet without the Prince of Denmark! As the Nuremberg trial of surviving German leaders after World War II made clear, the main achievement of such criminal prosecutions is not the punishment of disempowered leaders but political education through compiling undeniable evidence of the terrible wrongdoing of those accused and a demonstration in the course of the trial that the contrasting way of the victors is one of fairness and due process with respect to those who stand accused.

Again, we need to ask why this truncated, dysfunctional, politically illegitimate, and unprecedented approach was adopted as the framework for such a major judicial event, leading to the execution of the main culprit before evidence of his worst crimes of his regime could even be presented to a competent tribunal. The only credible explanation is that such an approach conformed to the political needs of the occupying power, and was imposed upon or accepted by the Iraqi government. A more adequate exposure of Saddam Hussein's crimes would have inevitably exposed American engagement with the regime and some measure of complicity with its crimes. Yet a more comprehensive trial would have seemingly served to strengthen the legitimacy of the Iraqi leadership elected, offsetting to some extent the delegitimizing impact of being perceived in Iraq as a dependent creature of the American occupation. Iraq was a strategic partner of the United States during the 1980s, the decade in which the worst excesses of Baathist rule took place, which incidentally included the persecution and execution of Shiite religious leaders. The exposure of this connection would certainly have generated some unwanted, further anti-American publicity in Iraq and around the world.

The U.S. relationship to Saddam Hussein's criminality is significant, and should not be disregarded because the events took place decades ago. The issues raised concern the relationship between geopolitical leadership and respect for the basic norms of international law. It was the United States that encouraged Iraq to attack Ayatollah Khomeini's Iran in 1980. It was the United States that supplied several of the components of the chemical weapons used against the Kurds, as well as a stream of dollar credits to facilitate Baghdad's drive to become a dominant military power in the region. It was the United States that used its diplomatic influence on the global stage to shield Baghdad from censure in the aftermath of these shocking events, and even dispatched Donald Rumsfeld to reassure Saddam Hussein that despite his notorious deeds nothing had changed so far as Washington was concerned. And later it was the United States in 1991, after Iraq was forced to withdraw from Kuwait, that either acquiesced in, or possibly even authorized, Saddam Hussein's bloody crackdown of the Kurds in the north and the marsh Arabs in the south of the country, having then had an interest in the unity of Iraq.

These historical realities help us understand why it was probably not *politically* possible to have a proper trial of Saddam Hussein at this time under these U.S./Iraqi auspices, but it was also not *politically* acceptable to create the sort of trustworthy international venue for prosecution and trial that would have exposed the full range of Saddam Hussein's criminality. The reliance on the Dujail incident as the basis for prosecution and punishment of Saddam Hussein must have seemed an ingenious solution from the perspective of the Americans who seemed to have controlled the process from behind the scenes whereby the Iraq Special Tribunal (IST) was established. The IST could be charged, as it was, with determining Saddam Hussein's criminality and punishment by examining the crimes associated with the Baathist period on a sequential basis, beginning with an incident that raised only internal Iraqi issues. Such a prosecution would undoubtedly produce a conviction that would be used to justify imposing the death penalty. Saddam Hussein would be removed from the scene before he had an opportunity to embarrass the American occupiers of Iraq. There is no doubt that Dujail did involve the commission of Crimes Against Humanity that, given the statute of the IST, warranted the maximum allowable punishment. A further peculiarity of the framework was the requirement that any death penalty be automatically appealed, with a decision rendered within thirty days, and that the punishment be carried out within an additional thirty days. Actually, Saddam Hussein was executed a mere five days after the mandatory appeal had been turned down, adding to suspicions that there was a special pressure to remove the former Iraqi leader from the scene as quickly as possible. Such haste in carrying out a death penalty is especially objectionable, as there exists no way to correct a mistake once the sentence has been carried out.

There were additional reasons why it was never appropriate to rush the process. To move from prosecution to execution so quickly, and by law, in a major political trial of this sort is unknown except in totalitarian states such as Stalin's Soviet Union or Hitler's Germany. To carry out an execution five days after the denial of an appeal from the sentence was to take from Saddam Hussein the thirty days that this already peculiar Iraqi law had fixed as the outer limit for carrying out the death sentence. To organize such a trial process while the country was enmeshed in a raging civil war and a resistance struggle further undermined the credibility of the process. If all this was not enough, there were other troubling features of the legal process. Most of those sitting in judgment on the court were Shiite partisans or Kurds without impressive credentials as jurists. And it is relevant that Saddam Hussein was removed from power and captured by an invading power that was itself guilty of waging a war in flagrant violation of the United Nations Charter, as well as in opposition to world public opinion. From many perspectives, those responsible for the invasion were as deserving of indictment, prosecution, and punishment as were the Iraqi defendants.

Rather than provide a milestone for the rule of law and Iraqi democracy, the trial and execution of Saddam Hussein raises high the banner of vindictive justice that obscured the very criminality that was supposedly being punished. It shifts anger from the accused to the accuser, and, incredibly, ceded the high moral ground to the criminal voice of Saddam Hussein. His farewell written message calling on all Iraqis to renounce hatred toward one another, and even toward their invader, expressed an admirable and timely moral sentiment that delivered a humane message. A remarkable feature of this entire legal drama was to redirect the compass of moral accountability away from Saddam Hussein at the endpoint of his life. Perhaps hidden beneath the politics of these events was an untold story of humanization. Saddam Hussein never showed remorse for any of his policies or deeds, but some disarming details have been revealed: he was respectful and appreciative toward his prison guards, he collected bread crusts from his prison food for birds, he wrote a rather magnanimous poem, and his demeanor in the presence of the hangman exhibited calm dignity. Of course, such behavior cannot exonerate the man for his abuses of power, but they do make us eager for a fuller account of how this historical figure evolved in the last stage of his life.

Perhaps, then, the worst result of this dreadfully crafted judicial process and punishment is that it deprives all of us of a needed closure with respect to the man and his deeds. Instead of having a full and authoritative account of Saddam Hussein's criminality and his evolution as a human being under accusation, we have a shadowy centaurian figure, half martyred and glorified, half reviled and abused. This saga was completed by the botched execution of his two fellow defendants in the Dujail trial, at least one of whom was beheaded.

The people of Iraq, especially, deserved better, but most unfortunately all indications suggest that this ugly episode addressing the crimes of the deposed dictator is a telling metaphor for the manner with which Nuri al-Maliki proposes to govern post-Baathist Iraq. Instead of establishing a clear discontinuity between the bad times of Saddam Hussein and the new governing process in Iraq, the whole drama of the execution seems a metaphor for the degree to which Iraq remains victimized by a criminalized form of governance, made that much worse by foreign occupation and an ongoing civil war. It is not surprising that more and more Iraqis, including those who suffered when Saddam Hussein was alive, now lament his removal from power, and are rushing across the borders of the country in search of a safe haven elsewhere. Many Iraqis recall that at least during Baathist rule there was order and security within the country, as well as political independence, and for much of the period notable social and economic progress.

10

Legality and Legitimacy
The Quest for Principled
Flexibility and Restraint

POINTS OF DEPARTURE

What follows is an attempt to acknowledge the complexity and relevance of debates about the relations between legality and legitimacy as it bears on political behavior. The opening section is intended to orient these international policy debates in wider traditions of political theory, particularly as it bears on the nature of sovereignty and the state. On this basis, the two prominent, recent instances of controversial recourse to war (Kosovo and Iraq) are considered from the perspective of legality and legitimacy, first as a matter of juridical evaluation and then from the perspective of international reputation. The focus throughout reflects a concern with the qualities of American global leadership since September 11, and how this leadership should or should not be guided by canons of legality.

Throughout the period between the end of World War II and the present periodic challenges have been directed at the core commitment of the United Nations Charter that prohibits unconditionally recourse to force other than in instances of self-defense strictly construed.[1] These challenges have commanded major attention in the last several years in the settings of two sets of global circumstances: alleged humanitarian emergencies and expanding claims of defensive necessity. In the first instance, the legal debate tends to be focused on the propriety of "humanitarian intervention," while in the second instance, the emphasis has been upon American claims and security policy since 9/11 that are associated with recourse to "preemptive war," or what is better known as anticipatory self-defense.

These developments have important policy and jurisprudential implications, and have been sharply contested in practice and doctrine. One important mode of legal reasoning that has emerged in both settings to defend or critique the contested use of force has rested on a distinction drawn between "legality" and "legitimacy." Much of the serious discussion, at least in the United States, has been so far devoted to the application of these ideas to the Kosovo War of 1999 and the Iraq War of 2003. In this chapter, these two controversial wars are considered from the perspective of legality and legitimacy. The domestic law historical background of this distinction is also superficially considered, as well as the jurisprudential implications of blurring the edges of legality by invoking guidelines of legitimacy. Finally, attention is given to whether the distinction performs a constructive role under present conditions of world order, and what might be done to reconstitute the domain of legality so as to minimize pressures to rely for justification on legitimacy, which simultaneously offer a juridical argument in support of a given course of action while violating the law.

In some senses, recourse to legitimacy as a supplement to legality is a discourse that parallels the revival of the just war doctrine, especially in thinking about the propriety of "war" as a response to the 9/11 attacks.[2] Indeed, supplying content and criteria for legitimating war resembles the process of validating war by reference to the just war doctrine. In this regard, invoking legitimacy as the basis for validating international uses of force acknowledges both the authority of law as serving normal needs of global society, and its dysfunctionality when extended to govern *selected* exceptional situations. But which circumstances, and by whom identified? And by whom appraised? Is not, in the end, the danger of relying on legitimacy to overcome the inadequacies of legality a means to assert the primacy of politics and the subordination of law?[3]

But why not, then, merely acknowledge that the law is violated for certain ethical and political reasons, and generalize such a framework? It is possible that *principled* violations of the Charter norm on force would serve an equivalent purpose to that of complementing legality with legitimacy. Yet to engage in behavior that is admittedly "illegal" seems to diminish respect for law more than to contend that incompleteness or new circumstances produce *reasonable* exceptions to law that should be constrained by principled considerations and treated as temporary. In this usage of "legitimacy" it might be better to think of the exception as *quasi-legal* rather than in the seminal usage of Carl Schmitt as *political*.

The distinction between legality and legitimacy originated and developed in the context of state/society relations, highlighting the significance of specific historical and structural circumstances of public order. The prominent assessment of this relationship between legality and legitimacy in late Weimar Germany sparked a complex and remarkably durable jurisprudential controversy about how to conceive of legality in circumstances where a political order is assaulted by an ultra-authoritarian movement such as the Nazis.[4] When dealing with the limits of legality within a state that possesses a functioning government the issues are fundamentally different. The main issue is whether the forms of legality provide the ultimate answer to the question of legitimacy, providing the citizens with final authority by way of legislative representation, or whether this legality should be tempered by societal norms interpreted by courts or subjected to emergency decrees issued by the source of "sovereign" authority, the head of state. In the historical context of Germany, the influence of legal positivism is often blamed for facilitating the rise of Naziism, encouraging the passivity and obedience of the German citizenry and the willingness of bureaucracy to preside over the destruction of democratic constitutionalism. But it seems doubtful that any view of law could have effectively obstructed the Nazi political onslaught associated with the rise of Hitler to absolute power, given the climate of popular opinion in crisis-ridden Germany. The legal arena in Germany, as well as theories about law, was certainly a site of struggle, but it was the inevitable prevalence of "the political" in periods of crisis rather than the choice of legal theory that determined the fate of Germany. Perhaps Germany was more susceptible to this dynamic of subservience to secular authority given its political culture, including the deep influence of Lutheranism, the late consolidation of state power, and its long experience of autocratic rule.

If we turn from domestic public order to world public order we discern dramatic differences. There are no governmental institutions beyond the state that can claim "sovereignty," in the sense of autonomous and ultimate authority to pronounce the law. The United Nations is best conceived as "a club of states," and is organized in such a way as to acknowledge geopolitical realities expressed formally by granting permanent membership in the Security Council and veto power to the five states that dominated world politics in 1945 when the UN was established. The International Court of Justice (ICJ), the judicial arm of the UN, has no general authority to decide disputes among states unless asked to do so or even to review contested decisions of the Security Council, possessing only a residual authority to issue "advisory opinions" if so requested by an organ of the Organization. No tradition of deference has emerged within the UN System to overcome the autonomy of leading states in relation to uses of force, although the efforts to oppose "aggression" have activated the UN from time to time.[5] Some legal scholars concluded that the legal prohibition embodied in the Charter had been seriously eroded or compromised by inconsistent patterns of practice, some reasonable, others not.[6] At the same time, the ICJ interpreted legality with respect to uses of force as specified by international law and the UN Charter as fully operative, and did not acknowledge any weakening of Charter norms as a result of the practice of states.[7] Additionally, there is widespread opposition to recent moves by the United States to view war as ultimately a discretionary instrument of foreign policy, as well as to the sort of unilateralism associated with the presidency of George W. Bush. Again, Kosovo and Iraq provide litmus tests for this push and pull.

Legality clarifies the core obligations relating to force, while legitimacy tries to identify *and delimit* a zone of exception that takes account of supposedly special circumstances. It is so far a problematic and controversial means of achieving flexibility, because the delimitation proposed lacks endorsement by the United Nations or acceptance by the governments of leading states. The legality/legitimacy discourse is largely an expression of concern in civil society about contested uses of international force, especially involving the United States. There is some international effort to move toward a more authoritative intergovernmental status for the distinction given its use with approval in the Report of the Independent International Commission on Kosovo, and considering the call by the UN secretary general for a resolution by the Security Council clarifying the Charter approach to uses of force under varying conditions. The official UN approach has been to insist that the Charter concept of legality is itself flexible enough to incorporate the *substance* of the Bush Doctrine on preemptive war, but not the *process* of unilateral invocation. "In Larger Freedom," the secretary general's comprehensive report to the Security Council on UN reform, drawing on recommendations made by an expert panel, insists that while preemptive war or anticipatory self-defense might be justifiable to address an emerging threat, that determination must be entrusted *without exception* to the Security Council.[8] Put this way it makes evident that the essential objection to American diplomacy since 9/11 is its unilateralism, but indirectly as well, as evident in the Iraq debate prior to the war, to the application of the doctrine in particular circumstances. Put differently, the United States tried hard to obtain approval for its claim to wage war against Iraq from the Security Council, but the Council refused, and then the United States acted in concert with its partners.

FORCE BEYOND LEGALITY: THE KOSOVO DEBATE

The debate occasioned by the Kosovo War of 1999 now seems overshadowed by the response to the 9/11 attacks, but the issues raised then with respect to the appropriateness of "humanitarian intervention" have a persisting relevance to the role of international law and the UNSC in setting *and suspending* limits on acceptable behavior by sovereign states in relation to international uses of force. At bottom the concern is with the method and style of embedding elements of morality, politics, and reasonableness in the interpretation of legal standards, whether this "loosening" of law is generally better done by stretching the meaning of the standards, that is, *internal* to the domain of "legality," or by acknowledging that it better preserves the core constraints of law (here the basic prohibition on nondefensive force) to acknowledge the limits of law by creating an *external* domain of exception, labeled "legitimacy."[9] Another way of expressing the inquiry is to consider under what conditions political and moral pressures for adjustment with respect to legal restraints should be dealt with by techniques of flexible interpretation and when these pressures should be handled by explicitly admitting that a gap exists between legality and legitimacy. If interpretative flexibility rejects textual guidance of carefully drafted treaty language, it undermines confidence in law as truly separate from politics and morality. It is this jurisprudential urge to sustain the authority of law as law that provides the inner strength of positivist orientations. However, if interpretative rigidity makes law incapable of adapting legal guidelines to changing circumstances in situations of widely perceived crisis, then law tends to be cast aside as "irrelevant" by power wielders and politically minded jurists or is upheld and regarded as "oppressive." This tension between the benefits of certainty and the need for flexibility is what inspires the quest for a golden means of interpretation that necessarily relies, however phrased, on the power to create exceptions. The goldenness of the process depends on explaining the exception as reasonable rather than arbitrary, and placing limitations based on principled criteria.[10] It contrast with the Schmitt view that law should give way to politics whenever there is present a clash, and that any stricter legalism, such as is espoused by democratic liberalism, involves a dangerous weakening of the state as a political actor that must protect society against its internal and external "enemies."

Drastic responses to this unavoidable dilemma arise whenever the moral and political imperatives of policy appear to exceed the limits of legality. Such responses rose to the surface in the course of the Kosovo debate. An influential response to the implications of the Kosovo War was developed by Michael Glennon, who proposed viewing the entire legal framework of constraint embodied in the United Nations Charter as having been sufficiently superseded by the present global setting to lose its restraining force, thereby allowing behavior to be authoritatively shaped by discretionary initiatives ("coalitions of the willing") until a new legal regime responsive to current realities of power and values can be established by the consent of major states.[11] A different accommodation to these same realities of power was proposed by Thomas Franck, who advocated a forthright repudiation of the legal constraint to explain the action taken in the circumstances of Kosovo.[12]

The now-infamous John Bolton, in contrast, acted as if the efforts of jurists to find a legal rationale for or against intervening in Kosovo were a waste of time, insisting instead that the United States should refrain from intervening in Kosovo *solely* because it had insufficient national interests at stake to warrant the risks and costs. If the assessment is based on such an extralegal calculation of interests, international law becomes almost totally irrelevant, except possibly for a dominant state such as the United States, which may or may not be concerned with its profile and reputation as a law-abiding global leader. Such a concern can work in both directions, either conveying a willingness to play the geopolitical game within the rule-governed framework of international law and the UN, or demonstrating its contempt for existing norms and institutions while claiming a freedom of maneuver with respect to such a framework for the sake of the greater public good.[13] The extreme version of this kind of politicized approach is to claim an exemption from legal constraint for itself while acting as an enforcer of the very same constraints with respect to those other states seen as challenging the established order of world politics. The Bush administration has adopted such a posture with respect to the accountability of political leaders for crimes under international law, insisting on an exemption for itself, while having the temerity to assist in the Iraqi preparation of the prosecution of Saddam Hussein and close associates as war criminals.

The specific circumstances prompting the Kosovo War have been frequently recounted. The historical context and short-term memory were definitely important. Serb brutality in Bosnia, climaxing in the massacre of some seven thousand Muslim males within the UN "safe haven" of Srebrenica in 1995 while UN peacekeepers looked on as spectators, was certainly a factor encouraging effective international action in the face of an imminent threat of another phase of ethnic cleansing in Kosovo. Possibly, as well, although more conjectural, an interest in confirming the vitality of the NATO alliance as it neared its fiftieth anniversary, despite the ending of the Cold War and the collapse of the Soviet Union, was also an encouragement for timely and effective intervention under NATO auspices. Beyond this, the growing perception of an emergent humanitarian emergency in Kosovo, associated with atrocities allegedly perpetrated by the Serbs against Kosovar civilians, combined with a stream of refugees, solidified public opinion in Europe and stiffened the will of European governments to take some protective action before the process of ethnic cleansing was under way in full force even without a mandate from the Security Council.[14] In effect, a humanitarian emergency highlighted by media attention was present in Kosovo posing a moral challenge. This challenge was reinforced by such political considerations as demonstrating NATO effectiveness, establishing an American military presence in the Balkans, and showing that the United States remained involved in Europe despite the ending of the Cold War.

Such a convergence of moral and political factors was not able to control fully the mechanisms of decision within the UN Security Council. Russia, traditionally aligned with Serbia, and China, uncomfortable about encroaching on sovereign rights, let it be known that any effort to obtain a mandate for military intervention within the Security Council would fail because of their veto. But without the approval of the Security Council even a humanitarian intervention would violate the Charter prohibition on recourse to nondefensive force. The U.S.-led pro-intervention countries were faced with a difficult choice: either abandon the Kosovar people to an oppressive regime imposed by Belgrade and apparently bent on ethnic cleansing to create a demographic balance more favorable to minority Serb domination or act in violation of the core obligation of the UN Charter to obtain advance approval for any use of international force that cannot be explained as self-defense against a prior armed attack. As we know, NATO chose to act, relying on the regional nature of the initiative, and the support of all neighbors except Greece, and seems to have rescued the Kosovar Albanian population, which comprised 90 percent of the totality. The intervention was effective, although criticized for its reliance on high-altitude bombing, its failure to do more to protect the Serb minority in the aftermath of the war, and its insufficient reconstruction effort. At the same time, the Security Council rejected a proposed resolution of censure relating to the intervention, and the UN accepted the task of working with the NATO occupying forces entrusted with peacekeeping operations, which could be viewed as a retrospective validation of the intervention by the UN, or at the very least, a refusal to censure the violation of the Charter. Of course, the refusal can itself be discounted as expression of *political* realities associated with the strength of the United States and its European partners in the Security Council rather than as a belated acknowledgement of either the *legality* or *legitimacy* of the intervention.

It was against this background that the Independent Commission on Kosovo believed that the best way to handle the mixture of contradictory legal, political, and moral pressures was to rely on a distinction between legality and legitimacy. In effect, the NATO intervention was viewed as *illegal* because of its irreconcilability with the UN Charter prohibition on nondefensive force, yet *legitimate* because of its effective response to an imminent humanitarian catastrophe. The need to rely on this extralegal justification was acknowledged in the Report as unfortunate, disclosing a deficiency in the legal regime governing the use of force, which suggested the importance of legal reform. Such reform is difficult within the UN setting because it is cumbersome to amend the Charter, but more fundamentally, because some major states distrust or oppose humanitarian rationales for intervention, and would surely withhold their consent from an expanded notion of permissible force even if under UN authority.[15] For these reasons, the recommendation to overcome the gap between legality and legitimacy seems unlikely to be heeded in the near future.

The Kosovo Commission additionally recommended a framework of principles that would, in effect, provide a quasi-legal framework to guide and assess legitimacy claims and undertakings. What was proposed consisted of a set of principles, which themselves depended on considerable interpretative discretion if applied to actual situations. The Kosovo Report puts forward three threshold principles and eight contextual principles that try to provide guidance as to *when* an intervention would be legitimate, and *how* such an intervention should be carried out to maintain its legitimate character.[16] The overall purpose of these principles is to depict conditions of what might be described as "humanitarian necessity" — that is, only by acting promptly and proportionately can an acutely vulnerable people or minority be protected against massive suffering. The principles make clear that the case for necessity must be strong, that diplomatic alternatives have been exhausted in good faith, and recourse to war is a last resort and undertaken in a manner that minimizes destructive effects for the civilian population being protected. In the Kosovo setting, these criteria were only partially met, and so the Kosovo War did not rank as high as it might have on the legitimacy scoreboard. There were doubts about whether the diplomatic efforts preceding the war were serious efforts to find a solution, there were some suspicion that the KLA had provoked the Yugoslav military forces in Kosovo so as to generate incidents that could be then reported to the world media as "atrocities," and there was much criticism of the failure of the international community to extend support to the nonviolent resistance efforts led by Ibrahim Rugova during the 1990s.[17]

A somewhat different approach to the Kosovo challenge was proposed by the International Commission on Intervention and State Sovereignty.[18] It tried to circumvent the rough edges of political disagreement by abandoning the antisovereignty language of humanitarian intervention, substituting the phrasing "the responsibility to protect." The outcome of both frameworks is similarly shaped by the formulation of a framework of principles for military intervention designed to get the job done, but minimize the use of force.[19] The frameworks are complementary in content and intention, with *The Responsibility to Protect* seemingly more directly incorporating the sort of language of guidance that is associated with the just war doctrine, and also more intent on changing Security Council practice. Its emphasis on what it calls "Right Authority" is designed to encourage the Security Council to reconsider its role under the Charter in light of the development of international human rights since the founding of the UN. The Security Council is encouraged strongly to discharge its responsibilities, but if it fails to do so, then action may be taken by a descending hierarchy of empowered actors: the General Assembly, regional and subregional actors, and finally, "concerned states." In light of the actuality of an impending humanitarian catastrophe, the main point is that external actors have an obligation to act in a timely and effective fashion. To bolster the capability of the Security Council to discharge this function and in direct response to the Kosovo prospect of vetos, the Report recommends that the five permanent members should agree not to use their veto if there exists otherwise majority support for taking protective action. Kofi Annan in his report on UN reform, titled *In Larger Freedom,* appears to endorse the approach advocated by *The Responsibility to Protect.* The secretary general asks rhetorically, "As to genocide, ethnic cleansing, and other such Crimes Against Humanity, are they not also threats to international peace and security, against which humanity should be able to look to the Security Council for protection?" He adds, "The task is not to find alternatives to the Security Council as a source of authority but to make it work better." And then listing some criteria resembling those proposed by the two commissions, Kofi Annan concludes, "I therefore recommend that the Security Council adopt a resolution setting out these principles and expressing its intention to be guided by them when deciding whether to authorize or mandate the use of force."[20]

Both reports, as well as the secretary general, offer constructive responses to the challenge, but it is unlikely, due to the underlying political differences that pertain to this subject matter, that anything formal will be agreed upon for some years. The impacts of 9/11 make such a prospect even more remote in one sense, but less important from another angle, given the likely continued decline in the willingness of major states, especially the United States, to use its power directly for the sake of overcoming a humanitarian catastrophe. The more immediate policy issue is whether the report of the Kosovo Commission or that of the Intervention and State Sovereignty Commission is more deserving of support. In my view the Kosovo Commission is to be preferred because it directly confronts the dilemma that arises at the outer limits of law when moral and political factors strongly favor moving beyond those limits. It also does not pretend that "intervention" is not "interventionary." But as earlier argued, both reports are constructive, move in generally the same direction, and should be reflected upon in addressing future contexts of humanitarian emergency in which interventionary responses are under consideration. The simmering genocidal circumstance in the Darfur region of Sudan is precisely such a context, but characterized by an absence of a sufficient political will on the part of major states to discharge "the responsibility to protect."[21]

LEGALITY, LEGITIMACY, AND THE IRAQ WAR

The main justifications for the Iraq War offered by the U.S. government prior to its onset were related to the threats posed by Iraq's possession of weapons of mass destruction (WMD), and secondarily, Iraq's failure to comply with a series of UN resolutions. This set of circumstances supposedly, according to official representations on behalf of American policy, validated a use of force despite the absence of explicit authorization. And this absence was itself contested by administration supporters who read into Security Resolution 1441 an implicit authorization to use necessary force to achieve Iraqi compliance with earlier UN directives.[22] Unlike Kosovo, where the factual grounds for claims of humanitarian necessity seemed widely accepted, the claims of defensive necessity relating to Iraq could not be convincingly made, and thus the claims of self-defense or implementation of UNSC resolutions were neither formally persuasive in the Security Council, nor accepted by public opinion either among states in the region of Iraq or in Europe, the locus of America's traditional allies. Opposition to the Iraq War was more intense elsewhere in the world, especially in Islamic countries where the conflict was viewed through the lens of "a clash of civilizations," neither more nor less. This skepticism has been vindicated by the failure to discover WMD, the main *pre-invasion* pretext for recourse to a preemptive war, the growing evidence that the U.S. government was resolved to invade and occupy Iraq quite apart from whether or not Baghdad complied with UN authority, the indications that oppressive circumstances in Iraq, while persisting, were not approaching an emergency phase (and had been far worse in prior years), and the absence of any clear evidence that the American occupation has been received by the majority of the Iraqi people as a welcomed liberation. In effect, there seemed insufficient grounds to validate the Iraq War because of its legality, and no persuasive reason to affirm its legitimacy.[23] In other words, the recommended approach to the Kosovo War, even if accepted, does not provide a justification for the Iraq War, but on the contrary supports the conclusion that it was both illegal and illegitimate.

Shortly before the start of the Iraq War, Anne-Marie Slaughter did attempt a variation explicitly modeled on the approach taken by the Kosovo Commission. Pointing out that the states favoring a use of force in Kosovo "sidestepped the United Nations completely and sought authorization for the use of force within NATO itself," she noted that "[t]he airwaves and newspaper opinion columns were filled with dire predictions that this move would fatally damage the United Nations as arbitrator of the use of force," but that after the generally successful outcome of the Kosovo War the Kosovo Commission found that "although formally illegal . . . the intervention was nonetheless legitimate in the eyes of the international community."[24] Writing days before the invasion, Slaughter saw a similar possibility for the American recourse to the war against Iraq but this could be established, if at all, only after the fact of an invasion. Slaughter somewhat surprisingly argued that ". . . the Bush administration has started on a course that could be called 'illegal but legitimate,' a course that could end up, paradoxically, winning United Nations approval for a military campaign in Iraq — though only after an invasion." This rather ingenious argument reasoned that the American recourse to the UN in search of approval was itself an implicit, although a conditional, endorsement of UN authority showing that the United States government would not act "without any reference to the United Nations at all." Slaughter sees this twilight zone of "compliance/violation" as part of "an unruly process of pushing and shoving toward a redefined role for the United Nations." In the end, despite the U.S. failure to receive authorization from the Security Council to initiate a war against Iraq ". . . the lesson that the United Nations and all of us should draw from the crisis" is this: "Overall, everyone involved is still playing by the rules. But depending on what we find in Iraq, the rules may have to evolve, so that what is legitimate is also legal." If playing by the rules means only that dubious claims to use force will first be vetted at the Security Council, and if not approved, will then be exercised, it limits the role of the UN to that of a debating society, where if the state seeking to engage in controversial behavior cannot make its case persuasively, it will proceed to act in any event. Slaughter's *approach* is untenable as it so seriously blurs the distinction between compliance and violation, disabling a critique from the perspective of either legality or legitimacy *in advance* of a challenged use of force. Reverting to the Kosovo precedent, it would seem that the case for legitimacy, in the face of illegality, was based on circumstances that *preceded* recourse to war. In my view, a retrospective construction of legitimacy as proposed by Slaughter provides an unacceptable validation of the primacy of geopolitics in relation to global governance.

Writing a year later, Slaughter applied the proposed approach, contending that her earlier analysis was based on the invasion of Iraq being "*potentially legitimate in the eyes of the international community*" if certain conditions were satisfied: finding WMD; a welcoming reception by the Iraqi people; and an acceptance of UN supervision of the occupation and political reconstruction of Iraq by the United States, the United Kingdom, and their array of lesser allies. Her entirely convincing conclusion in 2004 was that none of these conditions had been met, and thus the use of force against Iraq was illegal and illegitimate. Slaughter maintains that what Kosovo shows is that "[i]t is sometimes necessary to break the law to change it," and that the international community should respond by adapting the law to these changed circumstances associated with discharging the responsibility to protect." But she argues *after* the fact that "[t]he lesson of the invasion of Iraq is quite different," vindicating the opposition within the UN to the use of force by those governments that asked the United States to defer recourse to war until more evidence existed of a WMD presence in Iraq or more time for the UN inspection to produce an assessment of the Iraqi threat. Slaughter shares the view of the Bush administration that preemptive uses of force need to be made permissible in specified circumstances in view of the altered security threats posed after 9/11: "The world faces very different threats than it did in 1945." Yet for Slaughter this widening of the right of self-defense does not validate the abandonment of the core legal constraints of the Charter. In her words, "the most important lesson of the invasion of Iraq is that the safeguards built into the requirement of the *multilateral* authorization of the use of force by UN members are both justified and necessary. If nations seeking to use force cannot mount strong enough evidence of a security threat to convince a majority of the Security Council and to avoid a veto (provided that the veto is not clearly motivated by countervailing political interests), they should wait and try another way before sending in the troops."[25] I think Slaughter "before" and "after" discloses the difficulties of making a clear analysis of legality in circumstances of preemptive claims if the distinction between legality and legitimately is employed too loosely. In my view, the proposed American war against Iraq was definitively illegitimate as well as illegal *before* any use of force against Iraq was undertaken, and could not have been rendered retroactively legitimate regardless of whether WMD were found, the public welcomed the intervention, and the UN took over the postconflict occupation and reconstruction.[26] For Slaughter, in contrast, it would seem that a *potential* demonstration of legitimacy was a sufficient sign of adherence to the rules of world order even if such a claim should subsequently be shown as lacking a factual foundation. In my view, the claim to use force is only potentially legitimate if there can be made a *prior* demonstration of defensive necessity based on the imminence, plausibility, and severity of a security threat, with these conditions *normally* to be determined by a *multilateral* process, preferably by the Security Council. This is the approach now advocated by Kofi Annan, and the basis of the finding that the Kosovo War was illegal, yet legitimate.[27]

Slaughter seems to endorse a superficially similar approach but more closely considered, her views contain some significant variations. For Slaughter, if approval by the Security Council is thwarted by an actual or anticipated veto that is politically motivated, then recourse to force would be justified, even without UN approval. But she never clarifies how to identify a political motivation for an exercise of a veto. To this day, the U.S. government regards the French opposition to its effort to obtain a mandate for the invasion of Iraq as politically motivated. So long as the power of exception is a matter of decision by a hegemonic government, the limitations associated with the constraining guidelines are not likely to inhibit discretionary wars.

Beyond this, the possibility of retrospective legitimation opens wide the door to abuse of the legality/legitimacy approach. Perhaps a middle ground exists that rests on the provisional legitimacy of recourse to war — that is, where there is probable cause to suppose that the threshold criteria of legitimacy will be satisfied. In the instance of Iraq that would have meant untainted evidence of a massive WMD program, proof of strategic objectives by Baghdad that included support for global terror and future war plans, and an alienated Iraqi population that would welcome intervention (as the majority of the Kosovar citizenry clearly did). In my view, there was no way for the U.S. government to uphold the burden of persuasion prior to the invasion, and thus, unlike Slaughter, I would maintain that the position taken by the Bush administration was illegal and illegitimate from the outset, and not susceptible to being legitimated after the fact. At most, the degree of illegitimacy could have been considerably mitigated if large stockpiles of WMD had been discovered together with plans for future wars and if the Iraqi people had overwhelmingly welcomed the foreign forces as liberators. Then, and only then, could one credibly dismiss as "dead enders" the resisting elements in Iraq, as was done in the early stages of the occupation by Donald Rumsfeld.

A SECOND LEGITIMACY DEBATE IN PUBLIC POLICY CIRCLES

It is important to distinguish "legitimacy" as used to denote the status of the United States as global hegemon, and legitimacy as a benchmark of judgment with respect to a particular use of force that falls outside the orbit of legality. The two views of legitimacy may or may not be linked, depending on whether hegemonic legitimacy is associated, or not, with a reputation for generally adhering to international law. In the aftermath of the Iraq War, a debate has emerged in the mainstream on the nature of hegemonic legitimacy, and whether or not it presupposes law abidingness. This debate can be most usefully framed by presenting the views of a prominent neoconservative commentator on foreign affairs, Robert Kagan, and that of an equally prominent geopolitical realist, Robert W. Tucker (in collaboration with David Hendrickson).

The more intellectual neoconservatives acknowledge that the invasion of Iraq without a mandate from the Security Council cost the United States heavily in terms of perceived legitimacy, especially among European democratic states. This viewpoint has been most clearly expressed by Robert Kagan.[28] What is most interesting about Kagan's argument is that he de-links this loss of legitimacy from legality, and connects it with what he calls "the unipolar predicament" of having capabilities and vulnerabilities, but not the leadership to command adherence to defining policies. In Kagan's view it was this failure, abetted by clumsy diplomacy, that was exhibited by the split with traditional European allies in relation to the Iraq War. His point here is that the loss of legitimacy by the United States is not a consequence of Washington's refusal to have its policy shaped by reference to international law, a general posture of lawfulness, and deference to the United Nations. Kagan insists that this refusal has long characterized U.S. foreign policy, but that previously it did not produce political difficulties because America's traditional European allies were supportive.

It is Kagan's view that "[c]ontrary to much mythologizing on both sides of the Atlantic these days, the foundations of U.S. legitimacy during the Cold War had little to do with the fact that the United States had helped to create the UN or faithfully abided by the precepts of international law laid out in the organization's charter." In the same vein, "[i]t was not international law and institutions but the circumstances of the Cold War, and Washington's special role in it, that conferred legitimacy on the United States, at least within the West."[29] What led to this European acceptance of the legitimacy of American leadership were three pillars: the Soviet Union posed a strategic threat to Europe that could only be addressed by means of a European acceptance of American leadership; the Soviet Union was also a common ideological enemy enabling America to be the acknowledged leaders of "the free world"; and third, the structure of bipolarity meant that American power was kept in check by Soviet power, and this reassured Europeans that the United States would not be too reckless in pursuing its foreign policy (unlike the current circumstance of unchecked power in the relations between Europe and the United States).

These changed circumstances and their consequences for American hegemonic legitimacy came to a crisis in the run up to the Iraq War. Europe perceived no strategic threat arising from Iraq's behavior, and was deeply put off by the American insistence that such a strategic threat existed. At the same time, according to Kagan, the Europeans were disturbed by their inability to mount an effective opposition, nor to induce the United States to act only to the extent of UN authorization. Europeans viewed that their legitimacy was "an asset they have in abundance . . . they see it as a comparative advantage — the great equalizer in an otherwise lopsided relationship."[30] Kagan indicts the Europeans for their hypocrisy. He argues that Europe's central contention that the United States was dependent on the Security Council before it acted against Iraq was inconsistent with European support for evading the Security Council in order to proceed with humanitarian intervention in Kosovo back in 1999. Kagan's opposing thesis is as follows: "There are indeed sound reasons for the United States to seek European approval. But they are unrelated to international law, the authority of the Security Council, and the as-yet fabric of the international order. Europe matters to the United States because it and the United States form the heart of the liberal, democratic world."[31] From this perspective the prescription is simple: "The United States, in short, must pursue legitimacy in the manner truest to its nature: by promoting the principles of liberal democracy not only as a means to greater security but as an end in itself."[32] The question of whether or not the rift between two competing visions of world order can be healed, the one predominant in Europe and the other in the United States, depends in the last analysis on how they perceive the basic threat to world order: is it an exaggerated perception of the threat by the United States or an insufficient appreciation of it by Europe? Kagan regards this divergence as a "tragedy," and sides in the end with the American view, saying of the Europeans, "[i]n their effort to constrain the superpower, they might lose sight of the mounting dangers in the world, which are far greater than those posed by the United States."[33] There are from this perspective three main conclusions implied by Kagan's analysis: first of all, departures from legality are not of significant relevance to an assessment of legitimacy; second, legitimacy matters far more than legality in evaluating criticisms of foreign policy; and third, the American threat assessment, even if producing certain dysfunctional policies, is generally accurate, and should be regarded by European governments as a legitimate approach to world order in the period since 9/11. At the same time, Kagan acknowledges that it is not so regarded, and that part of the fault lies with the "maladroit" diplomacy of the Bush administration. In effect, Kagan would presumably like to see the Europeans respect the American view on the common threats posed to the established order of global security arising from Islamic terrorism and would encourage Washington to be more consultative and collegial in relation to European sensibilities when shaping its future foreign policy.

At issue is whether the disagreements that surface during the prewar debate on Iraq were primarily matters of diplomatic style or exhibited deep substantive differences. There is no doubt that the abrasive Bush approach, especially considering the earlier record of unilateralism and repudiation of lawmaking treaties, contributed to the image of the United States as a global leader of severely diminished legitimacy. But there were also significant substantive differences on the nature of the terrorist threat, and widely divergent interpretations as to whether the regime of Saddam Hussein should be regarded as part of the threat, and these differences could not have been removed by smoother diplomacy. In that sense, the Iraq War challenged the legitimacy of American global leadership in much more serious ways than were associated with objections to the Kosovo War of 1999 or the Afghanistan War.

Returning to the legality/legitimacy connection, Robert W. Tucker and David C. Hendrickson, with firm realist credentials, challenged the Kagan approach, mainly on the level of conceptualization.[34] It was the Tucker/Henrickson view, also expressed in an article published in *Foreign Affairs,* that the American fall from legitimacy was directly linked to its refusal to guide and justify its foreign policy by reference to international law. In their view, "[l]egitimacy arises from the conviction that state action proceeds within the ambit of law, in two senses: first, that action issues from rightful authority, that is, from the political institution authorized to take it; and second, that it does not violate a legal or moral norm."[35] They acknowledge that legitimacy is elusive as it is at least possible that illegal or unlawful action may on occasion be deemed legitimate, but despite this, their view is that "illegitimacy [is] a condition devoutly to be avoided."

The main burden of Tucker/Hendrickson's analysis is to take explicit issue with Kagan's view of how the United States sustained its legitimacy in the period of the Cold War. They argue that American legitimacy emerged out of four related features of its foreign policy — "its commitment to international law, its acceptance of consensual decision-making, its reputation for moderation, and its identification with the preservation of peace."[36] In contrast, they view each of these "pillars" of legitimacy to be severely weakened by the style and substance of American foreign policy during the Bush presidency. Tucker and Hendrickson acknowledge that there had been previous American initiatives that had challenged these principles, but that the overall posture of the country was one that maintained the link between legality and legitimacy, and that this was widely understood by our main allies in the world. In their view, American problems can be structurally understood in relation to its inability to handle "the unipolar moment" that emerged after the collapse of the Soviet Union. They also show the implausibility of initiating the Iraq War by invoking the so-called Bush Doctrine, claiming a right to wage preemptive wars. The absence of imminence of any threat, made all too clear by the failure to find WMD in Iraq, deprived the American policy of any plausible basis to argue either legality or legitimacy. But even more damaging from the Tucker/Hendrickson perspective was the evident indifference to legality: "In truth, the Bush administration did not care a fig for whether the war was lawful."[37] And further along this line was their conclusion that the U.S. government was now exhibiting "a fundamentally contemptuous attitude toward principles that had previously sustained U.S. legitimacy."[38]

Tucker and Hendrickson do not adopt an unconditional attitude toward legality, acknowledging that considerations of prudence and morality may justify unlawful conduct in exceptional circumstances. But in their view the Iraq War was not such an instance. Such illegal uses of force are "in fact unnecessary for U.S. security and actually imperil it." They argue that "containment and deterrence" had provided "a perfectly workable method of dealing with Saddam Hussein," while the occupation of Iraq has made "Americans much more insecure."[39] They are also critical of the Kosovo War, contending that the factual basis for claiming that an imminent humanitarian catastrophe justified the NATO intervention did not exist, but was fabricated on the basis of exaggerated accounts of Serb atrocities and disregard of KLA provocations.[40] In other words, maintaining legitimacy depends according to Tucker and Hendrickson on limiting departures from legality to situations of compelling necessity. The road back to legitimacy for the United States is a difficult one given current perceptions, but it is a vital part of restoring American security, as well as being of intrinsic benefit. Their closing words: ". . . the importance of legitimacy goes beyond its unquestionable utility . . . a good in itself. For its own sake, and for the sake of a peaceful international order, the nation must find its way back to that conviction again."[41]

Continuing the debate in the pages of *Foreign Affairs*, Kagan contends mainly that Tucker and Henrickson are now arguing a position that is inconsistent with their past acceptance of departures from legality, and are allowing their dissatisfaction with Bush's foreign policy to color their discussion of principle.[42] I think Kagan scores points here, but he fails to address the most fundamental issue, which is, under conditions of unipolarity, international law assumes a more important role than within global settings where countervailing centers of state power exist — providing the only available source of constraining discipline for the United States. This structural factor has been rendered more important by the sort of blunt approach that the Bush administration brings to diplomacy, virtually inviting other states to withhold support for American leadership on grounds of both legality and legitimacy. Kagan fails to deal with the bearing of extremist ideology in a context of unipolarity as aggravating the legitimacy crisis, and therefore understates the relevance of legality.

Kagan shares with Tucker and Hendrickson a deep concern about the loss of American legitimacy in world affairs, but insists that sustaining, losing, and regaining legitimacy has never been closely tied to a record of compliance with international law. In the end, Kagan thinks that more skillful diplomacy is all that is needed to restore American legitimacy as Washington is essentially correct about the nature of the post-9/11 world and what to do about it. It is my judgment that elevating style above substance will work to repair some of the damage, but that American legitimacy cannot be recovered until there is a strong sense that U.S. foreign policy is basically, although not invariably, constrained by respect for international law and the United Nations Charter.

THE FLEXIBILITY OF LAWYERS VERSUS THE FLEXIBILITY OF LAW

It is one thing to advocate a general adherence to legal guidelines, but it is quite another to translate this advocacy into agreed lines of behavior. There are always lawyers available to lend support to the preferred policy options of political leaders either motivated by careerist or nationalist goals. Never has this subordination of lawyers to the political mood been more obvious and blatant than during the Bush administration, but it is not a new phenomenon.[43] It should be acknowledged that long before George W. Bush arrived in the White House there were plenty of government lawyers available in Washington to justify casting aside the Geneva Conventions or to validate preemptive/preventive uses of force. It is this readiness to serve the power wielders that led the philosopher Immanuel Kant long ago to call international lawyers "miserable consolers."[44]

There is little doubt that it is difficult to attain the perspective of a detached and informed observer in the United States given the traumatizing effects of the 9/11 attacks, although with the passage of time that difficulty seems to have diminished. The proper assessment of legality needs to be outside the orbit of official rationalizations, but should not subscribe to legalistic understandings of law that are rigidly disconnected from context or changing circumstances. As legal expectations are always subject to interpretation, and are presumed to be consistent with prevailing ethical values and underlying security needs, there is room for considerable interpretative latitude without ever reaching the precarious domain of "illegal, but legitimate."[45]

In the setting of the main controversies of recent years, there is no evidence that torture provides the best source of information in the course of interrogating prisoners, and there is massive evidence that revelations of torture as official policy have damaged American security and contributed heavily to the decline in American legitimacy in both senses discussed above, that is, reputation for law abidingness, reputation as hegemonic leader. The pictures of abuse of detainees at Abu Ghraib and elsewhere in similar detention facilities suggest a pattern of sadistic behavior by guards condoned, if not induced and abetted, at the highest levels of the U.S. government. The portrayal of detention at Guantánamo contributes further to a portrait of depravity in dealing with the religious and human sensibilities of individuals under the total control of their captors and minders, aggravated by the realization that almost all of the captives lack any possible useful knowledge and many of whom are innocent of wrongdoing. A picture of gratuitous abuse emerges, connected to no reasonable purpose, and the result is damage to American legitimacy in both its wider and narrow senses. In other words, it is not only the Iraq War that provides the most notorious instance of illegal and illegitimate, but the general pattern of practices associated with the conduct of the Global War on Terror.

LEGALITY AND LEGITIMACY: THE DILEMMA RECONSIDERED

The ongoing preoccupation in political theory generated by Carl Schmitt's conceptualizations of legality and legitimacy have seldom explicitly influenced the application of such terminology to the *international* behavior and status of a sovereign state. The Schmitt perspective, arising in the context of emergent Nazi dictatorial rule, was supportive of the view that "legitimacy" was essentially an expression of political will that was inherently rooted in sovereignty, and took precedence over deference to "legality" in the internal and international operations of government. The sovereign should not be constrained by illusions about the primacy of law, which for Schmitt was the fatal flaw of liberal democracy. This way of deploying legality and legitimacy forms the background of discussion, but the foreground is associated with foreign policy debates about controversial uses of international force, or recourse to war.

These debates have been principally concerned about the propriety of the wars in Kosovo in 1999 and in Iraq since 2003. The earlier presentation of these debates was intended to convey the confused, even contradictory, history of legitimacy in both international relations and international law. In these intellectual settings legitimacy functions both as a statist benchmark of reputation and propriety, and as linked to legality. With respect to reputation, there is disagreement as to whether the reputation of a state, particularly a hegemonic actor, is or is not dependent on a record of compliance with international law, whether legitimacy is essentially concerned with diplomatic decorum as to responsible and effective uses of hegemonic power or is rooted, above all, in substantive behavior that exhibits respect for the core principles of international law.[46] For the Kosovo Commission invoking legitimacy was a means of endorsing an intervention on moral and political grounds that could not meet tests of legality. At the same time, it was hoped that the constraints of legality would be soon revised to incorporate the Kosovo precedent, thereby obviating future pressures to depart from these constraints. From these perspectives, reliance on legitimacy is a signal of the need and desirability of law reform.

In contrast, although invoking the approach of the Kosovo Commission, Anne-Marie Slaughter, writing in the tradition of international liberalism, supposes that if a state seeks legality, and is denied, as the United States was when it sought approval from the United Nations of its plan to wage war against Iraq, it could still *subsequently* be regarded as having acted legitimately if certain specified conditions were satisfied in the course of the war. Slaughter's eventual denial of legitimacy was not based on the illegality of recourse to a nondefensive war against Iraq, but on the failure of the Bush administration to demonstrate the accuracy of its own rationale for the war.

The recommended approach taken here is based on approval of the Kosovo Commission approach to the legality/legitimacy divide, but not to Slaughter's effort to allow legitimacy to be demonstrated after the fact. The positive role played by legitimacy is to impart a measure of flexibility with respect to the application of legal constraints on the use of international force in two, and only two, sets of circumstances: conditions of humanitarian necessity (Kosovo; Darfur, Sudan) and circumstances of defensive necessity (1967 War in the Middle East; Afghanistan War of 2002). As pointed out above, it is supportive of these views that the moral and political rationales for war in these two sets of circumstances have been endorsed by the UN secretary general and expert bodies as *already embodied* in the UN Charter if correctly understood. In other words, the gap between legality and legitimacy is not a matter of substantive standard, but interpretative clarity. Whether this is the proper approach to a concern about the limits of legality itself deserves further debate. By incorporating through interpretation changing circumstances, flexibility is achieved, but the clarity of an inhibiting text is definitely weakened. A motive for inflexibility in formulating constraints on the use of international force is to minimize the ambit of discretion available to governments, and thereby contribute to the basic undertaking of the United Nations "to save succeeding generations from the scourge of war."

There are no enduring solutions for these issues of war and peace that will recur in varying settings as history continues to unfold. It does seem that debating legality and legitimacy is one means to encourage deliberative reflection about controversial recourse to war to resolve international conflict. This reflection is needed in these contexts of decision to address the tension between a desired clarity in standards of constraint and a needed relief from such clarity in situations where moral and political imperatives are inconsistent with these constraints. The legality/legitimacy debate at its best, as in Kosovo, did perform this function. Since the September 11 attacks there have been renewed and more radical pressures directed at the framework of constraint understood as legality, but there has also been unprecedented resistance to these pressures by states and civil-society actors in relation to the Iraq War, including an international consensus that this particular war was both illegal and illegitimate. Whether this discourse based on legality/legitimacy will help frame future foreign-policy public debates is highly doubtful, but such considerations may influence professional assessments of future controversies over the use of force in various global settings.

11

Humanitarian Intervention?

Many developments account for the intensity of the recent debate concerning humanitarian intervention: the rise of humanitarian consciousness reinforced by an evolving sense of international accountability of political leaders; a post-Westphalian realization that ideas about territorial sovereignty need to be reconsidered in light of the various dimensions of globalization; suspicions that dominant states, especially the United States and its coalition partners, are using humanitarian pretexts to pursue otherwise unacceptable geopolitical goals and to evade legal prohibitions on the use of international force and the nonintervention norm; a series of high-profile instances (including Somalia, Bosnia, Rwanda, Kosovo, Darfur-Sudan) in which controversy arose about whether the international community was unacceptably doing too little or too much in response to a severe humanitarian emergency; and the post hoc rationalization of the Iraq War as allegedly justified on humanitarian grounds, rescuing the Iraqi people from tyranny, despite the absence of any prior authorization by the UN Security Council, the opposition of world public opinion, and the high levels of violence, strife, suffering, and destruction in Iraq. Additionally, the contextualization of global security in relation to the American-led struggle against megaterrorism has eroded claims of sovereignty on the part of states alleged to be havens of anti-Western political extremism. These developments also give rise to normative justifications of this erosion on the grounds that it produces humanitarian benefits (e.g., liberating women from an oppressive Taliban regime in Afghanistan, ridding Iraq of brutal dictator).

Two sets of responses stimulated by this series of developments pertain to the legal, ethical, and political status of humanitarian intervention: a statist response highlighted by reports of commissions composed of eminent persons and a civil-society response highlighted by case-by-case advocacy and criticism of action and inaction by the international community, along with various expressions of suspicion directed at self-serving accounts of motives on the part of intervening actors, with a particular concern associated with American claims to initiate wars in pursuit of its security without obtaining "a permission slip" from the United Nations.[1] It is not possible, especially after the Iraq War, to disentangle the U.S. government claim of right with respect to preemptive war from the diplomacy of the last decade or so associated with humanitarian intervention. The inhibitions on intergovernmental initiatives or on bodies constituted by "eminent persons" —

that is, persons prominently associated with governmental and intergovernmental careers — is such that these issues can only be addressed indirectly if at all.[2] This leaves the delicate task of disentangling geopolitics from humanitarianism to independent critical voices of opinion in global civil society.

What makes this subject matter challenging from a normative perspective of law and ethics is that it is neither beneficial to give a green light to interventionary diplomacy that proclaims humanitarian goals nor to absolutize the norm of non-intervention by posting a red light that prohibits humanitarian encroachments on sovereignty under all circumstances. What seems appropriate is a bright yellow light of caution, recognizing the danger of either allowing intervention to proceed under the humanitarian banner or the corresponding danger of insisting on nonintervention despite the existence of a genuine humanitarian emergency. Such a cautionary approach would seem to depend on an administering role for the United Nations, especially the Security Council. A precondition for a valid instance of humanitarian intervention is some explicit prior authorization by the UNSC. But suppose it is not forthcoming even in the face of a severe, unfolding humanitarian catastrophe? Can the UN General Assembly or a regional organization play a residual authorizing role? A coalition of the willing? Or in an extreme case of unfolding genocide or massive Crimes Against Humanity, should we not presume tacit acquiescence regionally and globally that amounts to authorization, or at least acquiescence? This was the case when India entered East Pakistan (now Bangladesh) in 1971 to stop Pakistani atrocities, Vietnam entered Cambodia in 1978 to end the reign of terror by the Khmer Rouge, and Tanzania entered Uganda in 1979 to depose the Idi Amin dictatorship. Each of these examples involved an intervention by a neighboring country, which seemed to act on the basis of strategic interests, but which also appeared to be motivated by genuine humanitarian concerns, or at the very least had the effect of rescuing a population enduring severe humanitarian abuse. Such a setting, mingling self-interest with humanitarianism, arouses suspicions in various quarters about the true intentions of the intervention, but if a humanitarian catastrophe is truly unfolding before the eyes of the world, it also should strengthen confidence that such an intervention is at least more likely to be effective. In effect, realist incentives reinforce the humanitarian rationale for violating sovereign rights. To assess whether this rationale is but a pretext for intervention, consideration should also be given to factors such as whether the intervening state withdraws shortly after the humanitarian emergency has ended, does not insist on establishing strategic bases or a long-term military presence, shows respect for the right of self-determination of the target country, and contributes significantly to the economic, political, and social reconstruction of the country in postconflict phases.

To grasp the contours of the contemporary debate, as a prelude to recommending an approach, the next two sections will consider, first, the perspectives of the official bodies appointed to set forth guidelines and resolve conceptual and doctrinal tensions, and then, the somewhat diverse civil-society perspectives that reflect the spectrum of views on how to balance deference to sovereign rights and concerns about geopolitical manipulations against the moral and political imperatives to prevent or mitigate an unfolding humanitarian catastrophe caused by political developments as distinct from catastrophes caused by natural disasters. The issue is complicated legally by the disposition in 1945 to reassure states joining the United Nations that the new organization would not intervene in matters "essentially within domestic jurisdiction" (Article 2[7] of the UN Charter), a provision widely understood to encompass abuses of a citizenry by its own government and even instances of civil strife and insurgency unless there was a genuine spillover of the violence to neighboring countries. Obviously, if the United Nations was denied the right to intervene, then states and regional actors possess no legal authority to use nondefensive force for such a purpose. Article 51 of the Charter creates an exception to the prohibition on recourse to force, but only with respect to authorizing a right of self-defense, and then appearing to limit this right to occasions where the state invoking self-defense has experienced a prior armed attack. In effect, humanitarian intervention appeared to be outlawed by the UN Charter as initially drafted. But the Charter is a constitutional document that evolves as community values change and emerging patterns of practice shape new understandings of the balance between the Westphalian autonomy of states and the expanding expectations that the international community will provide needed levels of global govenance. Integral to this shift in the direction of interventionary authority has been the unexpected rise of international human rights, and supportive notions and institutions of implementation, accountability, and even enforcement. The establishment in 2002 of the International Criminal Court is an institutional milestone in this process, although how far it will be able to realize its promise is uncertain, especially as its operation currently faces hostile opposition from the United States and China.

COMMISSION REPORTS AND THE PERSPECTIVES OF EMINENT PERSONS

The Kosovo War of 1999 was undertaken by NATO in reaction to a persuasive unfolding scenario of acute human rights violations, a massive exodus of refugees, and a plausible prospect of ethnic cleansing. The Albanian 90 percent majority population of Kosovo seemed at the mercy of the Serb minority, and given the then-recent experience of the war in Bosnia, culminating in the 1995 Srebrenica Massacre of about 7,000 Muslim males, it seemed reasonable to favor humanitarian intervention despite the absence of support on the part of more than one permanent member of the UN Security Council. NATO did represent the leading countries in Europe, but it was an alliance rather than a true regional organization, and in any event, lacked authority to engage in any kind of enforcement action in the absence of Security Council authorization. There were also undisclosed strategic motivations present associated with demonstrating the credibility of NATO as it approached the fiftieth anniversary of its founding in the aftermath of the Cold War. Also at stake was the willingness of the United States to provide leadership with respect to European security despite the absence of any external threat after the collapse of the Soviet Union.

It was this combination of circumstances that generated a highly visible debate about whether the Kosovo War should be regarded as a valuable precedent for future occasions of humanitarian intervention.[3] On the skeptical side was concern about setting a precedent that allowed recourse to war outside the scope of the right of self-defense and in the absence of an explicit mandate to intervene from the United Nations. On the positive side was the moral and political desirability of acting effectively in the face of a humanitarian emergency, confirmed in the Kosovo instance by a welcoming population and the rapid return of almost all of the Albanian Kosovar refugees. Shortly after the war, an Independent International Commission on Kosovo was established by the Swedish government, in consultation with the secretary general of the United Nations, to address these issues, as well as to consider the future for Kosovo.

The basic effort of the Kosovo Commission, which issued its report in 2000, was to offer an approach to addressing the doctrinal tension identified above. The report controversially suggested, first of all, that the Kosovo War was "legitimate, although illegal." In effect, this entailed an acceptance of the argument that a humanitarian emergency had actually existed, which made it morally and politically justified, and hence legitimate, to intervene militarily to protect the vulnerable Kosovar population. At the same time there was an acknowledgement that the intervention was illegal because it involved a nondefensive use of international force that had not been authorized in advance by the United Nations.[4]

This circumstance of "legitimate, although illegal" was admitted in the report to be confusing and unfortunate, but it seemed highly unlikely in the near future that the UN would formally revise its conceptions on the legality of force so as to overcome this tension. And yet it also seemed important for the international community to find the authority to act in the face of an unfolding humanitarian emergency as it had in Kosovo. One approach that was given attention at the time of the Kosovo intervention was to pronounce the law of the Charter to be essentially obsolete, and leave the decision to intervene, as in Kosovo, to an ad hoc coalition of the willing.[5] Such an assessment, in effect, prematurely gives up on the Charter effort to prohibit nondefensive wars of choice, a viewpoint that would exempt the invasion and subsequent occupation of Iraq from legal condemnation as a war of aggression. This "adjustment" unnecessarily concedes too much ground to geopolitical opportunism, as there are no criteria by which to assess whether the ad hoc coalition is a responsible actor capable and willing to confine its use of force to humanitarian goals. An alternative adjustment would involve the suspension of the veto, either by formal arrangement or informal patterns of practice, in instances of humanitarian emergency of the Kosovo or Darfur variety. This adjustment would be beneficial, and would have enabled the Kosovo intervention to receive authorization from the Security Council, circumventing the expected vetoes of China and Russia, while registering their concerns in open debate. This adjustment is not politically acceptable at the present time, as the tradeoff between sovereignty, geopolitics, and humanitarianism is understood and interpreted differently by permanent members of the Security Council. It is not only differing degrees of attachment to sovereign rights, but the accompanying suspicion that humanitarian claims are often pretexts for the pursuit of grand strategy by hegemonic actors, including imperial ambitions. In effect, diminishing the relevance of the veto is also an unlikely adjustment under present world conditions. Slightly less unlikely would be the evolution of a practice that allowed authorization to come from the General Assembly in those instances where a positive recommendation of humanitarian intervention was being blocked solely because of negative votes by one or two permanent members with veto powers.

The Kosovo Commission, acutely aware of these difficulties, advocated the legitimate but illegal approach, but only if it was used in conjunction with a principled framework that would test the worth of any particular claim of legitimacy.[6] The Kosovo Commission report sets forth eleven principles, divided into threshold principles and contextual principles that determine whether and to what extent the contention of legitimacy associated with the intervention is persuasive. There are three threshold principles, the first of which is that there are two sets of triggering circumstances: acute violations of human rights or of international humanitarian law; and state failure that exposes a population to mass suffering. The other two threshold principles insist that the intervention be undertaken for "the direct benefit of the victimized population" and that the method of intervention must be "reasonably calculated" to end the catastrophe as rapidly as possible and in a manner that protects civilians as a whole. There are eight further contextual principles: war must be a last resort; efforts to gain UN authorization must be undertaken in good faith; diligent efforts to resolve the conflict peacefully must be undertaken; some degree of multilateralism must guide the whole process; there should not exist a formal censure of the proposed intervention by either the Security Council or the International Court of Justice; the laws of war must be strictly upheld; the intervening states should obtain no territorial or special economic rewards, and should show a readiness to withdraw as soon as normalcy is restored; and sufficient resources should be made available during the postconflict phases to facilitate economic, social, and political reconstruction and development.[7] Such a checklist of principles is meant to pro-vide guidelines for policy and appraisal, and is obviously subject to wide varia-tions of interpretation in specific circumstances. Whether such considerations help to identify occasions for legitimate intervention and to shape its implemen-tation remains uncertain. Of course, as inaction in response to the unfolding and deepening humanitarian crisis in the Darfur region of Sudan illustrates, as Rhodesia did in 1994, no matter how legitimate the case for humanitarian inter-vention, absent political will on the part of those actors with the capacity to inter-vene, an effective international response will not be forthcoming. Paradoxically, it is one of the shadows cast upon claims of legitimacy — that is, the presence of strategic motives alongside the humanitarian considerations makes it more likely that *effective* action will be taken only in situations where the moral and politi-cal case for humanitarian intervention is reinforced by strategic incentives. In this sense, vulnerable peoples exposed to abuse and state failure in sub-Saharan Africa are not nearly as likely to be protected by an international initiative than those being victimized in regions that enjoy high geopolitical priorities as a result of either their resources or location.

A similar, but somewhat different tack was taken on interventionary diplo-macy by the Canadian initiative that led to the establishment of the Commission on Intervention and State Sovereignty, which issued an influential report under the title of "The Responsibility to Protect."[8] The report seeks to circumvent the controversy surrounding "humanitarian intervention" partly by adopting a dif-ferent language, and shifting the locus of inquiry from the victimized population to the role of the international community in such circumstances. In this spirit, it abandons the terminology of "humanitarian intervention" as unnecessarily provocative because it so frontally poses issues of sovereign rights and of uses of force by the most powerful states. By substituting the language of responsibility and protection, it is hoped that hot-button issues associated with interventionary diplomacy, evoking many bad memories of colonialism, can be circumvented, or at least mitigated. "The Responsibility to Protect" frames the undertaking by reference to four basic objectives: "to establish clearer rules, procedures and cri-teria for determining whether, when and how to intervene; to establish the legit-imacy of military intervention when necessary and after all other approaches have failed; to ensure that military intervention, when it occurs, is carried out only for purposes proposed, is effective, and is undertaken with proper concern to minimize human costs and institutional damage that will result; and to help eliminate, where possible, the causes of conflict while enhancing the prospects for durable and sustainable peace."[9] As with the Kosovo Commission's eleven principles, these objectives of the Canadian commission seem intended as rough guides to policy and assessment rather than to reinforce the red lines of inter-national law that pertain to uses of force and sovereignty. The engagement of national and international responsibility is inevitably related to political will, which is itself shaped by strategic interests, public opinion, media attention, and short-term memories of success and failures associated with prior intervention-ary undertakings. In the 1990s, the perceived failure of the American-led under-taking in Somalia contributed significantly to the refusal to support action by the United Nations in Rwanda despite the transparency of the genocidal dan-gers.[10] This refusal reflected both the sub-Saharan perceived absence of strategic interests by the dominant states and the realization that intervention could end up being costly in lives and resources and politically unpopular back home. In contrast, Kosovo in 1999 generated an American sense of strategic stakes, com-bined with a shift of tactics to diminish the risk of casualties for the intervening side, the memories associated with impotence arising from the feeble role of the UN in Bosnia a few years earlier, and the impulse to show that a regional mili-tary alliance and innovations in weaponry and doctrine would demonstrate that NATO was far more effective as an intervening actor than had been the United Nations.[11]

The Commission on Intervention and State Sovereignty was also intent on suggesting that responsibility be substituted for rights when it comes to the understanding of sovereignty, rendering a state that fails to protect its citizenry "irresponsible," and no longer entitled to unqualified deference with respect to unacceptable happenings within its territory. Such a rhetorical move is explained as needed to incorporate the rise of human rights, but also to take account of the then emergent perspective on security that involved thinking less about the secu-rity of the state (national security) and more about the security of people (human security).[12] The report also urges that the main organs of the United Nations take steps to endorse this approach, and to act accordingly, seeking to shape the politi-cal climate of opinion by formalizing at an intergovernmental and institutional level the consensus reached by the commission composed of eminent persons representative of the world as a whole and mostly associated with prominent careers in the governments of their respective countries.[13]

This report achieved considerable attention when issued, partly due to the energy of its co-chair, Gareth Evans, former foreign minister of Australia, and partly because it made a successful effort to find a less threatening, yet sensible and clear, way to discuss and fine-tune humanitarian intervention. The approach has been adopted by the Report of the Secretary General's High-Level Panel on Threats, Challenges and Change issued with considerable fanfare in November 2004. Two elements can be highlighted, firstly, the explicit abridgement of the nonintervention norm: "The principle of non-intervention in internal affairs cannot be used to protect genocidal acts or atrocities, such as large-scale viola-tions of international humanitarian law or large-scale ethnic cleansing, which can properly be considered a threat to international security and as such provoke action by the Security Council."[14] The report also recommends against any effort to alter the Charter language to accommodate this approach, contending that it is not necessary and likely not politically feasible. The report also declares that sovereignty is no longer operative as a shield for oppressive governments, suggesting that "[t]he successive humanitarian disasters in Somalia, Bosnia and Herzegovina, Rwanda, Kosovo and now Darfur, Sudan, have concentrated attention not on the immunities of sovereign Governments but their responsibilities, both to their own people and to the wider international community."[15] In this regard, "responsibility" has a dual face, upward to impose duties of protection on the organized international community, and downward to confirm obligations of territorial governance on the sovereign state. Of course, given the nature of international society, as well as its normative framework, major states are essentially exempted from such obligations, being too large to be held accountable either formally by legal censure or behaviorally by a world community intervention.

These developments await further incidents to determine whether their impact is mainly on the *style* of diplomatic language or affects, as well, *behavioral patterns of response*. What is excluded in these inquiries by credible individuals is the relevance, some would say the dominance, of geopolitics that seems crucial to the formation of political will in every particular instance, which in turn determines whether there is a strong prospect of an effective effort to insist on responsible behavior by governments and by the United Nations. The effects of the September 11 attacks on the global policy agenda, the dilatory response to Darfur, and the current leadership of the United States, which appears hostile to "humanitarian" nation-building (as contrasted with the enormous efforts undertaken by Washington in pursuance of strategic goals in Afghanistan and Iraq), combine to give an impression that humanitarian concerns and an ethos of human solidarity do not enjoy presently strong support from leading governments. The epic natural disaster caused by the South Asian tsunami of December 2004 temporarily encouraged a more hopeful picture about cooperative international efforts in response to a humanitarian crisis, but seems limited in influence to its special circumstances. From a realist perspective, the appeal of responding to a natural disaster is that costs and risks can be fixed with far greater certainty in advance, and no loss of life on the intervening side is likely. It is also worth noting that in the list of "humanitarian disasters" in the UN High-Level report neither Afghanistan nor Iraq are mentioned, despite the American efforts, especially in Iraq, to justify its use of force after the fact by reference to the undoubted oppressive conditions existing in both countries.

What is also missing, due to the eminence of the membership of these elite bodies, which tends to produce reports that reflect a preoccupation with the credibility of the findings and recommendations in mainstream intergovernmental circles, is the absence of any kind of critical bite that might offend those in power. There is a reluctance to name names, whether of states or individuals, and an unwillingness to address the distorting selectivity of geopolitics or to discuss the hidden motivations and incentives of the parties, especially as these relate to resources or investment opportunities. The UN High-Level Panel went further than usual, perhaps too far as far as institutional etiquette is concerned, when it included in its report a somewhat disguised criticism of American pretensions to provide for global security in the following language: "There is little evident international acceptance of the idea of security being best preserved by a balance of power, or by any single — even benignly motivated — superpower."[16] To find less veiled criticism or more ardent support for humanitarian intervention can only be found in civil society circles, especially those shaped by independent scholars who benefit from academic freedom. In this regard, those academic voices associated with think tanks and the like tend to reproduce the views of the blue-ribbon commissions, or even more narrowly, tailor their recommendations to the viewpoints held by current power wielders or their own major donors.[17]

DOMAINS OF DOUBT AND BELIEF: CIVIL-SOCIETY
PERSPECTIVES ON HUMANITARIAN INTERVENTION

Throughout the extensive literature on humanitarian intervention, almost all of it written by scholars living in the countries that do the intervening, either directly or through the agency of international institutions, one encounters a self-serving, moralistic rhetoric and tone. Michael Walzer has long served as a leading exponent of geopolitically conservative moralistic advocacy, including with respect to humanitarian intervention. In this spirit he writes, "[w]henever the filthy work can be stopped, it should be stopped. And if not by us, the supposedly decent people of this world, then by whom?"[18] According to another stalwart moralist of the established order, Michael Ignatieff, who is even more explicitly supportive than Walzer of the moral claims of the leading political actors in the current makeup of world order, criticism should be mostly directed at the reluctance to intervene, rather than with the supposedly incidental harm done by intervention.[19] Such views by independent scholars provide invaluable aid and comfort to the United States government and the former colonial states, casting them in the role of moral saviors of peoples trapped in barbaric circumstances. What such apologists for imperial prerogatives uniformly ignore is the historical record of cruel criminality on the part of these self-appointed, postcolonial guardians of world order. They also ignore the postinterventionary record of irresponsible withdrawal or the engagement with exploitative forms of reconstruction designed to ensure strategic control and economic benefits by way of lucrative investment contracts at the expense of the well being of the people.

Fortunately, the balance sheet on humanitarian intervention is being redrawn recently by several scholars who write from a critical perspective.[20] Anne Orfeld's *Reading Humanitarian Intervention* is a major contribution along these lines.[21] She effectively demonstrates the extent to which the perils of the present for societies experiencing humanitarian catastrophes are directly attributable to the legacy of colonial rule. The brunt of her trenchant analysis of humanitarian intervention focuses on the harm done to the society that is supposedly being helped to recover from atrocious circumstances, contending that it is neither collateral nor peripheral to the rescue operations. Orfeld shows that in the name of reconstruction, a capitalist set of constraints are imposed on a broken society that impairs its right of self-determination, as well as its sovereign control of resources, and prevents its leadership from adopting an approach to development that is beneficial to the people of the country rather than designed to make neoliberal foreign investors happy. The essence of her position is that "legal narratives" justifying humanitarian intervention have had the primary effect of sustaining "an unjust and exploitative status quo."[22]

The deepest criticism of humanitarian intervention as legal narrative is that it operates to revalidate violence by the strong and dominant against the weak and subordinate. In her provocative words,

> "the international community shares something with those fantasized others against which it constitutes itself. It shares a commitment to the wounding and excluding of marked others as its founding act. This fact helps to explain the vehemence with which those who identify with the international community come to disavow the leaders of "rogue" or "failed" national or tribal communities as less than human. This disavowal is necessary precisely because these communities in fact share that which the international community rejects as illegitimate: an originary violence deployed against those marked out on the grounds of race, ethnicity and gender. The attempts to disavow this lead to more violence."[23]

Orfeld contends that rather than accepting explanations of state failure and abuse based on ethnic tensions, extremist religion, and micronationalist and tribal rivalries, attention needs to be devoted to the strains imposed by the sort of brutalizing submission of labor and inequitable distribution of resources brought about by the disciplinary influence of neoliberal capitalism. The further contention here is that legal narratives of development and material progress, even human rights, are relied upon to mask unjust structural divisions based on class, gender, and race that are being deliberately perpetuated by power wielders, assisted in this dirty work at every stage by international lawyers available to provide a façade of legality.

Again, it is useful to reflect on Orfeld's carefully chosen words: "The imperial desire to know and to access 'other' peoples and territories is transformed through the practice of international law into a sense of expertise and authorization to speak about those who can be constructed as in need of 'our' help."[24] Such thinking encourages us to explore the hidden infrastructure of violent undertakings that proclaim their humanitarian credentials. This hidden infrastructure of economic and strategic self-interest manifests itself in a number of ways: by abandoning a society in shambles once the strategic objective of the intervenor has been achieved (for example, Afghanistan in 1989),[25] by sustaining an occupation without investing sufficiently in reconstruction (Bosnia, 1995; Kosovo, 1999), by seeking to establish strategic bases and economic privileges in a ravaged society (Iraq, 2003), by imposing a new leadership and a capitalist developmental template on the occupied country, thereby obstructing the right of self-determination, setting the stage for future political violence (almost every country that has been the site of humanitarian intervention since 1990), and turning loose a new generation of corrupt and authoritarian indigenous leaders who betray their own citizenry for the sake of their collaboration with foreign powers.

All of this contributes to sustaining a sort of "collective day-dream," as Edward Said describes the Orientalist process of visioning the other, which in the setting of humanitarian intervention allows the exploitative dominant side to sustain the illusion of moral distance between itself and evil out there at a distance. By so doing the intervening state(s), or their constructed "international community," represents itself by contrasting images arising from being "sovereign, civilized, autonomous, powerful and humane."[26] Such critical thinking is definitely a needed corrective to patterns of naive and uncritical liberal advocacy that has dominated mainstream discussions of humanitarian diplomacy, but does it go too far? When writing and speaking from the margins it is generally necessary to exaggerate to be heard at all, but then supercilious voices from the center respond knowingly that the criticism is "polemical," "utopian," and "irresponsible." At minimum, it is important to listen carefully to criticism from the margins, and then decide whether to correct for exaggeration.

Orfeld recognizes the anguishing dilemma posed by the choice between inhumane action and inhumane inaction, specifically in the face of the terrifying 1999 crisis in East Timor, when the Indonesian military engaged in and fomented massacres of a helpless civilian society that had been brutally colonized for the prior twenty-four years. Her point is that narrowing the issue to such a choice between action and inaction distorts the challenge facing analyst and advocate alike. Instead of evolving rationalizations for humanitarian intervention at the boiling point, it should be the work of international lawyers to point to the deforming legacies of colonial rule and hegemonic aspirations, and even more so to suggest alternative paths to development that will avoid the onset of catastrophe for a society and to shape postcatastrophic reconstruction in ways that produce a just and sustainable social, political, and economic order.[27] The lens of intervention, pro or contra, is too narrow to encompass the relevant terrain for a genuine humanitarian undertaking.

Ikechi Mgbeoji offers a parallel critique of conventional understandings of humanitarian intervention with specific reference to sub-Saharan Africa, using the experience of Liberia as a case that illuminates a far wider pattern afflicting the postcolonial destinies of much of the continent.[28] Mgbeoji situates the source of contemporary African troubles in the crude colonialist machinations of European states, culminating in the carving up of African natural communities into a series of artificial colonies at the 1884 to 1885 Berlin Conference. This resulted in a dynamic of emergence from the colonial experience with artificial polities that were vulnerable to disruption and a population unprepared for the exercise of constructive leadership at the level of the state. Mgbeoji also attributes blame to the kind of opportunistic African elites that took power in so many of these countries, often with connivance of the former colonial overlords, disclosing an overall pattern of coresponsibility: "I argue that the corrosion of the African psyche and the mutilation of precolonial African political structures laid the basis for the modern crises afflicting the continent. Beyond the pernicious legacy of European imperialism coupled with myopic, selfish, and impoverished leadership of the African elite, it seems clear that the solution to African political instability lies in a structural rearrangement of the African polity for the purpose of legitimate governance of African peoples."[29] In effect, the boundaries of the postcolonial state should not be treated as sacrosanct, especially when its effects are to bisect communities of solidarity. Mgbeoji shows how much the tragedy of Liberia is a product of this heritage of artificial boundaries that disregard the ethnic and tribal contours of peoples. Unlike Orfeld, Mgbeoji gives less significance to predatory capitalism, except as a byproduct of this unholy alliance between the colonialist background and a corrupt indigenous foreground. But like Orfeld, he repudiates the moralistic aura of Western interventionary diplomacy as an antidote to African primitiveness and barbarism.

Mgbeoji is worried about loosening the bonds of international law in the setting of African initiatives designed to address humanitarian catastrophes. He is not very positive about entrusting African regional actors with peacekeeping missions disconnected from supervision by the United Nations, using the troubling experience of Liberia to bolster a wider argument. In the end, Mgbeoji believes that so long as the underlying conditions in Africa are based on artificial ideas of statehood, humanitarian catastrophes will recur, and interventionary undertakings, even if properly guided, can do no more than provide temporary relief to a beleaguered society. To overcome this circumstance of what he calls "collective insecurity" will require a much more comprehensive approach that gets at the roots of conflict and hostility: ". . . the practice of a holistic concept of collective security and distributive social justice secured by legitimate state boundaries and good governance is the antidote to the civil conflicts ravaging the continent."[30] Mgbeoji makes it clear that part of the problem is the international practice of associating legitimate governance with control of the capital city by the leader and with an electoral process that often has only ritualistic significance, thereby circumventing the more fundamental sources of legitimacy associated with the existence of genuine political loyalty by the people and a corresponding commitment by the leadership to achieve social justice for the totality of the society. Such goals cannot be realized within the parameters of present African statehood, giving Mgeoji's argument a certain utopian edge, despite the power of his compelling assessment of the African situation, including the total inadequacy of a fire-fighting mentality with respect to the underlying crisis.

CONCLUDING OBSERVATIONS

The subject matter of humanitarian intervention has been foregrounded by the rise of human rights in a globalizing world. At the same time, the practice of rescuing populations raises a variety of *proximate* concerns about justification and effectiveness. It also raises more *fundamental* concerns associated with the causal onset of humanitarian emergencies and the impact of reconstructive efforts. There are two sets of responses that have been noted: the first consists of those who represent the established order, and seek to reconcile a sensitivity to the rights of independent states with actions designed to bring relief and rescue to peoples entrapped within oppressive or anarchic circumstances. These perspectives seek to make humanitarian intervention acceptable and operational, revising international law along the way, but without questioning underlying conditions or the motives of the intervenors. The second consists of critics of the established order that regard humanitarian intervention as a hypocritical exercise in postcolonial imperialism that not only fails to address basic issues generative of mass suffering, but may aggravate and intensify such suffering in specific cases by diverting attention from real causes and available cures.

This whole setting of debate has been complicated by the September 11 attacks on the United States, and the American response that has fused a new generation of real concerns about global security with a militarist push for global dominance by the currently hegemonic Western power. In this latter setting, as seen in Iraq since the American invasion of 2003, the humanitarian intervention argument is invoked as a cover for aggressive warfare and a prolonged hostile occupation. At the same time, the massive humanitarian catastrophe festering in Darfur has evoked widespread global concern, but only minimalist protective action, again confirming that where strategic interests are weak or conflicted, the needed political will for protective action will not be forthcoming no matter how grave and massive the unfolding tragedy and no matter how the intervention is sanitized by the language of protection. Rwanda redux.

The way forward is to proceed on complementary lines. Despite the difficulties and ambiguities of practice, it remains beneficial to counsel effective action in response to instances of ethnic cleansing, genocide, and widespread Crimes Against Humanity. It may be feasible to bring into being a volunteer, professional capability under the auspices of the United Nations that would be entrusted with the implementation of humanitarian diplomacy with reduced geopolitical interference. At the same time, it is essential to disseminate beyond academic circles the sorts of critical perspectives developed so powerfully by Orfeld and Mgbeoji, widening the orbit of understanding to encompass the *causes* of humanitarian catastrophe and the *effects* of both humanitarian intervention and adherence to the norm of nonintervention.

12

The Criminal Accountability of Leaders

At the Nuremberg Tribunals that followed World War II, the United States insisted that the surviving leaders of Nazi Germany and Imperial Japan be neither shot when captured nor set free, but rather prosecuted as war criminals in a court of law that gave those accused a full opportunity to present a defense. It had not been easy for Franklin Roosevelt to convince his British and Soviet counterparts, Winston Churchill and Josef Stalin, that this was the preferred course of action. Nuremberg and, even more so, the parallel tribunal established to prosecute Japanese political and military leaders, have been frequently criticized as "victors' justice," and so it was. At least, the victorious powers that managed the process in 1945 insisted that in the future the legal accountability of leaders would apply to the behavior of all sovereign states, and not just the losers. Justice Robert Jackson, the chief American prosecutor at Nuremberg, expressed this intention in his opening statement: "The ultimate step in avoiding periodic wars, which are inevitable in a system of international lawlessness, is to make statesmen responsible to law. And let me make clear that while this law is first applied against German aggressors, the law includes, and if it is to serve a useful purpose it must condemn, aggression by any other nation, including those which sit here now in judgment."[1]

However, there was a disturbing unwillingness by the victors of World War II to fulfill the expectations created by Jackson's statement, and perhaps there was never a serious intention to do so. The Nuremberg approach continues to lack credibility whenever it collides with the stubborn realities of geopolitics. The state system is still beholden to dominant states that insist on their prerogative to wage illegal and aggressive "wars of choice," thereby dangerously and often imprudently subordinating legality to a warped logic of political expediency. More carefully evaluated, adherence to the legal constraints on war making would have served most powerful countries well in recent years. International law encodes rules of diplomatic prudence as well as establishes a regime seeking to minimize the role of war, but the political mentality that dominates governmental elites in major states continues to view the war option as a discretionary aspect of sovereign rights.

Throughout the Cold War era, a series of initiatives rooted in civil society kept the Nuremberg flame flickering. These initiatives, based on acts of individual conscience, expressed the belief that leaders are legally and morally obliged to uphold international law in the area of war and peace. If they fail to do so, citizens have a right, even a duty, to refuse to participate in official policies even if ordered to do so.

This civic movement on behalf of official accountability climaxed in the latter stages of the Vietnam War and in relation to the nuclear arms race during the 1970s and 1980s. It produced antiwar heroes such as the Berrigan brothers (Daniel and Philip) and many young men who chose prison or indefinite exile rather than to obey orders to fight in Vietnam, orders that they considered illegal under international law. Religious leaders, including Martin Luther King Jr. and William Sloane Coffin, condemned the criminality of American policies in an influential book, *In the Name of America*.[2] Daniel Ellsberg explained his legally dubious release of the *Pentagon Papers* (which included many classified documents) as driven in large part by his reading of the Nuremberg Judgment. Telford Taylor, a respected and scholarly former military officer who was an important member of the prosecution team at Nuremberg, wrote a widely read indictment of American policy, *Nuremberg and Vietnam*.[3] The renowned British philosopher Bertrand Russell convened a tribunal in 1966 to examine charges of war crimes in Vietnam that included among its members leading intellectual figures in Europe, such as Jean-Paul Sartre and Simone de Beauvoir.

These and many other developments confirmed the role of an emergent global civil society in keeping alive the central idea that governments are not above the law, that those who represent the state are responsible for adhering to international law even in times of war and with respect to national security. There is no doubt that this civic trend was controversial, especially in the United States, but it kept alive a public consciousness that helped make possible a revival of Nuremberg Principles as active elements in the moral consciousness of contemporary society.

After decades of forgetfulness induced by the consuming rivalry of the Cold War era, there occurred in the 1990s a dramatic revival of the idea that neither states nor their leaders were above the law with respect to war making, genocide, and Crimes Against Humanity. The rebirth of the Nuremburg approach to war crimes began to reach intergovernmental circles. Some important indications of this included the establishment by the UN Security Council of special international criminal tribunals to address allegations of official crimes in the course of the breakup of the former Yugoslavia (1993) and arising from the massive killings in Rwanda (1994); the indictment by a Spanish court and the subsequent British detention for extradition of the now-deceased Chilean dictator Augusto Pinochet; the indictment of the late Slobodon Milosevic while he was still head of state in Yugoslavia, and his subsequent prosecution in The Hague; a worldwide movement of civil-society actors and states that led to the establishment in 2002 of a permanent international criminal court (ICC). This momentum, although resisted and weakened by some opposing trends, seemed to point to the gradual emergence of a law-governed world system that corresponded to the dynamics of economic and cultural globalization.

During the last century there have been two interacting traditions of support for international law, each with its own strengths and weaknesses. The *intergovernmental* tradition exhibiting a pattern of alternating assertiveness and neglect, as well as its opportunistic invocation in relation to adversaries and avoidance with respect to self and friends. The *transnational* civic tradition of support for legality often intensifies in response to intergovernmental irresponsibility. The intergovernmental level can gain public and media attention and impose punishments; its main weakness is inconsistent and highly selective implementation and the exemption of leaders of dominant and allied states from accountability. The civic level is more consistent than the intergovernmental, thereby filling a moral vacuum; but it lacks the authority or capacity to enforce its determinations, and has difficulty gaining mainstream public and media attention, much less credibility. Such developments as the establishment of the International Criminal Court and the Belgian national judicial experiment with "universal jurisdiction" in the 1990s were largely the work of collaborative efforts between a transnational coalition of NGOs and moderate governments working to strengthen the role of international law in the political governance of the planet.[4]

THE BUSH ERA

As soon as George W. Bush arrived at the White House, it became clear that issues of international accountability for war crimes would be handled in a highly partisan spirit that cast doubt on what had earlier seemed so promising in the immediately preceding period. Bush took the unprecedented step of withdrawing the American signature from the Rome Treaty leading to the establishment of the ICC in 2002, and then had the state department negotiate as many as one hundred bilateral treaties ensuring that no American citizens would ever be handed over to the ICC for prosecution.[5]

But at the same time, the United States government pushed harder than ever for the prosecution of Serbian political and military leaders thought to be responsible for war crimes in Bosnia and Kosovo. And in the context of Iraq, the U.S. government crafted a dubious Iraqi war-crimes procedure to prosecute Saddam Hussein in an inflamed setting that would virtually guarantee convictions without achieving any sense of justice. The mandate to impose a death sentence on defendants (which would not have been available if the trials had been in an international venue) further discredited this extreme example of what might be called "occupier's justice." This self-serving approach to criminal accountability has caused widespread public criticism of the United States, especially when its own behavior seems to violate so flagrantly the restraints on recourse to and the conduct of war making.

The American response to the attacks of September 11 has greatly complicated the situation. Even before September 11 American leaders were exhibiting a brazen form of geopolitical hubris. For example, back in 1988 George Bush Sr. said, "I will never apologize for the United States. I don't care what the facts are." This generalized ethos of unconditional nonaccountability was reiterated by his son, George Bush Jr., in the course of the 2004 State of the Union address: "America will never seek a permission slip to defend the security of our country." The clear implication of such defiant unilateralism is that the United States would never regard itself as constrained in its decisions to wage war on other countries by either the United Nations Charter or international law. More dramatically, the casting off of legal and ethical limits on American behavior, while insisting on such limits for enemies, conveyed to the world a dangerous rogue image of a belligerent and cynical imperial power aiming at world domination, accountable neither to rules nor public opinion.

Although it has proved hard to pin down the precise parameters of aggressive war,[6] the clear instances are easily discerned on the basis of the directives of the United Nations Charter. Articles 2(4) and 51 establish that it is impermissible to use force against another state except in circumstances of self-defense or in the furtherance of a mandate issued by a decision of the UN Security Council.[7] The essential idea in the Charter is that war making by a state against another state is aggression unless it can qualify as self-defense, which is deliberately defined narrowly in Article 51 of the Charter. Whatever the debates about the limits of self-defense, there is little responsible disagreement about the core obligation. There is no substantial doubt that the war against Iraq launched by the United States on March 20, 2003, was a flagrant instance of aggressive war.[8] Despite strenuous American efforts to persuade delegates with misleading evidence of Iraqi possession of weapons of mass destruction, the United States failed to obtain a mandate from the Security Council to use force against Iraq.[9] The Afghanistan War was also undertaken without a definite Security Council authorization, but at least there was a plausible case for American claims of a legitimate security urgency, a condition of defensive necessity created by the special character of the September 11 attacks, and the associated threats of future attacks. Although there were grounds for concern arising from stretching the law, there existed what appeared at the time to be a reasonable basis for a self-defense claim.[10] Unlike the Kosovo War, which also lacked a legal foundation, in Iraq there did not exist the mitigating circumstance of a humanitarian emergency or the legitimating influence of a regional consensus.[11] The Iraqi invasion represents a high point in American unilateralism that was hardly mitigated by the presence of some coalition partners. The invasion of Iraq struck a body blow at the authority of the United Nations, as well as to international law.

A NECESSARY STRUGGLE

There is little doubt that the Iraq War should be treated as an aggressive war that constitutes a Crime Against Peace. As such, those who planned and executed this war should be subject to indictment and prosecution if the Nuremberg framework were to be activated regardless of the power and influence of the accused state and its officialdom. Other crimes associated with the conduct of the war and the subsequent occupation should also give rise to accountability by reference to the laws of war and international humanitarian law.

With American backing, an Iraqi judicial procedure closely tied to the American occupation has made the crimes of Saddam Hussein and his chief lieutenants the subject of prosecution. These proceedings underscore the double standards at play when it comes to accountability for international crimes. The Iraqi trials also demonstrate that the United States government is not opposed on principled grounds to procedures of accountability for leaders of states so long as it can exempt its own officials and personnel, and those of its friends. Such a partisan posture creates an impression of extreme hypocrisy, and has the effect of reinforcing cynical views that holding individuals responsible for crimes of state is one more instance of the strong imposing their will on the weak whenever it serves their interests to do so. This is most unfortunate, as the acts of the powerful constitute the most dangerous threats to global public order. These need to be deterred and punished if the peoples of the world are to be better protected against the abuses of governments, and if global justice is to be perceived as a goal of international law rather than an offshoot of geopolitics.

These recent American policies have sparked a worldwide counterreaction of civic initiatives expressing a transnational consciousness in support of universal standards of accountability. As many as twenty distinct tribunals set up by civil-society actors have examined the criminality of various aspects of the Iraq War, with sessions in Japan, Britain, Belgium, the United States, Turkey, Germany, Sweden, and elsewhere. This "tribunal movement," unprecedented in global experience, expressed a worldwide sentiment of opposition to the Iraq War, and is an example of "globalization-from-below."

Global civil society is waging a struggle to extend the reach of criminal accountability that includes those leaders acting on behalf of dominant states. Especially in democratically organized states such as the United States, it is a matter of extending the rule of law to foreign as well as domestic policy. Such a development will not occur without a domestic cultural revolution that comes to appreciate that adherence to law is a necessary ingredient of power in the twenty-first century rather than being, as in the past, an impediment. The disasters of Vietnam and Iraq have untested potential to instruct the American people about the benefits of subjecting foreign policy to the discipline of international law. Whether such a learning process can occur rapidly enough to avoid further disasters may be the as yet unanswerable question that is likely to have a major bearing on the near future of world order. It is not just a matter of upgrading the relevance of law, but of downgrading the utility and acceptability of war as a policy option. Such downgrading might also lead to a reevaluation of current levels of overinvestment in an overwhelmingly dysfunctional war machine that is rarely used actively, and when used, generally produces costly results and widespread suffering and devastation. And contrary to near-mystical claims that the mere existence of this monster war machine makes world peace a possibility is the more objective assessment that more morally acceptable and financially conservative alternatives exist, and seem promising.

13

World Tribunal on Iraq
Truth, Law, and Justice

The World Tribunal on Iraq (WTI) was convened in Istanbul between June 24 and 27, 2005. It represented the culmination of a global effort that involved a series of earlier tribunal sessions devoted to pronouncing upon the legality and criminality of the Iraq War, and the related issues of personal accountability for those associated with the planning and carrying out of the war. This transnational initiative of civil society was organized by private citizens in various parts of the world, motivated by four main considerations: that the Iraq War was an ongoing massive "human wrong," essentially crimes responsible for inexcusable human suffering and societal devastation; that the initiation of the war flagrantly violated widely accepted norms of international law and morality; that the official institutions of state, region, and world, as well as the mainstream media, had remained silent spectators, exhibiting degrees of complicity with and a related unwillingness to challenge the ongoing wrongdoing; and that the officials responsible for the war had deceived and lied to build support for the war, creating information and knowledge gaps that deliberately undermined the inhibiting role in constitutional democracies of prudential legal and political checks on war making.[1]

The jurisprudential rationale for this initiative is the claim that citizens possess a residual right and duty to implement the norms of international law bearing on war and peace when official institutions fail to discharge their responsibilities. There is no formal foundation for this claim, but it follows from the wider Nuremberg logic that individuals have an obligation to do what is possible to oppose any aggressive war initiated and implemented in violation of the United Nations Charter and international law. In this sense, there is a law beyond that of sovereign states, which in extreme situations makes it appropriate to pass civic judgment on the official past and present policies of governments.[2]

Unlike with courts of law and the organs of the United Nations, the orientation of these citizen "tribunals" is to *confirm* the law, and draw the appropriate political and legal consequences, rather than to resolve factual controversies and assess the merits of a legal debate by heeding adversary positions in a spirit of fairness. The credibility of the process depends on the participation of high-profile individuals who possess an aura of moral authority. Persons who act as judges are often drawn from cultural and NGO circles, and generally lack credentials as lawyers or judges. The legal content of these tribunal proceedings is provided by expert testimony by jurists. The nature of the process is further clarified to avoid false pretenses by referring to the "judges" as "jurors" or even as "panelists." Unlike those of jurors in national legal systems, the qualifications of these jurors are based on their moral and political engagement, rather than any presumed neutrality with respect to the contested factual and legal issues. Despite this, it seems appropriate to associate their roles with that of jurors as their responses that form the judgment, or more modestly, "a declaration of conscience," are usually expressions of moral conviction and common sense, and do not purport to embody the technical expertise of courts of law operating within a constitutional system, although these assessments may include a belief in the relevance and authority of international law.

International law is important as a grounding for the moral and political claims associated with such a tribunal, but not for the purpose of discovering whether or not the challenged practices are legal. Although typically the accused state is invited by these tribunals to send an official representative to explain and defend the position of their government, it is without expectation that such an invitation will be accepted, and it never is. Governments, and intergovernmental institutions, above all the United Nations, ignore these tribunals, contending that they are worthless and irrelevant for several reasons: a lack of any formal governmental or intergovernmental mandate, a one-sided approach, and an outcome that is more or less predetermined. By and large, governments have been so far successful in discrediting these tribunals in most arenas of influential opinion making. The very existence of such a tribunal is generally ignored by the national media of the accused country despite the involvement of prominent and influential individuals. These tribunals often undertake a comprehensive inquiry into controversial and salient issues of public policy, which is followed by a reasoned explanation for the conclusions reached and the recommendations made. That is, the substantive outcome of these tribunals, in most instances, is worthy of attention, but due to the nongovernmental auspices of the activities, even their existence is overlooked if it is not explicitly condemned.

The WTI rested on a jurisprudence constructed by reference to prior tribunal initiatives that had taken place over the course of about four decades, although it also possessed some distinctive and original elements.[3] The organizers of the WTI explicitly acknowledged that they were inspired by the example of the Russell Tribunal established in 1967 at the initiative of the eminent British philosopher Bertrand Russell to consider charges of criminality associated with the role of the United States in the Vietnam War. It was then difficult to find a venue for such a controversial undertaking organized in the midst of the Cold War, but Denmark and Sweden were finally persuaded to allow these proceedings to take place within their territory. The panel of twenty-one jurors that constituted the

Russell Tribunal was chaired by Jean-Paul Sartre, and it included such prominent figures as Simone de Beauvoir, the American peace activist David Dellinger, the American writer James Baldwin, the German playwright Peter Weiss, and the black activist Stokely Carmichael. None of these individuals possessed any claim to adjudicative skills or even legal training. All were on record prior to the proceedings as being opposed to American aims in Vietnam. The published record of the two sessions of the Russell Tribunal even after the passage of time represents a generally accurate and comprehensive record of American wrongdoing in Vietnam, a judgment made on the basis of comparison with other influential accounts of the war. In this sense, although one-sided from the perspective of adversarial fairness, the results seem generally accurate, often unavailable elsewhere in comparable detail, and objective in the primary sense of truth-telling — that is, the evidence presented is honestly compiled and reflective of realities. The Russell Tribunal expressed a refusal by citizens of conscience to remain silent in the face of what they perceived to be blatant criminality that was carried on in a political atmosphere within the United States, which purported to be democratic but for many years carried on the Vietnam War without any significant debate and absent an adequate consideration of legal, moral, and political objections.[4]

One of the members of the Russell Jury was Lelio Basso, a prominent and prosperous Italian left jurist and legislator who believed that there existed a need for a permanent mechanism of inquiry and assessment in civil society, oriented around issues of global justice and the well being of peoples. Basso had established the Basso Foundation, which was devoted to these concerns, in Rome, and an early project of the Foundation was the creation of a Permanent Peoples' Tribunal (PPT) during the mid-1970s. Deliberately selecting the symbolic date of 1976, two hundred years after the American Declaration of Independence, the Basso initiative drafted what it called the Algiers Universal Declaration on the Rights of Peoples.[5] Over the next twenty years the PPT organized more than twenty sessions on a wide range of issues, including American intervention in several Central American countries, the oppressive government of Marcos in the Philippines, Soviet intervention in Afghanistan, the Armenian genocide, the independence struggle in Puerto Rico, and the plight of indigenous peoples in Amazonia, as well as an inquiry into the links between the IMF/World Bank and world poverty.

The staff of the Basso Foundation organized the sessions. Persons linked to the particular topic usually arranged the funding and preparation of the substantive materials. They prepared the witness list and handled any special forms of testimony. Some of these sessions were invaluable in compiling an authoritative record of wrongdoing, highlighting neglected instances of international criminality, and informing a wider public opinion about the policies of a particular government that seemed in violation of international law. In this latter instance, the proceedings of the PPT session devoted to wrongs associated with the Marcos regime when published in the Philippines became a best-seller in Manila, and according to Filipino activists contributed to the rise of "the people power movement" that managed to overthrow Marcos in 1986. The occasion of the tribunal led its organizers to gather in one place and at one time the most convincing evidence and allegations of wrongdoing that could be attributed to the accused government and its political and military leaders. Integral to the citizen tribunal process is subsequent publication and dissemination of the results, normally in book form, accompanied by forums arranged by those who were involved in organizing the tribunal. The Internet and alternative print media now function as principal, or at least co-equal, modes of dissemination throughout the world.

The inspirational basis of the WTI, other than earlier citizen efforts along the same lines, was the Nuremberg Tribunal, and the Nuremberg Principles that summarized the judgment, and were then embedded in international law. Important at Nuremberg were the intergovernmental blessings given to the principle that political and military leaders are not above the law, or exempt from criminal accountability. There are no exceptions.[6] True, Nuremberg (and Tokyo) were to some extent discounted as victors' justice with the apparent crimes of the victors located beyond the scope of permitted inquiry, but the American prosecutor, Justice Robert Jackson, made what has come to be known as the "Nuremberg Promise," that the principles laid down to judge the defendants at Nuremberg would subsequently be operative in relation to the future behavior of the victors.[7]

There is no doubt that for the period of the Cold War the Nuremberg Promise was broken in various ways by all of the governments that sat in judgment at Nuremberg, and further that the membership of the United Nations was largely complicit in repeated instances of "crimes of silence." But this promise made at Nuremberg was heeded by a variety of political activists, particularly in the setting of opposition to the Vietnam War, but also in relation to the development and deployment of nuclear weaponry and with respect to American interventions in Central America during the 1980s. And in this regard, the Russell Tribunal was a major innovative attempt to break the silence, and in Russell's own words bear "witness" to what was understood to be American lawlessness and criminality in Vietnam. It should also be noted that governments with the backing of the United Nations revived the Nuremberg Tradition during the 1990s on a number of fronts: the ad hoc tribunals to adjudge the criminality associated with the breakup of the former Yugoslavia and the Rwanda massacres; the worldwide movement of moderate governments and a coalition of NGOs to establish a permanent International Criminal Court; and a heightened reliance on national courts to enforce international criminal law, dramatized by the efforts to detain, extradite, and prosecute the former Chilean dictator, Augusto Pinochet.[8] Such an international climate that was pushing toward establishing an institutional foundation for holding the leadership of states criminally accountable for severe violations of international law gave an increased plausibility to the civic impulse to hold governments and their representatives to standards of accountability in the face of a prolonged aggressive war. The WTI is one expression of this public mood supportive of individual accountability of leaders that existed during the 1990s.

It is also relevant to an evalutation of the WTI to note that it had been preceded by an unprecedented level of public mobilization of antiwar sentiment prior to the Iraq War. The refusal of the United States and Britain to heed this opposition, and the failure of the United Nations to protect Iraq in the face of such illegal threats and uses of force, contributed to a sense of frustration and concern on the part of political activists around the world that led to the emergence of what has been described as "the tribunal movement," namely, the process of organizing tribunals on the Iraq War in various countries, followed by a final session in Istanbul that drew on the results of the earlier tribunal sessions, and offers the public a widely distributed assessment of the issues raised. The WTI proceedings received intense regional coverage, widespread Internet dissemination, and attracted representatives of alternative media from around the world. The WTI was the culmination of this unique organizing effort, which was worldwide in scope, and unprecedented in scale. Never before had sessions of this sort been organized to take place in sequence and in a variety of countries.

The WTI was organized more than two years after George W. Bush spoke on the flight deck of an American aircraft carrier lying off the coast of San Diego on May 1, 2003, with the banner reading "Mission Accomplished" unfurled in the background. Such a tribunal would in all probability never have been organized if indeed the mission had been accomplished as Bush then claimed. It was undoubtedly the intense and sustained Iraqi resistance to the American-led occupation of Iraq that created the opportunity and the incentive to make the elaborate arrangements associated with the tribunal movement. It was this same experience of extreme frustration in Washington after an expected quick victory that formed a crucial part of the Vietnam reality, which eventually led to the formation of the Russell Tribunal. In a deep sense, it is the failure of aggressive war policies to reach their goals on the ground that creates the time, the sense of urgency, and political space for making the huge investment of international effort by ordinary people with limited funds to organize and pay for such a tribunal. If either of these wars had been effectively concluded quickly, despite their aggressive character, it is doubtful that the political motivation would have been present to embark upon such a difficult organizational journey. Part of the civic motivation is the felt urgency of responding to ongoing patterns of violence and devastation that seem shocking both because of the suffering involved, the wrongfulness of the military undertaking, and the frustration arising from warfare that persists for years and serves no acceptable ends. Somewhat unrealistically, the tribunal project is associated with an effort to mobilize sufficient opposition to challenge the policies directly, or at least to heighten the aura of illegitimacy surrounding the war.[9]

The division of the world into sovereign states means that the site of such a tribunal requires either the "consent" or at least the acquiescence of a state. In this sense, holding such a tribunal presupposes a democratic climate if the undertaking is to enjoy any credibility. It would, for instance, have been seen as pure anti-Western propaganda if the Soviet Union had hosted the Russell Tribunal. The choice of Istanbul as the site of the WTI was itself notable, located outside of the main Western arenas, in a country that had not fully backed the American invasion although a longstanding strategic ally of the United States that was itself implicated in the war as its territory was used to launch air operations within Iraq by American planes based in Turkey. In this sense, Turkish society was deeply affected by the Iraq War. Located next to Iraq, Turkey was trying to work out its own diplomatic stance in relation to the European Union and the United States. The unobstructed occurrence of the WTI in Istanbul, made most visible nationally by front-page newspaper coverage, was itself evidence of the deepening of Turkish democracy and the confidence of its leadership in allowing such events to go forward on its territory. An initiative of this sort can only flourish within a democratic atmosphere, and can be understood as part of the struggle of citizens everywhere to oppose in a variety of ways gross human wrongs attributable to governments. And not only "citizens" in a narrow nationalistic sense, but in the terminology of the WTI, "citizens of conscience" — that is, those who belong to a borderless political community of like-minded persons that cannot be situated in space or on a map.

THE WORLD TRIBUNAL ON ISTANBUL: DEPICTING THE EVENT

The WTI was locally organized by a group of dedicated volunteers, mainly women, ordinary citizens in Turkey who normally worked on other jobs, arranging the whole event on a shoestring budget, contributing their own funds and relying on personal contacts to make this event happen. From the beginning, the WTI was both local and global, the latter in the form of an international coordinating committee with members from all over the world. And relations on this committee were generally cooperative, although at times experiencing tensions arising from personality clashes and differences in political style and priorities. The appropriate degree of Turkish leadership was a sensitive point of contention among the principal organizers, producing arguments about the agenda and format of the WTI. The main organizational responsibility was assumed by five Turkish women, assisted by a wider circle of Turkish and international advisers and helpers, operating through consensus and in a democratic spirit that at times appeared to endanger the process with logistical paralysis due to disagreements. As someone involved as an adviser from the initial planning stages, I had doubts all along as to whether this approach would succeed. It often seemed to me in some ways too spontaneous to pull off such an ambitious undertaking that was dependent on the participation of many internationally prominent persons. I had been involved with past endeavors of a similar kind, especially those organized by the Permanent Peoples' Tribunal in Rome during the 1980s, which seemed far more grounded professionally and fiscally, and had the benefit of a host organization with physical and staff facilities and in a position to ensure basic funding. Happily, I was wrong. The WTI turned out to be on almost all counts the most successful and influential event of this sort ever held. Interpreting this success is itself of political relevance, and possibly an indication that global civil society is indeed acquiring an increasing political agency, but not yet possessing the leverage and resources needed to challenge directly major governmental undertakings such as warfare initiated by the most powerful state in the world.

The WTI referred during its opening ceremony to the twenty earlier sessions that had inquired into the legality of the Iraq War as "hearings." These hearings were held in Barcelona, Brussels, Copenhagen, Genoa, Hiroshima, Lisbon, London, Mumbai, New York, Östersund, Paris, Rome, Seoul, Stockholm, Tunis, and several additional cities in Japan and Germany. There had never previously been such a global process. These various tribunals were both organized in response to particular national activism and a manifestation of a coordinated transnational antiwar coalition of social forces. The tribunal process had been preceded by the coordinated antiwar demonstrations that took place throughout the world on February 15, 2003. Those governments favoring an invasion of Iraq steadfastly ignored this extraordinary display of popular sentiment. Many thought such populist opposition to the Iraq policy to be a futile effort, especially if evaluated in relation to the declared objective of preventing the initiation of the Iraq War. These events were of greater political value if understood from longer perspectives as a form of antiwar and anti-imperial political educational initiative that was primarily concerned with ensuring that even if the Iraq War did get under way it would be widely understood globally as an illegitimate use of international force. Both these demonstrations and the tribunal process were expressions of what might appropriately be described as "moral globalization," expressing a concerted effort to mobilize outrage and public opinion with the main goal of shaping the climate of legitimacy with respect to the Iraq policy of the United States and its allies. The availability of the Internet makes this role feasible for global civil society because of the capacity to coordinate activities, share information, inform activists around the world, and create a global awareness of the outcome at no cost. An increasing skill in using information technology for this kind of transnational politics helps offset the disadvantages of low funding and poor coverage by influential media. The interest in the protection of human rights and support for humanitarian intervention in the face of genocide and severe Crimes Against Humanity are additional dimensions of what is being described here as moral globalization.[10]

The work of the WTI was divided between the Panel of Advocates and a Jury of Conscience. The Panel presented extensive evidence of war crimes; arranged the testimony of witnesses with special qualifications on various aspects of the war, especially relating to the suffering of the Iraqi people; and exposed the jury to a variety of expert accounts of the relevance of international law, as well as to critical interpretations of the geopolitical motivations that helped explain the real reasons for the invasion of Iraq. Again, the WTI blended a legal format with a partisan inquiry, signaling this approach by using the term "advocate" to describe the presentations to the jury. There was no pretense of neutrality or balance. The advocates were chosen for their familiarity with or exposure to the situation in Iraq, and because they were known and respected as critics of American policy in Iraq. The Jury of Conscience, which was as convinced about the underlying issues before the tribunal got under way as were the advocates, responded to the various presentations with unrehearsed questions, and after their deliberation and much internal discussion, issued a final unanimous assessment that was called the Declaration of the Jury of Conscience.

There were fifty-four presentations by advocates, including respected international law specialists such as Christine Chinkin and Phil Shiner, both from Britain, and Amy Bartholomew from Canada. In additionwere two former assistant secretary generals of the United Nations, Hans von Sponeck and Denis Halliday, both of whom had been high-level UN civil servants, and successively resigned their roles as administrators of the "Oil for Food Program" to protest the UN role in Iraq during the 1990s. They both believed that the UN sanctions program was responsible for inflicting indefensible suffering on the Iraqi people. Other advocates included several intellectual figures with world reputations, such as Samir Amin, Johan Galtung, and Joel Kovel. Perhaps the most moving presentations were made by several Iraqis who had held important posts in Iraqi civil society prior to the war, and traveled to Istanbul to participate in the WTI proceedings despite great security risks, given their expression of intense opposition to the occupation of their country.

There were seventeen members of the Jury of Conscience, presided over by the famed Indian novelist Arundhati Roy, who also made notable opening and closing statements on behalf of the jury. The members of the jury came from ten different countries and had a variety of backgrounds in the arts, education, and civil society. The only person with a legal background on the jury was one of the two American jurors, David Krieger, president of the Nuclear Age Peace Foundation, and even he was primarily known for his nonlegal writings on nuclear weapons and war. The credibility of the jury was based on the presence of citizens of conscience, notable in their own societies for social activism, moral courage, and political engagement, but with a variety of backgrounds ranging from Eve Ensler, creator of the "Vagina Monologues," to Murat Belge, a highly respected Turkish intellectual and newspaper columnist, to Chandra Muzaffar, a prominent NGO leader in Malaysia with a reputation for standing up to autocratic governments and for his eloquent commitment to Third World justice and Islamic moderation. In effect, the jury was, as it names suggests, an organ of conscience that made no pretense to be an expert legal body competent to apply international law. At the same time, to lift its views above morality and politics, great attention was given to the views of advocates that set forth a series of persuasive arguments relating to the legality of the Iraq War. The burden of this testimony, aside from the presentation of factual materials on the initiation and conduct of the war, was that those officials who were responsible decision makers and held leadership positions should be indicted and prosecuted as war criminals. The conclusions and analysis of the Declaration of the Jury of Conscience were substantiated by an International Law Appendix. This appendix does purport to meet professional standards, and is fully consistent with leading academic discussions that reach comparable conclusions.

Although speaking only for herself, Arundhati Roy expressed the ethos of the Jury when she said during the proceedings, "I don't think in . . . legal and bureaucratic terms . . . I didn't go down the road of questioning who we are or who we represent, because to me it was a bit like somebody asking me whether I had the legitimacy to write a novel. I mean, we're just a group of human beings, whether we are five or ten or fifteen or ten million. Surely, we have the right to express an opinion, and surely, if that opinion is irrelevant, surely, if that opinion is full of false facts, it will be treated as such, and if that opinion is, in fact, representative of the opinion of millions of people, it will become very huge."[11] In effect, the credibility of the WTI depends on its capacity for effective truth-telling that engages public opinion, and withstands fair-minded critical scrutiny.

In contrast to Roy, Jean-Paul Sartre validates the Russell Tribunal by reference to the unfulfilled expectations of the Nuremberg Promise and the need for some formal international institution to address such urgent and serious allegations of human wrongs. Sartre insists that "the legitimacy" of the Russell Tribunal derives equally from "its total powerlessness, and from its universality." Sartre somewhat misleadingly, I think, says that "the Russell Tribunal will have no other concern, in its investigations and conclusions, than to bring about a general recognition of the need for an international institution for which it has neither the means nor the ambition to be a substitute, whose essential role would be the resuscitation of the *jus contra bellum* which was still-born at Nuremberg — the substitution of ethical and juridical rules for the law of the jungle."[12] Surely, such a sentiment is naively optimistic about institutional developments. At this point the Nuremberg tradition has been somewhat resuscitated and the ICC established, but the geopolitical climate that prompted the Russell Tribunal is as war-prone and lawless as ever.

As coordinator of the Panel of Advocates I offered a more jurisprudential rationale for the WTI, its inception, process, and outcome, than was provided by Arundhati Roy. The fundamental explanation is that given by the Russell Tribunal and Permanent Peoples' Tribunal — namely, that where the international legal order fails to implement its own fundamental norms, then citizens and civil society have a residual right and responsibility to act in support of these norms and in opposition to aggressive warfare. Such action can take various legitimate forms, including critical speech, civil disobedience, tax refusal, formal legal challenges, nonviolent resistance, and civic commissions of inquiry and tribunals. This claim of authority is to some extent ex nihil — that is, without constitutional or positive law foundations. It rests on an ethos of concern and responsibility for fundamental law and morality, alive to the distinction between being a citizen and a subject, and expressive of the impulse to feel, think, and act as a global citizen in an increasingly globalizing world.

In response to the criticism that the WTI, and kindred initiatives, are one-sided "kangeroo courts," no better than civil-society show trials that mimic the legal charades of totalitarian regimes, a justification is offered here that such initiatives are characteristically only undertaken in the face of the most flagrant abuse of universally affirmed legal and moral norms, shocking to the conscience of humanity. The basic charge of the WTI was to document these charges of aggressive war and the commission of war crimes. Its intention was to mobilize public opposition to the persistence of such policies, and to contribute, however modestly, to a process for the rectification of wrongs. Over time, as well, with the expected publication of the WTI proceedings, the tribunal becomes a vehicle of moral and political education, as well as being itself a historic document that tells a story that mainstream narratives omit or slant.

There are also frequent derisive comments that such a tribunal has no standing to pass legal judgment, that its proposed course of recommended action lacks legal and political weight, and that such a faux tribunal usurps and confuses the role of established legal institutions and procedures. The argument made in support of the WTI emphasizes the reality of global civil society, and the responsibility of citizens since Nuremberg ("the Nuremberg Obligation") to do all that is possible to oppose crimes of state relating to war, including gathering evidence of criminality on the part of governmental officials and military commanders. Even before, Nuremberg President Franklin Roosevelt issued an appeal to the German people in the midst of the war to collect evidence of Nazi criminality.[13]

As far as the impact of the WTI is concerned, its success or failure is difficult to measure. The professed objective is to change the course of policy along
lines recommended, including holding the perpetrators accountable, as well as to
mobilize mass support for such demands throughout the world. In this instance,
the Declaration of Conscience condemned the invasion and occupation of Iraq
as illegal under international law, charged the governments of the United States
and the United Kingdom with the crime of aggression, a charge aggravated by
falsehoods and the manipulation of evidence to mislead public opinion, including willful misrepresentation of information by elected officials, and intensified
in the war itself by use of legally prohibited attacks on civilians and reliance on
forbidden weaponry, including shells and bombs containing depleted uranium.
The charges and findings were particularized in relation to governments, the UN
Security Council, corporate actors (including the media), and individuals who
acted on behalf of the responsible governments in relation to the Iraq War.

APPRAISING THE WTI

As an event intending to convey convincingly evidence of the main human
wrongs of the Iraq War, the WTI seems to have been highly effective at the time
of its staging. It received massive media coverage and Internet attention around
the world, especially in Turkey and elsewhere in the Middle East. It received no
coverage at all from influential media in the North, especially the United States.
Nevertheless, there were multiple TV and film crews attending the WTI, and
major newspapers and magazines in the Middle East, and throughout the Third
World, gave the WTI extensive coverage, including interviews with leading participants. The glamour, stature, and capacity of Arundhati Roy were certainly
one part of the story, as her picture appeared alongside interviews and profiles.
Turkish newspapers treated the WTI as a front-page story during the week of
its happening. I found that a Google search for the "World Tribunal on Iraq"
yields an astounding 1,950,000 items (as compared to 519,000 for the Nuremberg
Tribunal!). The Istanbul organizing committee, as well as the large number of
journalists representing alternate media, made important use of the Internet as
an organizing and mobilizing tool before, during, and after the proceedings.

In my view, the published proceedings of the WTI will provide the most comprehensive and persuasive indictment of the Iraq War yet available, and contribute to it an understanding of its wider ramifications. Its main value is educative
and as a consciousness-raising tool. It will almost certainly not be reviewed as
a notable book in the American media, and it will not be treated as a serious
scholarly contribution. At the same time, it will offer a compendium of the moral,
political, and legal arguments against the Iraq War and the policies that gave rise
to it. It is to be expected that most established centers of opinion are certain to

view the WTI proceedings through the sovereignty-coated lens of governmental law, and thus dismiss the evidence and findings as biased and partisan. In this sense, the WTI will be treated as authoritative for the more progressive sectors of global civil society, and as a frivolous gesture of political extremism by more established organs of opinion.

In relation to truth-telling, I believe the WTI proceedings will stand up well to independent scrutiny. I think the portrayal of the Iraq War by the WTI is essentially accurate from the perspectives of international politics, international law, and international morality. Its depictions of the damage inflicted and the suffering endured by the Iraqi people were graphic but well-documented and reliable.

The WTI is also an advance on prior efforts by civil society along the same lines. For one thing, women volunteers provided the main organizing energy. In contrast, both the Russell Tribunal and the PPT were dominated by men. The WTI locus in Turkey reflects the decentering of world order in relation to Europe and North America. For another, the Internet gave the WTI as an event, and its Declaration of Conscience, a truly global reach; as well, the presence of regional and alternative media ensured a much greater and immediate dissemination of the WTI proceedings than had been achieved by past initiatives of a comparable character. And finally, more than in past undertakings, the interplay of conscience, law, and morality was depicted in a sophisticated and persuasive way by the Panel of Advocates, and was embodied in a more politically persuasive form in the Declaration of the Jury of Conscience.

The WTI and the tribunal process that preceded and is likely to follow seems to be an important means for transnational organizing and mobilizing in relation to human wrongs. It is a flexible and fluid approach, the specific shape of which will vary from instance to instance, depending on the availability of resources, the perceived urgency of the situation, the priorities and temperament of the main organizers and participants, and wider attitudes of support or opposition in global civil society considered as a whole. The successful filming and publication in many languages of the proceedings is also important, as is the maintenance of a WTI Web site. There is little prospect that the formal governmental and intergovernmental framework of global political life will legitimate itself in relation to such human wrongs done under the cover of geopolitics in the foreseeable future. In this respect, even with the establishment of the ICC, most perpetrators of severe human wrongs continue to enjoy de facto impunity, being shielded by impenetrable walls of sovereign authority and rendered exempt by taking special protective measures reflecting the geopolitical clout of their governments.

Notes

CHAPTER 3: REVIVING PUNITIVE PEACE: THE SANCTIONS REGIME (1991–2003)

1. For an excellent overview that covers these issues, see Roger Normand and Christoph Wilcke, "Human Rights, Sanctions, and Terrorist Threats: The United Nations Sanctions against Iraq," *Transnational Law & Contemporary Problems* 11, no. 2 (Fall 2001): 299–343.
2. See Eric Schmitt, "U.S. Plan for Iraq Is Said to Include Attack on 3 Sides," *New York Times,* July 5, 2002; see also: editorial, "Battle Plans for Iraq," *New York Times,* July 6, 2002, A26.
3. A valuable overview has been provided by Sarah Graham-Brown, *Sanctioning Saddam: The Politics of Intervention in Iraq* (New York: I.B. Tauris, 1999).
4. See the early and respected assessment of the civilian impact of the sanctions imposed after the Gulf War by the Harvard Study Team that visited Iraq several times during 1991. Albert Acherio and others, "Effect of the Gulf War on Infant and Child Mortality in Iraq," *New England Journal of Medicine* 327: 931; see also *Unsanctioned Suffering: A Human Rights Assessment of United Nations Sanctions on Iraq,* Center for Economic and Social Rights, May 1996.
5. These two civil servants have become prominent civil-society campaigners against sanctions in the years following their resignation. See Denis Halliday and Hans von Sponeck, "The Hostage Nation: Former UN Relief Chiefs Hans von Sponeck and Denis Halliday Speak Out against an Attack on Iraq," *The Guardian,* 29 November 2001.
6. For rather contradictory accounts of this controversial inspection process under UN auspices, see Richard Butler, *The Greatest Threat: Iraq, Weapons of Mass Destruction and the Growing Crisis in Global Security* (New York: Public Affairs, 2000); Scott Ritter and others, *ENDGAME: Solving the Iraq Problem: Once and for All* (New York: Simon & Schuster, 1999); Tim Trevan, *Saddam's Secrets: The Hunt for Iraq's Hidden Weapons* (London, UK: HarperCollins, 1999).
7. As is consistently the case when liberal militarism seeks to appease the hard right, the criticisms of Clinton's foreign policy that have surfaced since 11 September have emphasized its reluctance to use force sufficiently to intimidate Islamic extremism. Bernard Lewis and Fouad Ajami have been particularly influential in mounting such lines of criticism, partly to support moves toward waging war against Iraq, and partly to give assent to the approach taken in the Afghanistan War.

8. For an argument along these lines, see Richard Falk, *The Great Terror War* (Northampton, MA: Olive Branch, 2003).

9. For text see White House Web site, www.whitehouse.gov.

10. For text see White House Web site, www.whitehouse.gov.

11. Compare George E. Bisharat, "Sanctions as Genocide," *Transnational Law & Contemporary Problems*, Vol. 11, No. 2, 379–425 (2001), with Joy Gordon, "When Intent Makes All the Difference in the World: Economic Sanctions on Iraq and the Accusation of Genocide," *Yale Human Rights & Development Law Journal* 5: 1–27 (2002). Gordon argues against the inference of genocide by stressing the degree to which specific intent is an essential element of the crime, and not present in relation to the sanctions policy.

12. See Javier Perez de Cueller, *Pilgrim for Peace: A Secretary General's Memoir* (New York: St. Martin's Press, 1997).

13. Ahtisaari, a respected international figure, revealing the conditions prevailing in Iraq when comprehensive sanctions were reimposed, wrote in the report: "The recent conflict has wrought near-apocalyptic results upon the economic infrastructure of what had been, until January 1991, a rather highly urbanized and mechanised society. Now, most means of modern life support have been destroyed or rendered tenuous. Iraq has, for some time to come, been relegated to a pre-industrial age, but with all the disabilities of post-industrial dependency on an intensive use of energy and technology." *Report to the Secretary-General on Humanitarian Needs in Kuwait and Iraq in the Immediate Post-Crisis Environment by a Mission Led by Mr. Martti Ahtisaari, Under-Secretary-General for Administration and Management 10-17 March 1991, UN SCOR, Annex, UN Doc. S/22366.*

14. See the devastating account based on these declassified documents by Thomas J. Nagy, "The Secret behind the Sanctions: How the US Intentionally Destroyed Iraq's Water Supply," *The Progressive*, August 2001; also Felicity Arbuthnot, "Allies Deliberately Poisoned Iraq's Public Water Supply in Gulf War," *Sunday Herald* (Scotland), 17 September 2001.

15. As Bisharat observes, 381 n. 11 fn. 4; beyond other considerations, Iraq's particular vulnerability to sanctions "was increased by its relative geographical isolation, its reliance on oil pipelines, and its limited shipping access, which made an embargo simple to enforce," citing Graham-Hughes, 73 n. 3, as source.

16. This statement was made in the course of the following exchange on *60 Minutes*: "We have heard that a half million children have died," said *60 Minutes* reporter Lesley Stahl, speaking of U.S. sanctions against Iraq. "I mean, that's more children than died in Hiroshima. And . . . and you know, is the price worth it?" To which Ambassador Albright replied, "I think this is a very hard choice, but the price . . . we think the price is worth it." Michael Schwartz, "U.S. Takes Selfish Stance in Relations throughout the World," *U-Wire*, 14 February 2001, available at http://www.uwire.com/content/topops021401001.htm.

17. The just war criteria are well expressed in the context of Iraq in an article primarily concerned with the prospect of war against Iraq, but are applicable to the sanctions discussion as well. See George Hunsinger, "Iraq: Stop the War," in *Robert McAfee Brown in Memoriam* (2003). See also Drew Christiansen and Gerard F. Powers, "Economic Sanctions and the Just-War Doctrine," in *Economic Sanctions: Panacea or Peacebuilding in a Post–Cold War World* (Boulder, CO: Westview Press, 1995), 97–117.

18. See Richard Garfield, "Health and Well-Being in Iraq: Sanctions and the Impact of the Oil-for-Food Program," *Transnational Law & Contemporary Problems* 11, no. 2: 277–98 (2001).

19. See helpful summary assessments by Sarah Graham-Brown, "Sanctions Renewed on Iraq," MERIP Information Note 96, May 14, 2002. See also George A. Lopez, "Toward Smart Sanctions on Iraq," *Policy Brief*, no. 5 (April 2001); Marc Lynch. "Smart Sanctions: Rebuilding Consensus or Maintaining Conflict?" *MERIP*, June 28, 2001.

20. Even *The Nation* endorsed an approach to Iraq that rests on renewed inspection and selective sanctions, partly as an alternative to war, partly as a containment plus strategy of meeting what it acknowledges to be an Iraqi threat. "War on Iraq Is Wrong," *The Nation*, June 19, 2002: 3–4.

21. See Bisharat and Joy articles referred to in note 11 for serious scholarly explorations of the relevance of genocide to the sanctions regime.

22. This position is fully developed in Falk, *The Great Terror War*, chapters 2 and 3.

CHAPTER 4

1. David Ray Griffin, *The New Pearl Harbor: Disturbing Questions about the Bush Administration And 9/11* (Northampton, MA: Interlink Publishing, 2004).

2. Most articulately advocated by Michael J. Glennon, *Limits of Law, Prerogatives of Power: Interventionism after Kosovo* (New York: Palgrave, 2001).

3. See John Yoo, *The Powers of War and Peace: The Constitution and Foreign Affairs after 9/11* (Chicago: University of Chicago Press, 2005).

4. These arguments are considered in Richard Falk, *The Great Terror War* (Northampton, MA: Interlink Publishers, 2003).

5. For a just war rationale of the war against terror see "Letter of American Intellectuals" (2002) and Jean Bethke Elshtein, *Just War against Terror: The Burden Of American Power In A Violent World* (New York: Basic Books, 2003); see also literature of the apologists for the Iraq War, including Fouad Ajami, *The Foreigner's Gift: The Americans, the Arabs, and the Iraqis in Iraq* (New York: Free Press, 2006) and Larry Diamond, *Squandered Victory: The American Occupation and the Bungled Effort to Bring Democracy to Iraq* (Henry Holt & Co., 2006).

6. A more balanced assessment of the timeline of provocations puts the onus on Israel. See Alexander Cockburn, "Hezbollah, Hamas, and Israel: Everything You Need to Know," *Counterpunch*, July 21, 2006. http://www.counterpunch.org/cockburn07212006.html.

7. Thomas Friedman, "New Power Struggle Emerging in the Middle East," *New York Times*, July 15, 2006.

8. Thomas Friedman, "Time for Plan B," *New York Times*, Aug. 6, 2006.

9. William Kristol, "Why Bush Should Go to Tel Aviv--And Confront Iran," *Financial Times*, July 16, 2006.

10. See Dan Plesch, "The End of the Beginning," Aug. 8, 2006. http://www.commentisfree.guardian.co.uk/dan_plesch/2006/08/post_2288.html.

11. See Newt Gingrich, "A Third World War," July 17, 2006. http://aei.ogr/publications/filter.all,pubID.24668/pub_detail.asp.

CHAPTER 5: WHAT FUTURE FOR THE UN CHARTER SYSTEM
OF WAR PREVENTION? REFLECTIONS ON THE IRAQ WAR

1. "President's Remarks at the United Nations General Assembly," Sept. 12, 2003, White House text.
2. For representative contributions, see Richard Falk, ed., *The Vietnam War and International Law,* 4 vols. (1968, 1969, 1972, 1976).
3. *The Kosovo Report: Conflict, International Response, Lessons Learned* (2000), 185–98; it should be mentioned that I was a member of the commission.
4. Such a practice could be regarded as an informal and substantive extension of the established practice of treating abstentions by permanent members as not blocking decisions by the Security Council despite the wording of Article 27(3) requiring "the concurring votes of the permanent members." Such a practice shows the degree to which the Security Council was able to contrive ways to overcome a paralysis that would have resulted from an interpretative approach based on textual fidelity, and it is impressive that this approach was established in the midst of the Cold War.
5. These three steps outlined in Kosovo Report, supra, note 3, 187.
6. A discussion of this challenge and the U.S. response is the theme of my book, Richard Falk, *The Great Terror War* (2003).
7. Initially fully depicted in "Remarks by the President at 2002 Graduation Exercise of the United States Military Academy," June 1, 2002; given a more enduring and authoritative status by their emphasis in the official White House document, *The National Security Strategy of the United States of America,* Sept. 2002, esp. chapter 5, 13–16.
8. See supra, note 1.
9. The most important Security Council resolutions were 678 (1990), 687 (1991), and, of course, 1441 (2002).
10. "President Bush's Prepared Remarks Declaring End to Major Combat in Iraq," text printed in *New York Times,* May 2, 2003, A14.
11. This position is most clearly articulated by Michael J. Glennon, *Why the Security Council Failed, Foreign Affairs* 82, no. 3: 16–35 (2003); the overall argument is more fully developed in Glennon's book *Limits of Law, Prerogatives of Power: Interventionism after Kosovo* (2001); also relevant, Anthony C. Arend and Robert J. Beck, *International Law and the Use of Force: Beyond the UN Charter Paradigm* (1993); A. Mark Weisbrud, *Use of Force: The Practice of States since World War II* (1997).
12. See Anne-Marie Slaughter, "Good Reasons for Going Around the U.N.," *New York Times,* March 18, 2003.
13. See Charles Krauthammer, "U.S. cleaning up Hussein's mess in Iraq," *Los Angeles Times,* May 16, 2003; Thomas I. Friedman, "Bored with Baghdad — Already," *New York Times,* May 18, 2003, §4, 13.
14. For the view that American moralism and legalism has had a detrimental impact on U.S. foreign policy during the first half of the twentieth century see George F. Kennan, *American Diplomacy 1900–1950* (1951); also Henry Kissinger, *Diplomacy* (1994), esp. 218–245, 762–835. For a more general interpretation of the Wilsonian component as a more widely conceived aspect of the overall American foreign-policy tradition, see Walter Russell Mead, *Special Providence: American Foreign Policy and How It Changed the World* (2001), 132–73.

15. Paul Kennedy, *The Rise and Fall of Great Power: Economic Change and Military Conflict 1500–2000* (1987).

16. For an argument along these lines, see Max Boot, "George Woodrow Bush: The President Is Becoming a Wilsonian Interventionist," *Wall Street Journal*, July 1, 2002.

17. Aside from identifying specific states as "the axis of evil" in the global setting of the war against terrorism, in his West Point speech the president included some strongly moralistic rhetoric of a visionary quality, quite inimical to the realist tradition. The following excerpt is indicative of the tone and message: "We are in a conflict between good and evil, and America will call evil by its name. By confronting evil and lawless regimes, we do not create a problem, we reveal a problem. And we will lead the world in opposing it." See supra, note 1.

18. See Richard Perle, "Thank God for the Death of the UN: Its Abject Failure Gave Us Only Anarchy. The World Needs Order," *The Guardian*, March 20, 2003.

19. For AN influential comprehensive presentation along these lines, see *The Responsibility to Protect: Report of the International Commission on Intervention and State Sovereignty* (2001).

20. Constructivism as an academic approach to the study of international relations is best explained by Alexander Wendt in his *Social Theory of International Politics* (1999).

21. For useful overviews of this trend see Sean Murphy, *Humanitarian Intervention: The United Nations in an Evolving World* (1996); Nicholas J. Wheeler, *Saving Strangers: Humanitarian Intervention in International Society* (2000).

22. For a well-crafted narrow doctrine of humanitarian intervention, see Jack Donnelly, *Universal Human Rights in Theory and Practice* (2nd ed., 2003), 242–60. For a generally skeptical set of reflections about claims of humanitarian intervention, see Aleksandar Jokic, ed., *Humanitarian Intervention: Moral and Philosophical Issues* (2003); for a somewhat more optimistic set of accounts, see J. L. Holzgrefe and Robert O. Keohane, eds., *Humanitarian Intervention: Ethical, Legal, and Political Dilemmas* (2003).

23. For important efforts, see Kosovo Report, note 3; *The Responsibility to Protect*, Report of the International Commission on Intervention and State Sovereignty (2001), 53–57; Lori Fisler Damrosch, "Concluding Remarks," in *Enforcing Restraint: Collective Intervention in Internal Conflicts*, ed. Lori Fisler Damrosch (1993), 348–67; and esp., Damrosch, "The Inevitability of Selective Response? Principles to Guide Urgent International Action," in *Kosovo and the Challenge of Humanitarian Intervention*, ed. Albrecht Schnabel and Ramesh Thakur (2001), 405–19.

24. It may be worth recalling the vigorous U.S. government objections to the Vietnamese intervention in Cambodia, and subsequent occupation, that disrupted the Khmer Rouge genocide. The American position repudiated the humanitarian considerations, emphasizing the Vietnamese violation of Cambodian sovereignty, urging immediate withdrawal despite the risk of regenerating a genocidal regime.

25. A more generalized view of the benefits arising from a law-oriented approach are well explained in Nicole Deller, Arjun Makhijani, and John Burroughs, eds., *Rule of Power or Rule of Law?* (2003).

26. See Oscar Schachter, "In Defense of International Rules on the Use of Force," 53 *U. Chi. L. Rev* 113 (1986).

27. The reference to failure is to challenge the central conclusion of Glennon's analysis, supra, note 11.

28. My assertion is in direct opposition to the inferences drawn by Robert Kagen in his influential book. See Kagen, *Of Paradise and Power: America and Europe in the New World Order* (2003).

CHAPTER 6: ENGAGING NORMATIVE CONSCIOUSNESS

1. I am not suggesting that international law is not itself part of the instrumental armory of dominant political actors, including the United States. For a preliminary statement, see R. Falk, "Orientalism and International Law: A Matter of Contemporary Urgency," in *Arab World Geographer*, 2004.

2. This rightist vision, put forward as a project, was articulated by many of the Bush inner circle in the notorious report of the Project for a New American Century prepared and issued some months before the 2000 elections. "Repairing America's Defenses," Project for a New American Century, Washington, D.C., 2000.

3. The idea of "recovery" is ambiguous, at once referring to the erosion of respect for international law and the UN associated with the Bush administration, but without any pretension that there ever existed a period in international political life when such normative constraint took precedence over the pursuit of vital national interests. What makes the notion of recovery attractive is the claim that the 1990s did witness progress in a number of areas toward a more reliable rule of law in world affairs, and any moves that would revive that spirit would compare favorably with the normative descent associated with post-9/11 behavior, especially by the United States.

4. For specification, see R. Falk, *The Declining World Order: America's Imperial Geopolitics* (New York: Routledge, 2004).

5. For Derrida and Habermas, see G. Borradori, *Philosophy in a Time of Terror: Dialogues with Jürgens Habermas and Jacques Derrida* (Chicago: University of Chicago Press, 2003); Homi K. Bhabha, *The Location of Culture* (New York & London: Routledge, 1994). I would also include some of the writings of Edward Said, including *Culture and Imperialism* (New York: Knopf, 1993).

6. R. Kagan, *Of Paradise and Power: America and Europe in the New World Order* (New York: Knopf, 2003).

7. See Z. Brzezinski, *The Choice: Global Domination or Global Leadership* (New York: Basic, 2004); Amitai Etzioni, *From Empire to Community: A New Approach to International Relations* (New York: Palgrave, 2004); Anne-Marie Slaughter, *A New World Order* (Princeton, NJ: Princeton University Press, 2004).

8. For invaluable counterpoint to the American emphasis in the setting, consider the following work, which is oriented around the role of international law in relation to the development agenda. Balakrishnan Rajagopal, *International Law from Below: Development, Social Movements, and Third World Resistance* (Cambridge, UK: Cambridge University Press, 2003).

9. George W. Bush, "Commencement Address," West Point, NY, U.S. Military Academy, June 2002.

10. Most coherently set forth in the White House document, "National Security Strategy of the United States of America," issued September 2002; more crudely depicted
in David Frum and Richard Perle, *An End to Evil: How to Win the War on Terror*
(New York: Random House, 2003).

11. See definition in Article 53 of the Vienna Convention on the Law of Treaties: ". . . a
peremptory norm of general international law is a norm accepted and recognized by
the international community of States as a whole as a norm from which no deroga-
tion is permitted and which can be modified only by a subsequent norm of general
international law having the same character."

12. See UN General Assembly Res. 95, adopted 11 Dec. 1946, "Affirmation of the Principles of International Law Recognized by the Charter of the Nuremberg Tribunal."

13. For assessments, see E. Barkun, *The Guilt of Nations: Restitution and Negotiating
Historic Injustices* (New York: Norton, 2000); R. Falk, note 3, 107–36.

14. The American pursuit of global dominance preceded 9/11, but relied primarily on
economistic and idelogoical expansion. For an argument to this effect, see R. Falk,
Predatory Globalization: A Critique (Cambridge, UK: Polity, 2000).

15. Francis Anthony Boyle, *World Politics and International Law* (Durham, NC: Duke
University Press, 1985); Boyle, *Foundations of World Order: The Legalist Approach
to International Relations* (Durham, NC: Duke University Press, 1999).

16. These issues explored in detail with respect to the approach taken by the *New York
Times* to the relevance of international law. Howard Friel and Richard Falk, *The
Record of the Paper: How the NY Times Misrepresents US Foreign Policy* (London:
Verso, 2004).

CHAPTER 7: DEMYSTIFYING IRAQ

1. David Campbell, "Beyond Choice: The Ontopolitics of Critique," in Jenny Edkins,
ed., "The Ethics of Engagement," *Journal of International Relations* (2005).

2. See John Hart Ely, *War and Responsibility: Constitutional Lessons of Vietnam and
Its Aftermath* (Princeton, NJ: Princeton University Press, 1993); also Ely, *Democracy
and Distrust: A Theory of Judicial Review* (Cambridge, MA: Harvard University Press,
1980).

3. For overview, see Shadia Drury, *Leo Strauss and the American Right* (New York:
St. Martin's Press, 1999); see also James Atlas, "A Classicist's Legacy: New Empire
Builders," *New York Times,* May 4, 2003, §4, 1, 4.

4. See Walter Russell Mead, *Power, Terror, Peace, and War* (New York: Knopf, 2004)
83–105, 152–54.

5. For an attempt at a normative assessment of international relations that is neither
Wilsonian or neocon, see Richard Falk, *On Humane Governance: Toward a New
Global Politics* (Cambridge, UK: Polity, 1995); Falk, *The Declining World Order:
America's Imperial Geopolitics* (New York: Routledge, 2004).

6. "Repairing America's Defenses," Project for a New American Century, Washington, D.C., September 2000.

7. Instructive works on democracy are Robert A. Dahl, *Democracy and Its Critics*
(New Haven, CT: Yale University Press, 1980); David Held, *Democracy and the
Global Order* (Cambridge, UK: Polity, 1995).

8. Document issued by the White House under this title with a covering letter by
President Bush, and dated September 2002.

9. *The 9/11 Commission Report: Final Report of the National Commission on Terrorist Attacks upon the United States*, authorized edition (New York: Norton, 2004); see also the scathing attack by Benjamin DeMott, "Whitewash as Public Service: How the 9/11 Commission Defrauds the Nation," *Harpers*, October 2004, 35–45.

10. See transcript of conversation with Jim Lehrer, *The News Hour*, September 11, 2003.

11. For indictments of administration policy on this basis, see Richard A. Clarke, *Against All Enemies: Inside America's War on Terror* (New York: Free Press, 2004); Anonymous, *Imperial Hubris: Why the West Is Losing the War on Terror* (Washington, D.C., 2004).

12. This reasoning is well illustrated in Robert Kagan, *Of Paradise and Power: America and Europe in the New World Order* (New York: Viking, 2003).

13. See David Ray Griffin, *The New Pearl Harbor: Disturbing Questions about the Bush Administration and 9/11* (Northampton, MA: Interlink, updated edition, 2004).

14. This distinction is clumsily rejected by Robert Baer in his review of the Griffin book, shoring up the legitimacy of the Bush response to 9/11, and confining criticism to allegations of burearcratic incompetence. See Baer, "Dangerous Liaisons," *The Nation*, Sept. 27, 2004, 38–40.

15. See especially the celebrated essay by Noam Chomsky entitled "The Responsibility of Intellectuals," reprinted in Chomsky, *American Power and the New Mandarins: Historical and Political Essays* (New York: Pantheon, 1969) 323–66; also highly relevant is the work of Edward Said, see Said, *Representations of the Intellectual* (New York: Pantheon, 1994).

16. See Jacques Derrida, *Aporias* (Stanford, CA: University of Stanford Press, 1993).

17. See Daniel Ellsberg, *Secrets: A Memoir of Vietnam and the Pentagon Papers* (New York: Viking, 2002).

18. Among notable attempts, see David Held, *Global Covenant: The Social Alternative to the Washington Consensus* (Cambridge, UK: Polity, 2004); Amitai Etzioni, *From Empire to Community: A New Approach to World Order* (New York, Palgrave, 2004); also Falk, *The Declining World Order*, n. 5.

19. This assessment is powerfully developed in Ikechi Mgbeoji, *Collective Insecurity: The Liberian Crisis, Unilateralism, & Global Order* (Vancouver, BC: UBC Press, 2003).

CHAPTER 8: DEMOCRATIZING THE MIDDLE EAST

1. This argument is effectively made by Jim Garrison, *America As Empire: Global Leader or Global Power?* (San Francisco, CA: Berrett-Kohler, 2004).

2. New York, NY: G. P. Putnam, 2004.

CHAPTER 10: LEGALITY AND LEGITIMACY: THE QUEST FOR PRINCIPLED FLEXIBILITY AND RESTRAINT

1. Thomas M. Franck, "Who Killed Article 2(4)? Or: Changing Norms Governing the Use of Force by States," 64 *Amer J Int'l L* 109 (1970); Louis Henkin, "The Reports of the Death of Article 2(4) Are Greatly Exaggerated," 65 *Amer J Int'l L* 544 (1971).

2. Jean Bethke Elshtain, *Just War against Terror* (New York: Basic Books, 2003); Michael Walzer, *Arguing about War* (New Haven, CT: Yale University Press); Richard Falk, *The Great Terror War* (Northampton, MA: Interlink Press, 2003).

3. The locus classicus for such discussions is Carl Schmitt, *Legality and Legitimacy*, trans. John P. McCormick (Durham, NC: Duke University Press, 2004).

4. For a fascinating account, see David Dyzenhaus, *Legality and Legitimacy: Carl Schmitt, Hans Kelsen and Hermann Heller in Weimar* (Oxford, UK: Oxford University Press, 1997).

5. Instances where the UNSC has applied Charter norms to oppose aggression in an effective manner include the Korean War (1950–52), The Suez Operation (1956), and the Gulf War (1991).

6. Anthony Clark and Robert J. Beck, *International Law & the Use of Force* (London: Routledge, 1993); A. Mark Weisburd, *Use of Force: The Practice of States since World War II* (University Park: Pennsylvania State University Press, 1997).

7. Case Concerning Military and Paramilitary Activities in and against Nicaragua (Nicaragua v. United States) 1986 International Court of Justice Reports 14.

8. "In Larger Freedom: Towards Development, Security and Human Rights for All," Report of the Secretary General, A/59/2005, 21 March 2005, para. 122–26.

9. The issue is much discussed recently in political and legal theory in relation to the statist thinking of Carl Schmitt and now Geogio Agamben. See particularly Agamben, *State of Exception* (Chicago: University of Chicago Press, 2005).

10. See *Kosovo Report* (Independent International Commission on Kosovo) (Oxford: Oxford University Press, 2000), esp. 192–95 (hereinafter cited as Kosovo Report.

11. Michael J. Glennon, *Limits of Law; Prerogatives of Power: Interventionism after Kosovo* (New York: Palgrave, 2001).

12. Thomas M. Franck, "Break It, Don't Fake It," *Foreign Affairs* 78: 116–22 (1999).

13. Richard Perle, "Thank God for the death of the UN: Its Abject Failure Gave Us Only Anarchy," *Guardian*, 20 March 2003.

14. Particularly influential was the incident in the Kosovo village of Recak on January 15, 1999, where Yugoslav military forces killed some 45 Kosovars, allegedly civilians, although Serbs claim that the casualties were the result of a skirmish with the KLA, and were paramilitary combat officers. See Kosovo Report, 81, 83.

15. There were also independent skeptics. Noam Chomsky, *The New Military Humanism: Lessons from Kosovo* (Monroe, ME: Common Courage Press, 1999). For a wider, deeper skepticism about claims of humanitarian intervention see Anne Orfeld, *Reading Humanitarian Intervention: Human Rights and the Use of Force in International Law* (Cambridge, UK: Cambridge University Press, 2003); as well, the domestic jurisdiction provision of the UN Charter, Article 2(7), can be understood as a deliberate legal obstacle to preclude the UN from endorsing humanitarian intervention.

16. Kosovo Report 193–95; also Appendix A.

17. On Rugova see Kosovo Report, 43–65.

18. "The Responsibility to Protect," Report of the International Commission on Intervention and State Sovereignty, 2001.

19. Report, note 18, xii–xiii, and appendix B.

20. All references in this paragraph are to "In Larger Freedom," cited *in* note 8, A/59/2005, para. 122–26.

21. See Report of the International Commission of Inquiry on Darfur to the United Nations Secretary General (Pursuant to UNSC Res. 1564, 18 Sept 2004), Geneva, 25 January 2005; Scott Straus, "Darfur and the Genocide Debate," *Foreign Affairs* 84, no. 1: 123–33 (2005).

22. For definitive statements of U.S. government official arguments along these lines, see William H. Taft IV and Todd F. Buchwald, "Preemption, Iraq, and International Law," John Yoo, "International Law and the War in Iraq," and Ruth Wedgewood, "The Fall of Saddam Hussein: Security Council Mandates and Preemptive Self-Defense," in *Future Implications of the Iraq Conflict,* selections from the *American Journal of International Law,* September 2003.

23. For comprehensive assessments along these lines, see C/G. Weeramantry, *Armageddon or Brave New World? Reflections on the Hostilities in Iraq* (Ratmalana, Sri Lanka: Weeramantry International Centre, 2nd ed., 2005); Domenic McGoldrick, *From 9-11 to the Iraq War 2003* (Oxford, UK: Hart Publishing, 2004), esp. 24–86; see also R. Falk and David Krieger, eds., *The Iraq Crisis and International Law* (Santa Barbara, CA: Nuclear Age Peace Foundation, 2003).

24. Slaughter, "Good Reasons for Going Around the U.N.," *New York Times,* March 18, 2003.

25. All quotes in this paragraph are from Slaughter, "The Use of Force in Iraq: Illegal and Illegitimate," *ASIL Proceedings 2004,* 262–63.

26. Richard Falk, "The Iraq War and the Future of International Law," in prior note, 263–66.

27. See text at note 8; also Kofi Annan, Address by the Secretary General. Kofi Annan, UN Doc. SG/SM/8891, September 23, 2003.

28. "America's Crisis of Legitimacy," *Foreign Affairs* 83, no. 2: 65–87.

29. Id. at 67.

30. Id. at 72.

31. Id. at 84.

32. Id. at 85.

33. Id. at 87.

34. "The Sources of American Legitimacy," *Foreign Affairs* 83, no. 6: 18–32 (2004).

35. Id. at 18.

36. Id. at 24.

37. Id. at 26.

38. Id. at 23.

39. Id. at 29.

40. Id. at 30–31.

41. Id. at 32.

42. "A Matter of Record: Security, Not Law, Established American Legitimacy," *Foreign Affairs* 84, no. 1: 170–73 (2005).

43. See Mark Danner, *Torture and Truth: America, Abu Ghraib, and the War on Terror* (New York: New York Review of Books, 2004); also Lisa Hajjar, "What's the Matter with Yoo?" and R. Falk, "Law, Lawyers, Liars and the Limits of Professionalism," papers presented at the 2005 Law & Society Annual Meeting, June 2–5, 2005, Las Vegas, Nevada.

44. "Perpetual Peace," in *Kant on History,* ed. Lewis White Beck (Indianapolis, IN: Bobbs-Merrill, 1963), 85–135, 99. See also the Busiris scene in Jean Giradoux, *Tiger at the Gates* (New York: Oxford University Press, 1955), 43–47.

45. This issue has been decisively elaborated by Harold Lasswell and Myres S. McDougal in their influential article, "The Identification and Appraisal of Diverse Systems of Public Order," reprinted in McDougal, *Studies in World Public Order* (New Haven, CT: Yale University Press, 1960), 3–41; for the wider issues associated with interpretative discretion, see Myres S. McDougal, Harold D. Lasswell, and James C. Miller, *The Interpretation of Agreements and World Public Order* (New Haven, CT: Yale University Press, 1967).

46. See generally, Thomas M. Franck, *The Power of Legitimacy among Nations* (New York: Oxford University Press, 1990).

CHAPTER 11: HUMANITARIAN INTERVENTION?

1. The phrase was first used by President Bush in the 2004 State of the Union address to Congress: "America will never seek a permission slip to defend the security of our country." White House, January 20, 2004; see also "National Security Strategy of the United States of America," White House, September 2002, for authoritative statement of the American claim to initiate a preemptive war whenever it perceives a security threat.

2. For discussion of the political constraints relevant to the operation of such international commissions, see Richard Falk, "Liberalism at the Global Level: Solidarity vs. Cooperation," in Eivind Hovden and Edward Keene, eds., *The Globalization of Liberalism* (New York: Palgrave, 2002) 75–98.

3. I leave aside legal and moral criticisms of the war relating to the reliance on tactics of waging the war mainly by high-altitude bombing, and the failure of occupying forces to avoid reverse ethnic cleansing and other abuses of the Serb minority, especially immediately following the cessation of hostilities.

4. See *Kosovo Report: Conflict, International Responses, Lessons Learned*, Independent International Commission on Kosovo (Oxford, UK: Oxford University Press, 2000).

5. Most fully argued by Michael J. Glennon, *Limits of Law, Prerogatives of Power* (New York: Palgrave, 2001). See also Glennon, "Why the Security Council Failed," *Foreign Affairs* 82(3): 16–35 (2003).

6. See also the criteria for intervention set forth by the Danish Institute of International Affairs: serious violations of human rights or international humanitarian law; a failure by the UNSC to act; a multilateral basis for action undertaken; only necessary and proportionate force used; "disinterestedness" of the intervening states. *Humanitarian Intervention: Legal and Political Aspects*, Danish Institute of International Affairs, Copenhagen, 1999, pp. 106–111. This was the first attempt to provide a systematic, principled framework for humanitarian intervention.

7. Report, pp. 193–195.

8. Published by the International Development Research Centre, Ottawa, Canada, 2001.

9. P. 11; the report also sets forth its own set of guidelines that resembles in most respects the eleven principles listed by the Kosovo Report, as well as borrows from the language and approach used in the just war tradition. Pp. 12–13.

10. For an excellent overview of these various cases arising in the 1900s that produced either action or inaction on the part of the international community, see Nicholas J. Wheeler, *Saving Strangers: Humanitarian Intervention in International Society*

(Oxford, UK: Oxford University Press, 2000); for an important sympathetic assessment of the UN response to the Rwanda crisis, see Michael Barnett, *Eyewitness to Genocide: The UN and Rwanda* (Ithaca, NY: Cornell University Press, 2002).

11. See Michael Walzer, *Arguing about War* (New Haven, CT: Yale University Press, 2004), esp. 87–91.

12. P. 13; also Lloyd Axworthy, as Minister of External Affairs in Canada, made a special effort to introduce the idea of human security into the discourse of statecraft. Axworthy's important contributions to thinking about security are well expressed in his book *Navigating the World: Canada's Global Future* (Toronto: Knopf Canada, 2003).

13. P. 74; the membership of the commission is discussed on pp. 77–79.

14. UN Report, 65.

15. P. 65; see p. 66 endorsement of "the emerging norm that there is a collective international responsibility to protect" but seeming to confine its implementation to the Security Council, thereby indirectly invalidating the residual authority of such other actors as regional organizations or coalitions of the willing." There is also presented a checklist of five criteria designed to provide a framework for principled action, and resembling the lists earlier discussed.

16. UN Report, Sec. 186; the skepticism relating to balance of power appears to be an elliptical repudiation of the realist approach to world order, and when combined with the rejection of hegemonic or imperial geopolitics appears to imply support for a norm-based, UN-centered approach.

17. For a standard academic set of inquiries that situates itself within the mainstream of the American/UK debate on interventionary diplomacy, see J.L. Holzgrefe and Robert O. Keohane, eds., *Humanitarian Intervention: Ethical, Legal, and Political Dilemmas* (Cambridge, UK: Cambridge University Press, 2003). Two additional valuable edited collections are Deen K. Chaterjee and Don E. Scheid, eds., *Ethics and Foreign Intervention* (Cambridge, UK: Cambridge University Press, 2003) and Jonathan Moore, ed., *Hard Choices: Moral Dilemmas in Humanitarian Intervention* (Lanham, MD: Rowman & Littlefield, 1998).

18. Walzer, note 11, 81.

19. Michael Ignatieff, "The Burden," *New York Times Magazine*, Jan. 5, 2003, 22–27, 50–54.

20. As with so much critical writing in international relations, Noam Chomsky has authored the seminal text repudiating the humanitarian claims of the United States. See Chomsky, *The New Military Humanism: Lessons from Kosovo* (Monroe, ME: Common Courage Press, 1999).

21. Orfeld, *Reading Humanitarian Intervention: Human Rights and the Use of Force in International Law* (Cambridge, UK: Cambridge University Press, 2003).

22. Orfeld, 11.

23. Orfeld, 68.

24. Orfeld, 79.

25. The aftermath of the 2002 Afghanistan War is more ambiguous. Certainly, the American effort to achieve economic and political reconstruction of the ravaged country has been flawed, and insufficient. At the same time, U.S. troops have remained, Kabul at least has been secured, and national elections have been held. Of course, the motivation in Afghanistan is complex, as the Taliban remains a political force in parts of the country and the general context of the struggle against

Al Qaeda means that there exists a strategic objective of ensuring that Afghanistan does not become again a base for anti-American extremism encourages a continuing involvement by the United States. Ironically, an apparent consequence of the intervention is a revival of the poppy crop.

26. Orfeld, 204.
27. A brilliant corrective to those who think of colonialism as of only historical interest because it is past is provided by Derek Gregory, *Colonial Present* (Malden, MA: Blackwells, 2004).
28. *Collective Insecurity: The Liberian Crisis, Unilateralism, & Global Order* (Vancouver: UBC Press, 2003).
29. Mgbeoji, 1.
30. Mgbeoji, 142.

CHAPTER 12: THE CRIMINAL ACCOUNTABILITY OF LEADERS

1. In R. Falk, G. Kolko, and R. J. Lifton, eds., *Crimes of War* (New York: Random House, 1971), 85; also Karl Jaspers, *The Question of German Guilt* (New York: Capricorn, 1961).
2. *In the Name of America* (New York: Clergy and Laymen Concerned about Vietnam, 1968).
3. Telford Taylor, *Nuremberg and Vietnam: An American Tragedy* (Chicago: Quadrangle Books, 1970).
4. See John Borneman, ed., *The Case of Ariel Sharon and the Fate of Universal Jurisdiction* (Princeton, NJ: Princeton Institute for International and Regional Studies Monograph Series, No. 2, 2004). Stephen Macedo, ed., *Universal Jurisdiction* (Philadelphia: University of Pennsylvania Press, 2005).
5. The signature of a treaty does not bind the party; ratification does, and there was never a prospect that the U.S. Congress would ratify the treaty establishing the ICC. Bush's withdrawal of signature was a domestic and international signal of the American repudiation of the whole process of establishing an international institution addressing issues of accountability.
6. See UNGA Res. 3314, 14 Dec. 1974; text in Weston, doc., 232; Article 1 of the resolution associates "aggression" with "the use of armed force against the sovereignty, territorial integrity or political independence of another State, or in any manner inconsistent with the Charter of the United Nations."
7. It was such a mandate that gave a color of legality to the Gulf War in 1991.
8. This assessment of the illegality with respect to the Iraq War has been overwhelmingly confirmed by mainstream international law specialists. A representative panel at the 2004 Annual Meeting of the American Society of International Law composed of Anne-Marie Slaughter, Thomas M. Franck, James Crawford, Mary Ellen O'Connell, and myself unanimously reached such a conclusion of illegality. See, "Iraq, One Year Later," *Proceeding of the 98th Annual Meeting of the American Society of International Law*, 2004, 261–74.
9. See feeble efforts by American officials to invoke earlier Security Council resolutions to support legality of the Iraqi invasion. For discussion see ASIL Proceedings, Note 8, 263–69.

10. Discussed in Falk, *The Great Terror War* (Northampton, MA: Olive Branch Press, 2003), 61–72. Even though the war had a legal basis, it was undertaken in a manner that makes its legality questionable, and quite possibly imprudent as well. The main legal doubts concerned the absence of a clear Security Council authorization and the failure by the U.S. government to treat war as a last resort.

11. See analysis to this effect in the report of the Kosovo Commission. *Kosovo Report* (Oxford, UK: Oxford University Press, 2000) at 163–98.

CHAPTER 13: WORLD TRIBUNAL ON IRAQ: TRUTH, LAW, AND JUSTICE

1. For text of the "Downing Street Memo," see Richard Falk, Irene Gendzier, and Robert Jay Lifton, eds., *Crimes of War: Iraq* (New York: Nation Books, 2006), 126–29; Christopher Scheer, Robert Scheer, and Laksmi Chaudhry, *The Five Biggest Lies Bush Told Us about Iraq* (New York: Akashic Books/Seven Stories Press, 2003); for more general consideration see John Hart Ely, *War and Responsibility: Constitutional Lessons of Vietnam and Its Aftermath* (Princeton, NJ: Princeton University Press, 1993); see also Pierce O'Donnell, *In Time of War: Hitler's Terrorist Attack on America* (New York: New Press, 2005).

2. On Nuremberg logic see Falk, Gendzier, and Lifton, note 1, 55–76.

3. There were some earlier notable initiatives along the same lines in relation to an inquiry into the Reichstag Fire in Nazi Germany and the Moscow show trials described in a useful study of the entire subject by Arthur Jay Klinghoffer and Judith Apter Klinghoffer, *International Citizens' Tribunals*, New York: Palgrave, 2002.

4. For a complete record of the Russell Tribunal, see John Duffett, ed., *Against the Crime of Silence: Proceedings of the International War Crimes Tribunal* (New York: Simon & Schuster, 1968), especially the opening statements of Noam Chomsky, Bertrand Russell, and Jean-Paul Sartre, xiii–xxix, 3–4, 14–16, 40–45.

5. For text of Algiers Declaration, see Burns H. Weston, Richard Falk, and Hilary Charlesworth, eds., *Supplement of Basic Documents to International Law and World Order*, 3rd. ed. (St. Paul, MN: West Publishing, 1997), 473.

6. Compare the current raging debate relating to U.S. practices in Iraq and with respect to the rejection of the International Criminal Court. For range of criticisms of U.S. governmental claims of exception and exemption from the perspective of international law, see Amy Bartholomew, ed., *Empire's Law: The American Imperial Project and the "War to Remake the World"* (London, UK: Pluto Press, 2006). For an earlier influential argument against encumbering global diplomacy with unrealistic efforts to impose international legal accountability for war making on political leaders of this line of international law, see Hedley Bull, "The Grotian Conception of International Society," in Herbert Butterfield and Martin Wight, eds., *Diplomatic Investigations* (Cambridge, MA: Harvard University Press, 1968), 50–73; and more recently, Jack L. Goldsmith and Eric A. Posner, *The Limits of International Law* (New York: Oxford University Press, 2005).

7. Opening Statement, Richard Falk, Gabriel Kolko, Robert Jay Lifton, eds., *Crimes of War* (New York Random House, 1971), 85.

8. See Stephen Macedo, ed. *Universal Jurisdiction* (Philadelphia: University of Pennsylvania Press, 2005); Reed Brody and Michael Ratner, eds., *The Pinochet Papers: The Case against Augusto Pinochet in Spain and Britain* (The Hague, Netherlands: Kluwer, 2001); Roger Burbach, *The Pinochet Affair: State Terrorism and Global Justice* (London, UK: Zed Books, 2003).

9. There is a parallel set of civil society initiatives by way of these tribunals that is based on exposing *historic* wrongs, rather than ongoing war, such as associated with the travails of indigenous peoples, of slavery, of unacknowledged historic genocides (e.g., Armenia). The Permanent Peoples' Tribunal had many sessions devoted to such issues. Usually there exists a strong connection between representatives of the victim communities and the initiative undertaken to raise levels of awareness on the part of a wider public with respect to a human wrong that is treated as part of a forgotten or romanticized past by the wider public, but remains an open wound for those who identify with the victims as survivors or decendants. One of the most moving, and vivid, of such accounts is Peter Balakian's *The Burning Tigris: The Armenian Genocide and America's Response* (New York: HarperCollins, 2003). See also Iris Chang, *The Rape of Nanking: The Forgotten Holocaust of World War II* (New York: Basic Books, 1997).

10. See *The Responsibility to Protect*, Report of the International Commission on Intervention and State Sovereignty (Ottawa, Canada: International Development Research Centre, 2001); Geoffrey Robertson, *Crimes against Humanity: The Struggle for Global Justice* (New York: New Press, 2000).

11. Roy statement reprinted in Falk, Gendzier, and Lifton, 159–63, n. 1, at 162.

12. All quotes from Sartre in Duffett, 40–45, n. 4.

13. Text of statement by Roosevelt in Falk, Kolko, and Lifton, 76–77.

Index